MATHEMATICS WORKBOOK FOR THE SAT*

*"SAT" and "Scholastic Aptitude Test" are registered trademarks of the College Entrance Examination Board. This book has been prepared by Arco Publishing, Inc., which bears sole responsibility for its contents.

MATHEMATICS WORKBOOK FOR THE SAT

BRIGITTE SAUNDERS, M.A.
Department of Mathematics
Great Neck South Senior High School
Great Neck, New York

with

DAVID FRIEDER, M.A. and **MARK WEINFELD, M.S.**
Co-Directors, MATHWORKS, New York City

ARCO PUBLISHING, INC.
NEW YORK

Second Edition, Second Printing, 1985

Published by Arco Publishing, Inc.
215 Park Avenue South, New York, N.Y. 10003

Copyright © 1985 by Arco Publishing, Inc.
Copyright © 1980 by Brigitte Saunders
All rights reserved. No part of this book may
be reproduced, by any means, without permission
in writing from the publisher, except by a
reviewer who wishes to quote brief excerpts in
connection with a review in a magazine or
newspaper.

Library of Congress Cataloging in Publication Data

Saunders, Brigitte.
  Mathematics workbook for the SAT.

  Summary: A mathematics workbook dealing with decimals,
fractions, percent, algebra, geometry, roots, and
radicals, designed to prepare high school students for the
SAT. Includes practice tests.
    1. Mathematics—Examinations, questions, etc.
2. Scholastic aptitude test. [1. Mathematics—
Examinations, questions, etc. 2. Scholastic aptitude
test—Study guides] I. Frieder, David. II. Weinfeld, Mark.
III. Title.
QA43.S28   1985   513'.14'076   84-18584
ISBN 0-668-06138-3 (Paper Edition)

Printed in the United States of America

This book is dedicated to the students of Great Neck South Senior High School, who have made my many years of teaching there so rewarding. Special thanks must go to my son, Danny, for his suggestions, help, and patience during my months of writing. Also, to David, Dad, Mom, and Mother for their continued support.

Contents

To the Student   xi

1. Operations with Integers and Decimals   1

Diagnostic Test • Addition of Integers • Subtraction of Integers • Multiplication of Integers • Division of Integers • Addition or Subtraction of Decimals • Multiplication of Decimals • Division of Decimals • The Laws of Arithmetic • Estimating Answers • Solutions to Tests and Exercises

2. Operations with Fractions   17

Diagnostic Test • Addition and Subtraction • Multiplication and Division • Reducing Fractions • Operations with Mixed Numbers • Comparing Fractions • Complex Fractions • Solutions to Tests and Exercises

3. Verbal Problems Involving Fractions   32

Diagnostic Test • Solutions to Tests and Exercises

4. Variation   43

Diagnostic Test • Ratio and Proportion • Direct Variation • Inverse Variation • Solutions to Tests and Exercises

5. Percent   56

Diagnostic Test • Fractional and Decimal Equivalents of Percents • Finding a Percent of a Number • Finding a Number When a Percent Is Given • To Find What Percent One Number Is of Another • Percents Greater Than 100 • Solutions to Tests and Exercises

6. Verbal Problems Involving Percent   70

Diagnostic Test • Percent of Increase or Decrease • Discount • Commission • Profit and Loss • Taxes • Solutions to Tests and Exercises

7. Averages — 85

Diagnostic Test • Simple Average • To Find a Missing Number When an Average Is Given • Weighted Average • Solutions to Tests and Exercises

8. Concepts of Algebra—Signed Numbers and Equations — 95

Diagnostic Test • Signed Numbers • Solution of Linear Equations • Simultaneous Equations in Two Unknowns • Quadratic Equations • Equations Containing Radicals • Solutions to Tests and Exercises

9. Literal Expressions — 110

Diagnostic Test • Solutions to Tests and Exercises

10. Roots and Radicals — 118

Diagnostic Test • Addition and Subtraction of Radicals • Multiplication and Division of Radicals • Simplifying Radicals Containing a Sum or Difference • Finding the Square Root of a Number • Solutions to Tests and Exercises

11. Factoring and Algebraic Fractions — 128

Diagnostic Test • Reducing Fractions • Addition or Subtraction of Fractions • Multiplication and Division of Fractions • Complex Algebraic Fractions • Using Factoring to Find Missing Values • Solutions to Tests and Exercises

12. Problem Solving in Algebra — 142

Diagnostic Test • Coin Problems • Consecutive Integer Problems • Age Problems • Investment Problems • Fraction Problems • Mixture Problems • Motion Problems • Work Problems • Solutions to Tests and Exercises

13. Geometry — 167

Diagnostic Test • Areas • Perimeter • Right Triangles • Coordinate Geometry • Parallel Lines • Triangles • Polygons • Circles • Volumes • Similar Polygons • Solutions to Tests and Exercises

14. Inequalities — 198
Diagnostic Test • Algebraic Inequalities • Geometric Inequalities • Solutions to Tests and Exercises

15. Quantitative Comparisons — 210
Diagnostic Test • Solutions to Tests and Exercises

16. Practice Tests

Practice Test A — 225

Practice Test B — 237

Practice Test C — 247

Solutions to Practice Tests — 256

To The Student

The following text is designed as a self-teaching text in preparation for college entrance examinations. At the beginning of each chapter, you will find a diagnostic test consisting of ten questions. Try this test before you read the chapter. Answers will be found at the end of the chapter. If you get eight to ten questions right, you may skip that chapter and go right on to the next diagnostic test at the beginning of the following chapter. Or perhaps you would like to skim the instructional material anyway, just for review, but not bother with the practice exercises. If you get five to seven questions right, you might do the practice exercises only in the sections dealing with problems you missed. If you get less than five questions right, you need to work very carefully through the entire chapter.

After working through a specific chapter, you will find a similar test at the end. Try this and your score should now be almost perfect. Look once again at any instructional material dealing with errors you made before proceeding to the next section.

Working diligently through every chapter in this manner will strengthen your weaknesses and clear up any mathematical confusions. Completely worked-out solutions to all practice exercises will be given at the end of each chapter.

Operations with Integers and Decimals

DIAGNOSTIC TEST

Answers on page 13

1. Find the sum of 683, 72, and 5429
   (A) 5184   (B) 6184   (C) 6183   (D) 6193   (E) 6284

2. Subtract 417 from 804
   (A) 287   (B) 388   (C) 397   (D) 387   (E) 288

3. Find the product of 307 and 46
   (A) 3070   (B) 14,082   (C) 13,922   (D) 13,882   (E) 14,122

4. Divide 38,304 by 48
   (A) 787   (B) 798   (C) 824   (D) 1098   (E) 1253

5. Add 6.43 + 46.3 + .346
   (A) 14.52   (B) 53.779   (C) 53.392   (D) 53.076   (E) 1452

6. Subtract 81.763 from 145.1
   (A) 64.347   (B) 64.463   (C) 63.463   (D) 63.337   (E) 63.347

7. Multiply 3.47 by 2.3
   (A) 79.81   (B) 7.981   (C) 6.981   (D) 7.273   (E) 7.984

8. Divide 2.163 by .03
   (A) 7210   (B) 721   (C) 72.1   (D) 7.21   (E) 0.721

9. Find $3 - 16 \div 8 + 4 \times 2$
   (A) 9   (B) $2\frac{1}{3}$ (C) 10   (D) 18   (E) $\frac{2}{3}$

10. Which of the following is closest to $\frac{8317 \times 91}{217 \times .8}$?
    (A) 4   (B) 40   (C) 400   (D) 4000   (E) 40,000

In preparing for the mathematics section of your college entrance examination, it is most important to overcome any fear of mathematics.

2 OPERATIONS WITH INTEGERS AND DECIMALS

The level of this examination extends no further than relatively simple geometry. Most problems can be solved using only arithmetic. By reading this chapter carefully, following the sample problems, and then working on the practice problems in each section, you can review important concepts and vocabulary, as well as familiarize yourself with various types of questions. Since arithmetic is basic to any further work in mathematics, this chapter is extremely important and should not be treated lightly. By doing these problems carefully and reading the worked-out solutions, you can build the confidence needed to do well.

1. ADDITION OF INTEGERS

In the process of addition, the numbers to be added are called *addends*. The answer is called the *sum*. In writing an addition problem, put one number underneath the other, being careful to keep columns straight with the units' digits one below the other. If you find a sum by adding from top to bottom, you can check it by adding from bottom to top.

Example: Find the sum of 403, 37, 8314 and 5

Solution: 403
           37
         8314
            5
         ————
         8759

Practice 1

Answers on page 13

1. Find the sum of 360, 4352, 87, and 205

(A) 5013   (B) 5004   (C) 5003   (D) 6004   (E) 6013

2. Find the sum of 4321, 2143, 1234, and 3412

(A) 12,110   (B) 11,011   (C) 11,101   (D) 11,111   (E) 11,110

3. Add 56 + 321 + 8 + 42

(A) 427   (B) 437   (C) 517   (D) 417   (E) 527

4. Add 99 + 88 + 77 + 66 + 55

(A) 384   (B) 485   (C) 385   (D) 375   (E) 376

5. Add 1212 + 2323 + 3434 + 4545 + 5656

(A) 17,171   (B) 17,170   (C) 17,160   (D) 17,280   (E) 17,270

2. SUBTRACTION OF INTEGERS

The number from which we subtract is called the *minuend*. The number which we take away is called the *subtrahend*. The answer in subtraction is called the *difference*.

If 5 is subtracted from 11, the minuend is 11, the subtrahend is 5 and the difference is 6.

Since we cannot subtract a larger number from a smaller one, we often must borrow in performing a subtraction. Remember that when we borrow, because of our base 10 number system, we reduce the digit to the left by 1, but increase the right-hand digit by 10.

Example: 54
        − 38

Since we cannot subtract 8 from 4, we borrow 1 from 5 and change the 4 to 14. We are really borrowing 1 from the tens column and, therefore, add 10 to the ones column. Then we can subtract.

Solution: 4 ¹4
         − 3 8
         ─────
           1 6

Sometimes we must borrow across several columns.

Example: 503
        − 267

We cannot subtract 7 from 3 and cannot borrow from 0. Therefore we reduce the 5 by one and make the 0 into a 10. Then we can borrow 1 from the 10, making it a 9. This makes the 3 into 13.

Solution: 4 ¹0 3   4 9 ¹3
         − 2 6 7   − 2 6 7
                   ─────────
                     2 3 6

Practice 2   Answers on page 13

1. Subtract 803 from 952

(A) 248   (B) 148   (C) 249   (D) 149   (E) 147

2. From the sum of 837 and 415, subtract 1035

(A) 217   (B) 216   (C) 326   (D) 227   (E) 226

3. From 1872 subtract the sum of 76 and 43

(A) 1754   (B) 1838   (C) 1753   (D) 1839   (E) 1905

4. Find the difference between 237 and 732

(A) 496   (B) 495   (C) 486   (D) 405   (E) 497

5. By how much does the sum of 612 and 315 exceed the sum of 451 and 283?

(A) 294　(B) 1661　(C) 293　(D) 197　(E) 193

3. MULTIPLICATION OF INTEGERS

The answer to a multiplication problem is called the *product*. The number being multiplied is called a *factor* of the product.

When multiplying by a number containing two or more digits, place value is extremely important when writing partial products. When we multiply 537 by 72, for example, we multiply first by 2 and then by 7. However, when we multiply by 7, we are really multiplying by 70 and therefore leave a 0 at the extreme right before we proceed with the multiplication.

Example:
```
    537
     72
   1074
  37590
  38664
```

If we multiply by a three-digit number, we leave one zero on the right when multiplying by the tens digit and two zeros on the right when multiplying by the hundreds digit.

Example:
```
     372
     461
     372
   22320
  148800
  171492
```

Practice 3

Answers on page 14

Find the following products.

1. 526 multiplied by 317

(A) 156,742　(B) 165,742　(C) 166,742　(D) 166,748　(E) 166,708

2. 8347 multiplied by 62

(A) 517,514　(B) 517,414　(C) 517,504　(D) 517,114　(E) 617,114

3. 705 multiplied by 89

(A) 11,985　(B) 52,745　(C) 62,705　(D) 62,745　(E) 15,121

4. 437 multiplied by 607

(A) 265,259 (B) 265,219 (C) 265,359 (D) 265,059 (E) 262,059

5. 798 multiplied by 450

(A) 358,600 (B) 359,100 (C) 71,820 (D) 358,100 (E) 360,820

4. DIVISION OF INTEGERS

The number being divided is called the *dividend*. The number we are dividing by is called the *divisor*. The answer to the division is called the *quotient*. When we divide 18 by 6, 18 is the dividend, 6 is the divisor and 3 is the quotient. If the quotient is not an integer, we have a *remainder*. The remainder when 20 is divided by 6 is 2, because 6 will divide into 18 evenly, leaving a remainder of 2. The quotient in this case is $6\frac{2}{6}$. Remember that in writing the fractional part of a quotient involving a remainder, the remainder becomes the numerator and the divisor the denominator.

When dividing by a single-digit divisor, no long division procedures are needed. Simply carry the remainder of each step over to the next digit and continue.

Example: $6 \overline{)5\ 8^43^1 4^2 4}$ with quotient $9\ 7\ 2\ 4$

Practice 4

Answers on page 14

1. Divide 391 by 23

(A) 170   (B) 16   (C) 17   (D) 18   (E) 180

2. Divide 49,523,436 by 9

(A) 5,502,605   (B) 5,502,514   (C) 5,502,604
(D) 5,502,614   (E) 5,502,603

3. Find the remainder when 4832 is divided by 15

(A) 1   (B) 2   (C) 3   (D) 4   (E) 5

4. Divide 42,098 by 7

(A) 6014   (B) 6015   (C) 6019   (D) 6011   (E) 6010

5. Which of the following is the quotient of 333,180 and 617?

(A) 541   (B) 542   (C) 549   (D) 540   (E) 545

5. ADDITION OR SUBTRACTION OF DECIMALS

The most important thing to watch for in adding or subtracting decimals is to keep all decimal points underneath each other. The proper placement of the decimal point in the answer will be in line with all the decimal points above.

Example: Find the sum of 8.4, .37 and 2.641

Solution: 8.4
          .37
       2.641
     11.411

Example: From 48.3 subtract 27.56

Solution: 4 $\overset{7}{8}$. $\overset{12}{3}$ 10
         2 7 . 5 6
         2 0 . 7 4

In subtraction, the upper decimal must have as many decimal places as the lower, so we must fill in zeros where needed.

Practice 5

Answers on page 15

1. From the sum of .65, 4.2, 17.63, and 8, subtract 12.7
   (A) 9.78   (B) 17.68   (C) 17.78   (D) 17.79   (E) 18.78

2. Find the sum of .837, .12, 52.3, and .354
   (A) 53.503   (B) 53.611   (C) 53.601   (D) 54.601   (E) 54.611

3. From 561.8 subtract 34.75
   (A) 537.05   (B) 537.15   (C) 527.15   (D) 527.04   (E) 527.05

4. From 53.72 take the sum of 4.81 and 17.5
   (A) 31.86   (B) 31.41   (C) 41.03   (D) 66.41   (E) 41.86

5. Find the difference between 100 and 52.18
   (A) 37.82   (B) 47.18   (C) 47.92   (D) 47.82   (E) 37.92

6. MULTIPLICATION OF DECIMALS

In multiplying decimals, we proceed as we do with integers, using the decimal points only as an indication of where to place a decimal point in the product. The number of decimal places in the product is equal to the sum of the number of decimal places in the numbers being multiplied.

Example: Multiply .375 by .42

Solution: .375
            .42
            ───
            750
           15000
           ─────
           .15750

Since the first number being multiplied contains three decimal places and the second number contains two decimal places, the product will contain five decimal places.

To multiply a decimal by 10, 100, 1000, etc., we need only to move the decimal point to the right the proper number of places. In multiplying by 10, move one place to the right (10 has one zero), by 100 move two places to the right (100 has two zeros), by 1000 move three places to the right (1000 has three zeros), and so forth.

Example: The product of .837 and 100 is 83.7

Practice 6

Answers on page 15

Find the following products.

1. 437   (A) 1.0488   (B) 10.488   (C) 104.88
    .24   (D) 1048.8   (E) 10,488

2. 5.06   (A) .3542   (B) .392   (C)   3.92
    .7   (D) 3.542   (E) 35.42

3. 83   (A) 12.45   (B) 49.8   (C) 498
    1.5   (D) 124.5   (E) 1.245

4. .7314 (A) .007314   (B) .07314   (C) 7.314
    100   (D) 73.14   (E) 731.4

5. .0008 (A) .000344   (B) .00344   (C) .0344
    4.3   (D) 0.344   (E) 3.44

7. DIVISION OF DECIMALS

When dividing by a decimal, always change the decimal to an integer by moving the decimal point to the end of the divisor. Count the number of places you have moved the decimal point and move the dividend's decimal point the same number of places. The decimal point in the quotient will be directly above the one in the dividend.

Example: Divide 2.592 by .06

Solution: $.06 \overline{)2.592}$ = 43.2

To divide a decimal by 10, 100, 1000, etc., we move the decimal point the proper number of places to the *left*. The number of places to be moved is always equal to the number of zeros in the divisor.

Example: Divide 43.7 by 1000

Solution: The decimal point must be moved three places (there are three zeros in 1000) to the left. Therefore our quotient is .0437

Sometimes division can be done in fraction form. Always remember to move the decimal point to the end of the divisor (lower part of fraction) and then the same number of places in the dividend (upper part of fraction).

Example: Divide $\dfrac{.0175}{.05} = \dfrac{1.75}{5} = .35$

Practice 7

Answers on page 15

1. Divide 4.3 by 100

   (A) .0043   (B) 0.043   (C) 0.43   (D) 43   (E) 430

2. Find the quotient when 4.371 is divided by .3

   (A) 0.1457   (B) 1.457   (C) 14.57   (D) 145.7   (E) 1457

3. Divide .64 by .4

   (A) .0016   (B) 0.016   (C) 0.16   (D) 1.6   (E) 16

4. Find $.12 \div \dfrac{2}{.5}$

   (A) 4.8   (B) 48   (C) .03   (D) 0.3   (E) 3

5. Find $\dfrac{10.2}{.03} \div \dfrac{1.7}{.1}$

   (A) .02   (B) 0.2   (C) 2   (D) 20   (E) 200

8. THE LAWS OF ARITHMETIC

Addition and multiplication are *commutative* operations, as the order in which we add or multiply does not change an answer.

Example: $4 + 7 = 7 + 4$
$5 \cdot 3 = 3 \cdot 5$

Subtraction and division are not commutative, as changing the order does change the answer.

Example: $5 - 3 \neq 3 - 5$
$20 \div 5 \neq 5 \div 20$

Addition and multiplication are *associative*, as we may group in any manner and arrive at the same answer.

Example: $(3 + 4) + 5 = 3 + (4 + 5)$
$(3 \cdot 4) \cdot 5 = 3 \cdot (4 \cdot 5)$

Subtraction and division are not associative, as regrouping changes an answer.

Example: $(5 - 4) - 3 \neq 5 - (4 - 3)$
$(100 \div 20) \div 5 \neq 100 \div (20 \div 5)$

Multiplication is *distributive* over addition. If a sum is to be multiplied by a number, we may multiply each addend by the given number and add the results. This will give the same answer as if we had added first and then multiplied.

Example: $3(5 + 2 + 4)$ is either $15 + 6 + 12$ or $3(11)$.

The *identity for addition* is 0 since any number plus 0, or 0 plus any number, is equal to the given number.

The *identity for multiplication* is 1 since any number times 1, or 1 times any number, is equal to the given number.

There are no identity elements for subtraction or division. Although $5 - 0 = 5$, $0 - 5 \neq 5$. Although $8 \div 1 = 8$, $1 \div 8 \neq 8$.

When several operations are involved in a single problem, parentheses are usually included to make the order of operations clear. If there are no parentheses, multiplication and division are always performed prior to addition and subtraction.

Example: Find $5 \cdot 4 + 6 \div 2 - 16 \div 4$

Solution: The + and − signs indicate where groupings should begin and end. If we were to insert parentheses to clarify operations, we would have $(5 \cdot 4) + (6 \div 2) - (16 \div 4)$, giving $20 + 3 - 4 = 19$.

Practice 8

Answers on page 15

1. Find $8 + 4 \div 2 + 6 \cdot 3 - 1$
   (A) 35 (B) 47 (C) 43 (D) 27 (E) 88

2. $16 \div 4 + 2 \cdot 3 + 2 - 8 \div 2$
   (A) 6 (B) 8 (C) 2 (D) 4 (E) 10

3. Match each illustration in the left-hand column with the law it illustrates from the right-hand column.

   a. $475 \cdot 1 = 475$
   b. $75 + 12 = 12 + 75$
   c. $32(12 + 8) = 32(12) + 32(8)$
   d. $378 + 0 = 378$
   e. $(7 \cdot 5) \cdot 2 = 7 \cdot (5 \cdot 2)$

   u. Identity for Addition
   v. Associative Law of Addition
   w. Associative Law of Multiplication
   x. Identity for Multiplication
   y. Distributive Law of Multiplication over Addition
   z. Commutative Law of Addition

9. ESTIMATING ANSWERS

On a competitive examination, where time is an important factor, it is essential that you be able to estimate an answer. Simply round off all answers to the nearest multiples of 10 or 100 and estimate with the results. On multiple-choice tests, this should enable you to pick the correct answer without any time-consuming computation.

Example: The product of 498 and 103 is
(A) 5124 (B) 501,294 (C) 51,294
(D) 31,674 (E) 817,324

Solution: 498 is about 500. 103 is about 100. Therefore the product is about (500) (100) or 50,000 (Just move the decimal point two places to the right when multiplying by 100). Therefore the correct answer is C.

Example: Which of the following is closest to the value of
$$\frac{4831 \cdot 710}{2314}$$
(A) 83 (B) 425 (C) 1600 (D) 3140 (E) 6372

Solution: Estimating, we have $\frac{(5000)(700)}{2000}$. Dividing numerator and denominator by 1000, we have $\frac{5(700)}{2}$ or $\frac{3500}{2}$, which is about 1750. Therefore we choose answer C.

Practice 9

Answers on page 16

Choose the answer closest to the exact value of each of the following problems. Use estimation in your solutions. No written computation should be needed. Circle the letter before your answer.

1. $\dfrac{483 + 1875}{119}$

   (A) 2   (B) 10   (C) 20   (D) 50   (E) 100

2. $\dfrac{6017 \cdot 312}{364 + 618}$

   (A) 18   (B) 180   (C) 1800   (D) 18,000   (E) 180,000

3. $\dfrac{783 + 491}{1532 - 879}$

   (A) .02   (B) .2   (C) 2   (D) 20   (E) 200

Retest

Answers on page 16

1. Find the sum of 86, 4861, and 205
   (A) 5142   (B) 5132   (C) 5152   (D) 5052   (E) 4152

2. From 803 subtract 459
   (A) 454   (B) 444   (C) 354   (D) 344   (E) 346

3. Find the product of 65 and 908
   (A) 59,020   (B) 9988   (C) 58,920   (D) 58,020   (E) 59,920

4. Divide 66,456 by 72
   (A) 903   (B) 923   (C) 911   (D) 921   (E) 925

5. Find the sum of .361 + 8.7 + 43.17
   (A) 52.078   (B) 51.538   (C) 51.385   (D) 52.161   (E) 52.231

6. Subtract 23.17 from 50.9
   (A) 26.92   (B) 27.79   (C) 27.73   (D) 37.73   (E) 37.79

7. Multiply 8.35 by .43
   (A) 3.5805   (B) 3.5905   (C) 3.5915   (D) 35.905   (E) .35905

OPERATING WITH INTEGERS AND DECIMALS

8. Divide 2.937 by .11
   (A) .267   (B) 2.67   (C) 26.7   (D) 267   (E) 2670

9. Find $8 + 10 \div 2 + 4 \cdot 2 - 21 \div 7$
   (A) 17   (B) 23   (C) 18   (D) 14   (E) $\frac{5}{7}$

10. Which of the following is closest to $\dfrac{2875 + 932}{5817 \div 29}$
    (A) .2   (B) 2   (C) 20   (D) 200   (E) 2000

OPERATIONS WITH INTEGERS AND DECIMALS 13

SOLUTIONS TO PRACTICE EXERCISES

Diagnostic Test

1. (B) 683
        72
      5429
      ————
      6184

2. (D) $8\overset{79}{\cancel{04}}$
         417
         ———
         387

3. (E)   307
          46
        ————
        1842
       12280
       —————
       14,122

4. (B)   798
         48)38304
             336
             ———
             470
             432
             ———
             384
             384

5. (D) 6.43
       46.3
        .346
       ——————
       53.076

6. (D) $14\overset{4\,10\,9}{\cancel{5.1\cancel{0}0}}$
        81.763
        ——————
        63.337

7. (B)   3.47
          2.3
         ————
         1041
         6940
         ————
         7.981

8. (C)   72.1
        .03)2.163

9. (A) 3 − (16 ÷ 8) + (4 × 2) = 3 − 2 + 8 = 9

10. (D) Estimate $\dfrac{8000 \cdot 100}{200 \cdot 1}$ = 4000

Practice 1

1. (B) 360   2. (E) 4321   3. (A)   56   4. (C) 99
       4352   2143   321   88
         87   1234   8   77
        205   3412   42   66
       ————   ————   ———   55
       5004   11,110   427   ———
                                                              385

5. (B) 1212
        2323
        3434
        4545
        5656
       ——————
       17,170

Practice 2

1. (D) $9\overset{4}{\cancel{5}}{}^{1}2$ 2. (A)   837   3. (C)   76 $18\overset{6}{\cancel{7}}2$
         −803   +415   +43   −119
         ————   —————   ———   ————
          149                    $12\overset{4}{\cancel{5}}{}^{1}2$ 119   1753
                                 −1035
                                 —————
                                   217

14 OPERATING WITH INTEGERS AND DECIMALS

4. (B) $\overset{6\ \overset{12}{\cancel{3}}}{7\cancel{3}2}$
   -237
   $\overline{495}$

5. (E) 612
   $+315$
   $\overline{927}$

   451
   $+283$
   $\overline{734}$

   $\overset{8}{\cancel{9}}{}^{1}27$
   -734
   $\overline{193}$

Practice 3

1. (C) 526
   317
   ────
   3682
   5260
   157800
   ──────
   166,742

2. (A) 8347
   62
   ─────
   16694
   500820
   ──────
   517,514

3. (D) 705
   89
   ─────
   6345
   56400
   ─────
   62,745

4. (A) 437
   607
   ─────
   3059
   262200
   ──────
   265,259

5. (B) 798
   450
   ─────
   39900
   319200
   ──────
   359,100

Practice 4

1. (C) $\begin{array}{r}17\\23\overline{)391}\\\underline{23}\\161\\\underline{161}\end{array}$

2. (C) $\begin{array}{r}5{,}502{,}604\\9\overline{)49{,}523{,}436}\end{array}$

3. (B) $\begin{array}{r}322\text{ Remainder }2\\15\overline{)4832}\\\underline{45}\\33\\\underline{30}\\32\\\underline{30}\\2\end{array}$

4. (A) $\begin{array}{r}6014\\7\overline{)42098}\end{array}$

5. (D) Since the quotient, when multiplied by 617, must give 333,180 as an answer, the quotient must end in a number which, when multiplied by 617, will end in 0. This can only be (D), since 617 times (A) would end in 7, (B) would end in 4, (C) in 3, and (E) in 5.

OPERATIONS WITH INTEGERS AND DECIMALS   15

Practice 5

1. (C)   .65 $\overset{2\ 9}{\cancel{3}\cancel{0}}.48$ 2. (B)   .837   3. (E) $5\overset{5}{\cancel{6}}1.\overset{7}{\cancel{8}}\overset{}{1}0$
        4.2   −1 2.7 0   .12   3 4.7 5
       17.63   1 7.7 8   52.3   5 2 7.0 5
        8.   .354
       30.48   53.611

4. (B)   4.81   53.72   5. (D) $\overset{9\ 9\ 9}{1\cancel{0}\cancel{0}.\cancel{0}\cancel{0}}0$
        +17.5   − 22.31   − 5 2.1 8
        22.31   31.41   4 7.8 2

Practice 6

1. (C)   437   2. (D)   5.06   3. (D)   8 3
          .24   .7   1.5
         1748   3.542   41 5
         8740   83 0
        104.88   124.5

4. (D) .7314   Just move decimal point   5. (B)   .0008
         100   two places to right.   4.3
        73.14   24
                                                     320
                                                   .00344

Practice 7

1. (B) Just move decimal point two places to left, giving .043 as the answer.

2. (C) $\overset{14.57}{.3\overline{)4.371}}$ 3. (D) $\overset{1.6}{.4\overline{)64}}$

4. (C) $.12 \div \dfrac{2.0}{.5} = .12 \div 4 = .03$

5. (D) $\dfrac{10.20}{.03} \div \dfrac{1.7}{.1} = 340 \div 17 = 20$

Practice 8

1. (D) $8 + (4 \div 2) + (6 \cdot 3) - 1$
        $= 8 + 2 + 18 - 1 = 27$

16 OPERATING WITH INTEGERS AND DECIMALS

2. (B) $(16 \div 4) + (2 \cdot 3) + 2 - (8 \div 2)$
   $= 4 + 6 + 2 - 4 = 8$

3. $(a, x)(b, z)(c, y)(d, u)(e, w)$

Practice 9

1. (C) Estimate $\dfrac{500 + 2000}{100} = \dfrac{2500}{100}$

   $= 25$, closest to 20.

2. (C) Estimate $\dfrac{6000 \cdot 300}{400 + 600} = \dfrac{1{,}800{,}000}{1000}$

   $= 1800$

3. (C) Estimate $\dfrac{800 + 500}{1500 - 900} = \dfrac{1300}{600}$

   $=$ about 2

Retest

1. (C) 86
        4861
         205
        ────
        5152

2. (D) 803
         459
        ────
         344

3. (A)   908
           65
         ─────
          4540
         54480
         ─────
         59,020

4. (B) 923
     72)66456
        648
        ───
        165
        144
        ───
         216
         216

5. (E)   .361
        8.7
       43.17
       ─────
       52.231

6. (C) $0.90
        23.17
        ─────
        27.73

7. (B)   8.35
          .43
         ────
         2505
        33400
        ─────
        3.5905

8. (C)   26.7
       .11)2.937
            22
            ──
            73
            66
            ──
            77
            77

9. (C) $8 + (10 \div 2) + (4 \cdot 2) - (21 \div 7)$
   $= 8 + 5 + 8 - 3 = 18$

10. (C) Estimate $\dfrac{3000 + 1000}{6000 \div 30} = \dfrac{4000}{200} = 20$

Operations with Fractions

Work out each problem in the space provided. Circle the letter before your answer.

DIAGNOSTIC TEST

Answers on page 28

1. The sum of $\frac{3}{5}$, $\frac{2}{3}$ and $\frac{1}{4}$ is
 (A) $\frac{1}{2}$ (B) $\frac{27}{20}$ (C) $\frac{3}{2}$ (D) $\frac{91}{60}$ (E) $1\frac{5}{12}$

2. Subtract $\frac{3}{4}$ from $\frac{9}{10}$.
 (A) $\frac{3}{20}$ (B) 1 (C) $\frac{3}{5}$ (D) $\frac{3}{40}$ (E) $\frac{7}{40}$

3. The number 582,354 is divisible by
 (A) 4 (B) 5 (C) 8 (D) 9 (E) 10

4. $\frac{5}{6} \div (\frac{4}{3} \cdot \frac{5}{4})$ is equal to
 (A) 2 (B) $\frac{50}{36}$ (C) $\frac{1}{2}$ (D) $\frac{36}{50}$ (E) $\frac{7}{12}$

5. Subtract $32\frac{3}{5}$ from 57.
 (A) $24\frac{2}{5}$ (B) $25\frac{3}{5}$ (C) $25\frac{2}{5}$ (D) $24\frac{3}{5}$ (E) $24\frac{1}{5}$

6. Divide $4\frac{1}{2}$ by $1\frac{1}{8}$.
 (A) $\frac{1}{4}$ (B) 4 (C) $\frac{8}{9}$ (D) $\frac{9}{8}$ (E) $3\frac{1}{2}$

7. Which of the following fractions is the largest?
 (A) $\frac{1}{2}$ (B) $\frac{11}{16}$ (C) $\frac{5}{8}$ (D) $\frac{21}{32}$ (E) $\frac{3}{4}$

8. Which of the following fractions is closest to $\frac{2}{3}$?
 (A) $\frac{11}{15}$ (B) $\frac{7}{10}$ (C) $\frac{4}{5}$ (D) $\frac{1}{2}$ (E) $\frac{5}{6}$

17

18   OPERATIONS WITH FRACTIONS

9. Simplify $\dfrac{4 - \frac{9}{10}}{\frac{2}{3} + \frac{1}{2}}$.

(A) $\dfrac{93}{5}$ (B) $\dfrac{93}{35}$ (C) $\dfrac{147}{35}$ (D) $\dfrac{147}{5}$ (E) $\dfrac{97}{35}$

10. Find the value of $\dfrac{\frac{1}{a} + \frac{1}{b}}{\frac{1}{a} - \frac{1}{b}}$ when a = 3, b = 4.

(A) 7   (B) 2   (C) 1   (D) $\frac{1}{7}$ (E) $\frac{2}{7}$

1. ADDITION AND SUBTRACTION

To add or subtract fractions, they must have the same *denominator*. To add several fractions, this common denominator will be the least number into which each given denominator will divide evenly.

Example: Add $\frac{1}{2} + \frac{1}{3} + \frac{1}{4} + \frac{1}{5}$

Solution: The common denominator must contain two factors of 2 to accommodate the 4, and also a factor of 3 and one of 5. That makes the least common denominator 60. Change each fraction to sixtieths by dividing the given denominator into 60 and multiplying the quotient by the given numerator.

$$\frac{30}{60} + \frac{20}{60} + \frac{15}{60} + \frac{12}{60} = \frac{77}{60} = 1\frac{17}{60}$$

When only two fractions are being added, a shortcut method can be used: $\dfrac{a}{b} + \dfrac{c}{d} = \dfrac{ad + bc}{bd}$. That is, in order to add two fractions, add the two cross products and place this sum over the product of the given denominators.

Example: $\frac{4}{5} + \frac{7}{12}$

Solution: $\dfrac{4(12) + 5(7)}{5(12)} = \dfrac{48 + 35}{60} = \dfrac{83}{60} = 1\dfrac{23}{60}$

A similar shortcut applies to the subtraction of two fractions:

$$\dfrac{a}{b} - \dfrac{c}{d} = \dfrac{ad - bc}{bd}.$$

Example: $\dfrac{4}{5} - \dfrac{7}{12} = \dfrac{4(12) - 5(7)}{5(12)} = \dfrac{48 - 35}{60} = \dfrac{13}{60}$

Practice 1

Answers on page 28

Work out each problem in the space provided. Circle the letter before your answer.

1. The sum of $\frac{1}{2} + \frac{2}{3} + \frac{3}{4}$ is

   (A) $\frac{6}{9}$ (B) $\frac{23}{12}$ (C) $\frac{23}{36}$ (D) $\frac{6}{24}$ (E) $2\frac{1}{3}$

2. The sum of $\frac{5}{17}$ and $\frac{3}{15}$ is

   (A) $\frac{126}{255}$ (B) $\frac{40}{255}$ (C) $\frac{8}{32}$ (D) $\frac{40}{32}$ (E) $\frac{126}{265}$

3. From the sum of $\frac{3}{4}$ and $\frac{5}{6}$ take the sum of $\frac{1}{4}$ and $\frac{2}{3}$.

   (A) 2 (B) $\frac{1}{2}$ (C) $\frac{36}{70}$ (D) $\frac{2}{3}$ (E) $\frac{5}{24}$

4. Subtract $\frac{3}{5}$ from $\frac{9}{11}$.

   (A) $-\frac{12}{55}$ (B) $\frac{12}{55}$ (C) 1 (D) $\frac{3}{8}$ (E) $\frac{3}{4}$

5. Subtract $\frac{5}{8}$ from the sum of $\frac{1}{4}$ and $\frac{2}{3}$.

   (A) 2 (B) $\frac{3}{2}$ (C) $\frac{11}{24}$ (D) $\frac{8}{15}$ (E) $\frac{7}{24}$

2. MULTIPLICATION AND DIVISION

In multiplying fractions, always try to cancel any denominator with any numerator to keep your numbers as small as possible. Remember that if all numbers cancel in the numerator, you are left with a numerator of 1. The same goes for the denominator. If all numbers in both numerator and denominator cancel, you are left with $\frac{1}{1}$ or 1.

Example: Multiply $\frac{3}{5} \cdot \frac{15}{33} \cdot \frac{11}{45}$

Solution: $\dfrac{\cancel{3}}{5} \cdot \dfrac{\cancel{15}}{\cancel{33}} \cdot \dfrac{\cancel{11}}{\cancel{45}_{3}} = \dfrac{1}{15}$

In dividing fractions, we invert the number following the division sign and multiply.

Example: Divide $\frac{5}{18}$ by $\frac{5}{9}$

Solution: $\dfrac{\cancel{5}}{\cancel{18}_{2}} \cdot \dfrac{\cancel{9}}{\cancel{5}} = \dfrac{1}{2}$

OPERATIONS WITH FRACTIONS

Practice 2

Answers on page 29

Work out each problem in the space provided. Circle the letter before your answer.

1. Find the product of $\frac{3}{2}$, 6, $\frac{4}{9}$ and $\frac{1}{12}$.
   (A) 3   (B) $\frac{1}{3}$ (C) $\frac{14}{23}$ (D) $\frac{1}{36}$ (E) $\frac{5}{12}$

2. Find $\frac{7}{8} \cdot \frac{2}{3} \div \frac{1}{8}$.
   (A) $\frac{3}{14}$ (B) $\frac{7}{96}$ (C) $\frac{21}{128}$ (D) $\frac{14}{3}$ (E) $\frac{8}{3}$

3. $\frac{3}{5} \div (\frac{1}{2} \cdot \frac{3}{10})$ is equal to
   (A) 4   (B) $\frac{1}{4}$ (C) $\frac{12}{5}$ (D) $\frac{5}{12}$ (E) $\frac{12}{15}$

4. Find $\frac{2}{3}$ of $\frac{7}{12}$.
   (A) $\frac{7}{8}$ (B) $\frac{7}{9}$ (C) $\frac{8}{7}$ (D) $\frac{8}{9}$ (E) $\frac{7}{18}$

5. Divide 5 by $\frac{5}{12}$.
   (A) $\frac{25}{12}$ (B) $\frac{1}{12}$ (C) $\frac{5}{12}$ (D) 12   (E) $\frac{12}{5}$

3. REDUCING FRACTIONS

All fractional answers should be left in lowest terms. There should be no factor which can still be divided into numerator and denominator. In reducing fractions involving very large numbers, it is helpful to tell at a glance whether or not a given number will divide evenly into both numerator and denominator. Certain tests for divisibility assist with this.

If a number is divisible by	Then
2	it ends in 0, 2, 4, 6, or 8
3	the sum of the digits is divisible by 3
4	the number formed by the last 2 digits is divisible by 4
5	the numbers ends in 5 or 0
6	the number meets the tests for divisibility by 2 and 3
8	the number formed by the last 3 digits is divisible by 8
9	the sum of the digits is divisible by 9

OPERATIONS WITH FRACTIONS 21

Example: By what single digit number should we reduce $\frac{135,492}{428,376}$?

Solution: Since both numbers are even, they are at least divisible by 2. The sum of the digits in the numerator is 24. The sum of the digits in the denominator is 30. Since these sums are both divisible by 3, each number is divisible by 3. Since these numbers meet the divisibility tests for 2 and 3, they are each divisible by 6.

Example: Reduce to lowest terms: $\frac{43672}{52832}$

Solution: Since both numbers are even, they are at least divisible by 2. However, to save time, we would like to divide by a larger number. The sum of the digits in the numerator is 22, so it is not divisible by 3. The number formed by the last two digits of each number is divisible by 4, making the entire number divisible by 4. The numbers formed by the last three digits of each number is divisible by 8. Therefore, each number is divisible by 8. Dividing by 8, we have $\frac{5459}{6604}$

Since these numbers are no longer even and divisibility by 3 was ruled out earlier, there is no longer a single digit factor common to numerator and denominator. It is unlikely, at the level of this examination, that you will be called on to divide by a two-digit number.

Practice 3

Answers on page 29

Work out each problem in the space provided. Circle the letter before your answer.

1. Which of the following numbers is divisible by 5 and 9?

(A) 42,235   (B) 34,325   (C) 46,505   (D) 37,845   (E) 53,290

2. Given the number 83,21p, in order for this number to be divisible by 3, 6, and 9, p must be

(A) 4   (B) 5   (C) 6   (D) 0   (E) 9

3. If n! means n(n-1)(n-2) ... (4)(3)(2)(1), so that 4! = (4)(3)(2)(1) = 24, then 19! is divisible by

(I) 17   (II) 54   (III) 100   (IV) 39

(A) I and II only   (B) I only   (C) I and IV only
(D) I, II, III, and IV   (E) none of the above

4. The fraction $\frac{432}{801}$ can be reduced by dividing numerator and denominator by

(A) 2   (B) 4   (C) 6   (D) 8   (E) 9

5. The number 6,862,140 is divisible by

(I) 3   (II) 4   (III) 5

(A) I only   (B) I and III only   (C) II and III only
(D) I, II and III   (E) III only

4. OPERATIONS WITH MIXED NUMBERS

To add or subtract mixed numbers, it is again important to find common denominators. If it is necessary to borrow in subtraction, you must borrow in terms of the common denominator.

Example: $23\frac{1}{3} - 6\frac{2}{5}$

Solution: $23\frac{1}{3} = 23\frac{5}{15}$
$-6\frac{2}{5} = -6\frac{6}{15}$

Since we cannot subtract $\frac{6}{15}$ from $\frac{5}{15}$, we borrow $\frac{15}{15}$ from 23 and rewrite our problem as

$22\frac{20}{15}$
$-6\frac{6}{15}$

In this form, subtraction is possible, giving us an answer of $16\frac{14}{15}$.

Example: Add $17\frac{3}{4}$ to $43\frac{3}{5}$

Solution: Again we first change the fractions to a common denominator. This time it will be 20.

$17\frac{3}{4} = 17\frac{15}{20}$
$+43\frac{3}{5} = +43\frac{12}{20}$

When adding, we get a sum of $60\frac{27}{20}$, which we change to $61\frac{7}{20}$.

To multiply or divide mixed numbers, always change them to improper fractions first.

Example: Multiply $3\frac{3}{5} \cdot 1\frac{1}{9} \cdot 2\frac{3}{4}$

Solution: $\frac{\cancel{18}^2}{\cancel{5}} \cdot \frac{\cancel{10}^2}{\cancel{9}} \cdot \frac{11}{\cancel{4}_2} = 11$

Example: Divide $3\frac{3}{4}$ by $5\frac{5}{8}$

Solution: $\frac{15}{4} \div \frac{45}{8} = \frac{\cancel{15}}{\cancel{4}} \cdot \frac{\cancel{8}^{2}}{\cancel{45}_{3}} = \frac{2}{3}$

Practice 4

Answers on page 29

Work out each problem in the space provided. Circle the letter before your answer.

1. Find the sum of $1\frac{1}{6}$, $2\frac{2}{3}$ and $3\frac{3}{4}$.
   (A) $7\frac{5}{12}$ (B) $6\frac{6}{13}$ (C) $7\frac{7}{12}$ (D) $6\frac{1}{3}$ (E) $7\frac{1}{12}$

2. Subtract $45\frac{5}{12}$ from 61.
   (A) $15\frac{7}{12}$ (B) $15\frac{5}{12}$ (C) $16\frac{7}{12}$ (D) $16\frac{5}{12}$ (E) $17\frac{5}{12}$

3. Find the product of $32\frac{1}{2}$ and $5\frac{1}{5}$.
   (A) 26   (B) 13   (C) 169   (D) $160\frac{1}{10}$ (E) $160\frac{2}{7}$

4. Divide $17\frac{1}{2}$ by 70.
   (A) $\frac{1}{4}$ (B) 4   (C) $\frac{1}{2}$ (D) $4\frac{1}{2}$ (E) $\frac{4}{9}$

5. Find $1\frac{3}{4} \cdot 12 \div 8\frac{2}{5}$.
   (A) $\frac{2}{5}$ (B) $\frac{5}{288}$ (C) $2\frac{1}{5}$ (D) $\frac{1}{2}$ (E) $2\frac{1}{2}$

5. COMPARING FRACTIONS

There are two methods by which fractions may be compared to see which is larger (or smaller).

Method I—Change the fractions to the same denominator. When this is done, the fraction with the larger numerator is the larger fraction.

Example: Which is larger, $\frac{5}{6}$ or $\frac{8}{11}$?

Solution: The least common denominator is 66.

$\frac{5}{6} = \frac{55}{66}$ $\frac{8}{11} = \frac{48}{66}$

Therefore, $\frac{5}{6}$ is the larger fraction.

Method II—To compare $\frac{a}{b}$ with $\frac{c}{d}$, compare the cross products as follows:

If $ad > bc$, then $\frac{a}{b} > \frac{c}{d}$

24 OPERATIONS WITH FRACTIONS

If ad < bc, then $\frac{a}{b} < \frac{c}{d}$

If ad = bc, then $\frac{a}{b} = \frac{c}{d}$

Using the example above, to compare $\frac{5}{6}$ with $\frac{8}{11}$, compare 5 · 11 with 6 · 8. Since 5 · 11 is greater, $\frac{5}{6}$ is the larger fraction.

Sometimes, a combination of these methods must be used in comparing a series of fractions. When a common denominator can be found easily for a series of fractions, Method I is easier. When a common denominator would result in a very large number, Method II is easier.

Example: Which of the following fractions is the largest?

(A) $\frac{3}{5}$ (B) $\frac{21}{32}$ (C) $\frac{11}{16}$ (D) $\frac{55}{64}$ (E) $\frac{7}{8}$

Solution: To compare the last four, we can easily use a common denominator of 64.

$\frac{21}{32} = \frac{42}{64}$ $\frac{11}{16} = \frac{44}{64}$ $\frac{55}{64}$ $\frac{7}{8} = \frac{56}{64}$

The largest of these is $\frac{7}{8}$. Now we compare $\frac{7}{8}$ with $\frac{3}{5}$ using Method II. 7 · 5 > 8 · 3, therefore $\frac{7}{8}$ is the greatest fraction.

Practice 5

Answers on page 30

Work out each problem in the space provided. Circle the letter before your answer.

1. Arrange these fractions in order of size, from largest to smallest: $\frac{4}{15}$, $\frac{2}{5}$, $\frac{1}{3}$.

(A) $\frac{4}{15}$, $\frac{2}{5}$, $\frac{1}{3}$　　(B) $\frac{4}{15}$, $\frac{1}{3}$, $\frac{2}{5}$　　(C) $\frac{2}{5}$, $\frac{1}{3}$, $\frac{4}{15}$
(D) $\frac{1}{3}$, $\frac{4}{15}$, $\frac{2}{5}$　　(E) $\frac{1}{3}$, $\frac{2}{5}$, $\frac{4}{15}$

2. Which of the following fractions is the smallest?

(A) $\frac{3}{4}$　　(B) $\frac{5}{6}$　　(C) $\frac{7}{8}$　　(D) $\frac{19}{24}$　　(E) $\frac{13}{15}$

3. Which of the following fractions is the largest?

(A) $\frac{3}{5}$　　(B) $\frac{7}{10}$　　(C) $\frac{5}{8}$　　(D) $\frac{3}{4}$　　(E) $\frac{13}{20}$

4. Which of the following fractions is closest to $\frac{3}{4}$?

(A) $\frac{1}{2}$　　(B) $\frac{7}{12}$　　(C) $\frac{5}{6}$　　(D) $\frac{11}{12}$　　(E) $\frac{19}{24}$

5. Which of the following fractions is closest to $\frac{1}{2}$?

(A) $\frac{5}{12}$　　(B) $\frac{8}{15}$　　(C) $\frac{11}{20}$　　(D) $\frac{31}{60}$　　(E) $\frac{7}{15}$

6. COMPLEX FRACTIONS

To simplify complex fractions, fractions which contain fractions within them, multiply every term by the lowest number needed to clear all fractions in the given numerator and denominator.

Example: $\dfrac{\frac{1}{6} + \frac{1}{4}}{\frac{1}{2} + \frac{1}{3}}$

Solution: The lowest number into which 6, 4, 2 and 3 will divide is 12. Therefore, multiply every term of the fraction by 12 to simplify the fraction.

$$\frac{2+3}{6+4} = \frac{5}{10} = \frac{1}{2}$$

Example: $\dfrac{\frac{3}{4} - \frac{2}{3}}{1 + \frac{1}{2}}$

Solution: Again, we multiply every term by 12. Be sure to multiply the 1 by 12 also.

$$\frac{9-8}{12+6} = \frac{1}{18}$$

Practice 6

Answers on page 30

Work out each problem in the space provided. Circle the letter before your answer.

1. Write as a fraction in lowest terms: $\dfrac{\frac{2}{3} + \frac{1}{6} + \frac{1}{4}}{\frac{2}{3} - \frac{1}{2}}$

   (A) $\frac{13}{2}$ (B) $\frac{7}{2}$ (C) $\frac{13}{14}$ (D) $\frac{4}{13}$ (E) $\frac{49}{12}$

2. Simplify: $\dfrac{\frac{5}{6} - \frac{2}{3}}{\frac{5}{12} - \frac{1}{6}}$

   (A) $\frac{5}{12}$ (B) $\frac{5}{6}$ (C) $\frac{2}{3}$ (D) $\frac{1}{6}$ (E) $\frac{7}{12}$

3. Find the value of $\dfrac{\frac{1}{a} + \frac{1}{b}}{\frac{1}{ab}}$ when a = 2 and b = 3.

   (A) $\frac{5}{6}$ (B) 5   (C) $4\frac{1}{6}$ (D) $1\frac{1}{5}$ (E) $2\frac{2}{5}$

26 OPERATIONS WITH FRACTIONS

4. Find the value of $\dfrac{\frac{1}{a} + \frac{1}{b}}{\frac{1}{ab}}$ when $a = \frac{1}{2}$ and $b = \frac{1}{3}$.

   (A) $\frac{5}{6}$ (B) 5 (C) $4\frac{1}{6}$ (D) $1\frac{1}{5}$ (E) $2\frac{2}{5}$

5. Find the value of $\dfrac{2\frac{1}{3}}{5\frac{1}{2} + 3\frac{1}{3}}$.

   (A) $\frac{4}{17}$ (B) $\frac{21}{25}$ (C) $\frac{7}{6}$ (D) $\frac{12}{51}$ (E) $\frac{14}{53}$

Retest

Answers on page 30

Work out each problem in the space provided. Circle the letter before your answer.

1. The sum of $\frac{4}{5}$, $\frac{3}{4}$ and $\frac{1}{3}$ is

   (A) $\frac{8}{12}$ (B) $\frac{113}{60}$ (C) $\frac{1}{5}$ (D) $\frac{10}{9}$ (E) $\frac{11}{6}$

2. Subtract $\frac{2}{3}$ from $\frac{11}{15}$.

   (A) $\frac{3}{4}$ (B) $\frac{7}{5}$ (C) $\frac{5}{7}$ (D) $\frac{1}{15}$ (E) $\frac{1}{3}$

3. If 52,34p is divisible by 9, the digit represented by p must be

   (A) 1   (B) 2   (C) 3   (D) 4   (E) 5

4. $(\frac{3}{5} + \frac{1}{4}) \div \frac{34}{15}$ is equal to

   (A) $\frac{5}{3}$ (B) $\frac{5}{8}$ (C) $\frac{8}{3}$ (D) $\frac{8}{5}$ (E) $\frac{3}{8}$

5. Subtract $62\frac{2}{3}$ from 100.

   (A) $37\frac{1}{3}$ (B) $38\frac{1}{3}$ (C) $37\frac{2}{3}$ (D) $38\frac{2}{3}$ (E) $28\frac{2}{3}$

6. Divide $2\frac{2}{5}$ by $4\frac{8}{10}$.

   (A) 2   (B) $\frac{1}{2}$ (C) $\frac{288}{25}$ (D) $\frac{25}{288}$ (E) $2\frac{1}{4}$

7. Which of the following fractions is the smallest?

   (A) $\frac{7}{12}$ (B) $\frac{8}{15}$ (C) $\frac{11}{20}$ (D) $\frac{5}{6}$ (E) $\frac{2}{3}$

8. Which of the following fractions is closest to $\frac{1}{4}$?

   (A) $\frac{4}{15}$ (B) $\frac{3}{10}$ (C) $\frac{3}{20}$ (D) $\frac{1}{5}$ (E) $\frac{1}{10}$

9. Simplify: $\dfrac{\frac{5}{2} + \frac{2}{3}}{\frac{3}{4} + \frac{5}{6}}$

(A) 2 (B) $\frac{1}{2}$ (C) 12 (D) $\frac{1}{4}$ (E) 4

10. Find the value of $\dfrac{\frac{1}{ab}}{\frac{1}{a} + \frac{1}{b}}$ when a = 4, b = 5.

(A) 9 (B) 20 (C) $\frac{1}{9}$ (D) $\frac{1}{20}$ (E) $\frac{9}{40}$

SOLUTIONS TO PRACTICE EXERCISES

Diagnostic Test

1. **(D)** Change all fractions to sixtieths.
$$\frac{36}{60} + \frac{40}{60} + \frac{15}{60} = \frac{91}{60}$$

2. **(A)** $\dfrac{9}{10} - \dfrac{3}{4} = \dfrac{36 - 30}{40} = \dfrac{6}{40} = \dfrac{3}{20}$

3. **(D)** The sum of the digits is 27, which is divisible by 9.

4. **(C)** $\dfrac{5}{6} \div \left(\dfrac{4}{3} \cdot \dfrac{5}{4}\right) = \dfrac{5}{6} \div \dfrac{5}{3} = \dfrac{\cancel{5}}{\cancel{6}_2} \cdot \dfrac{\cancel{3}}{\cancel{5}} = \dfrac{1}{2}$

5. **(A)** $\begin{aligned} 57 &= 56\tfrac{5}{5} \\ 32\tfrac{3}{5} &= 32\tfrac{3}{5} \\ \hline &24\tfrac{2}{5} \end{aligned}$

6. **(B)** $\dfrac{9}{2} \div \dfrac{9}{8} = \dfrac{\cancel{9}}{\cancel{2}_1} \cdot \dfrac{\cancel{8}^4}{\cancel{9}} = 4$

7. **(E)** Use a common denominator of 32.

$\dfrac{1}{2} = \dfrac{16}{32}$ $\dfrac{11}{16} = \dfrac{22}{32}$ $\dfrac{5}{8} = \dfrac{20}{32}$ $\dfrac{21}{32}$

$\dfrac{3}{4} = \dfrac{24}{32}$

Of these, $\dfrac{3}{4}$ is the largest.

8. **(B)** Use a common denominator of 30.

$\dfrac{11}{15} = \dfrac{22}{30}$ $\dfrac{7}{10} = \dfrac{21}{30}$ $\dfrac{4}{5} = \dfrac{24}{30}$ $\dfrac{1}{2} = \dfrac{15}{30}$

$\dfrac{5}{6} = \dfrac{25}{30}$

Since $\dfrac{2}{3} = \dfrac{20}{30}$, the answer closest to $\dfrac{2}{3}$ is $\dfrac{7}{10}$.

9. **(B)** Multiply every term of the fraction by 30.
$$\dfrac{120 - 27}{20 + 15} = \dfrac{93}{35}$$

10. **(A)** $\dfrac{\tfrac{1}{3} + \tfrac{1}{4}}{\tfrac{1}{3} - \tfrac{1}{4}}$

Multiply every term by 12.
$$\dfrac{4 + 3}{4 - 3} = 7$$

Practice 1

1. **(B)** Change all fractions to twelfths.
$$\dfrac{6}{12} + \dfrac{8}{12} + \dfrac{9}{12} = \dfrac{23}{12}$$

2. **(A)** Use the cross product method.
$$\dfrac{5(15) + 17(3)}{17(15)} = \dfrac{75 + 51}{255} = \dfrac{126}{255}$$

3. **(D)** $\dfrac{3}{4} + \dfrac{5}{6} = \dfrac{18 + 20}{24} = \dfrac{38}{24} = \dfrac{19}{12}$

$\dfrac{1}{4} + \dfrac{2}{3} = \dfrac{3 + 8}{12} = \dfrac{11}{12}$

$\dfrac{19}{12} - \dfrac{11}{12} = \dfrac{8}{12} = \dfrac{2}{3}$

4. **(B)** $\dfrac{9}{11} - \dfrac{3}{5} = \dfrac{45 - 33}{55} = \dfrac{12}{55}$

5. **(E)** $\dfrac{1}{4} + \dfrac{2}{3} = \dfrac{3 + 8}{12} = \dfrac{11}{12}$

$\dfrac{11}{12} - \dfrac{5}{8} = \dfrac{88 - 60}{96} = \dfrac{28}{96} = \dfrac{7}{24}$

OPERATIONS WITH FRACTIONS   29

Practice 2

1. (B) $\dfrac{\cancel{2}}{\cancel{2}} \cdot \dfrac{\cancel{6}}{1} \cdot \dfrac{\cancel{4}^{\,2}}{\cancel{9}_{\,3}} \cdot \dfrac{1}{\cancel{12}_{\,2}} = \dfrac{1}{3}$

2. (D) $\dfrac{7}{\cancel{8}} \cdot \dfrac{2}{3} \cdot \dfrac{\cancel{8}}{1} = \dfrac{14}{3}$

3. (A) $\dfrac{3}{5} \div \dfrac{3}{20}$

   $\dfrac{\cancel{3}}{\cancel{5}} \cdot \dfrac{\cancel{20}^{\,4}}{\cancel{3}} = 4$

4. (E) $\dfrac{\cancel{2}}{3} \cdot \dfrac{7}{\cancel{12}_{\,6}} = \dfrac{7}{18}$

5. (D) $\dfrac{\cancel{5}}{1} \cdot \dfrac{12}{\cancel{5}} = 12$

Practice 3

1. (D) The digits must add to a number divisible by 9. All answers are divisible by 5. $3+7+8+4+5 = 27$, which is divisible by 9.

2. (A) The sum of the digits must be divisible by 9 and the digit must be even. $8+3+2+1 = 14$. Therefore, we choose (A) because $14 + 4 = 18$, which is divisible by 9.

3. (D) $19! = 19 \cdot 18 \cdot 17 \cdot 16 \ldots 3 \cdot 2 \cdot 1$. This is divisible by 17, since it contains a factor of 17. It is divisible by 54, since it contains factors of 9 and 6. It is divisible by 100, since it contains factors of 10, 5, and 2. It is divisible by 39, since it contains factors of 13 and 3.

4. (E) The sum of the digits in both the numerator and denominator are divisible by 9.

5. (D) The sum of the digits is 27, which is divisible by 3. The number formed by the last two digits is 40, which is divisible by 4. The number ends in 0 and is therefore divisible by 5.

Practice 4

1. (C) $1\frac{1}{6} = 1\frac{2}{12}$
   $2\frac{2}{3} = 2\frac{8}{12}$
   $3\frac{3}{4} = 3\frac{9}{12}$
   $\overline{6\frac{19}{12}} = 7\frac{7}{12}$

2. (A) $61 \phantom{\tfrac{5}{12}} = 60\frac{12}{12}$
   $\underline{45\frac{5}{12} = 45\frac{5}{12}}$
   $15\frac{7}{12}$

3. (C) $\dfrac{\cancel{65}^{\,13}}{\cancel{2}} \cdot \dfrac{\cancel{26}^{\,13}}{\cancel{5}} = 169$

4. (A) $17\dfrac{1}{2} \div 70 = \dfrac{35}{2} \div 70 = \dfrac{\cancel{35}}{2} \cdot \dfrac{1}{\cancel{70}_{\,2}} = \dfrac{1}{4}$

5. (E) $\dfrac{\cancel{7}}{\cancel{4}} \cdot \dfrac{\cancel{12}^{\,3}}{1} \cdot \dfrac{5}{\cancel{42}_{\,2}} = \dfrac{5}{2} = 2\frac{1}{2}$

Practice 5

1. (C) $\frac{2}{5} = \frac{6}{15}$ $\quad \frac{1}{3} = \frac{5}{15}$

2. (A) To compare (A), (B), (C), and (D), use a common denominator of 24.

   $\frac{3}{4} = \frac{18}{24}$ $\quad \frac{5}{6} = \frac{20}{24}$ $\quad \frac{7}{8} = \frac{21}{24}$ $\quad \frac{19}{24}$

   Of these, $\frac{3}{4}$ is the smallest. To compare $\frac{3}{4}$ with $\frac{13}{15}$, use cross products. Since $(3)(15) < (4)(14)$, $\frac{3}{4} < \frac{13}{15}$. Therefore, (A) is the smallest.

3. (D) To compare (A), (B), (D), and (E), use a common denominator of 20.

   $\frac{3}{5} = \frac{12}{20}$ $\quad \frac{7}{10} = \frac{14}{20}$ $\quad \frac{3}{4} = \frac{15}{20}$ $\quad \frac{13}{20}$

   Of these, $\frac{3}{4}$ is the largest. To compare $\frac{3}{4}$ with $\frac{5}{8}$ use cross products. Since $(3)(8) > (4)(5)$, $\frac{3}{4}$ is the larger fraction.

4. (E) Use a common denominator of 24.

   $\frac{1}{2} = \frac{12}{24}$ $\quad \frac{7}{12} = \frac{14}{24}$ $\quad \frac{5}{6} = \frac{20}{24}$ $\quad \frac{11}{12} = \frac{22}{24}$

   $\frac{19}{24}$

   Since $\frac{3}{4} = \frac{18}{24}$, the answer closest to $\frac{3}{4}$ is (E), $\frac{19}{24}$.

5. (D) Use a common denominator of 60.

   $\frac{5}{12} = \frac{25}{60}$ $\quad \frac{8}{15} = \frac{32}{60}$ $\quad \frac{11}{20} = \frac{33}{60}$ $\quad \frac{31}{60}$

   $\frac{7}{15} = \frac{28}{60}$

   Since $\frac{1}{2} = \frac{30}{60}$, the answer closest to $\frac{1}{2}$ is (D), $\frac{31}{60}$.

Practice 6

1. (A) Multiply every term of the fraction by 12.

   $$\frac{8 + 2 + 3}{8 - 6} = \frac{13}{2}$$

2. (C) Multiply every term of the fraction by 12.

   $$\frac{10 - 8}{5 - 2} = \frac{2}{3}$$

3. (B) $\frac{\frac{1}{2} + \frac{1}{3}}{\frac{1}{6}}$ Multiply every term by 6.

   $$\frac{3 + 2}{1} = 5$$

4. (A) $\frac{1}{\frac{1}{2}} = 2$ $\quad \frac{1}{\frac{1}{3}} = 3$ $\quad \frac{1}{\frac{1}{6}} = 6$

   $$\frac{2 + 3}{6} = \frac{5}{6}$$

5. (E) $\frac{\frac{7}{3}}{\frac{11}{2} + \frac{10}{3}}$ Multiply every term by 6.

   $$\frac{14}{33 + 20} = \frac{14}{53}$$

Retest

1. (B) Change all fractions to sixtieths.

   $\frac{48}{60} + \frac{45}{60} + \frac{20}{60} = \frac{113}{60}$

2. (D) $\frac{11}{15} - \frac{2}{3} = \frac{11}{15} - \frac{10}{15} = \frac{1}{15}$

3. (D) The sum of the digits must be divisible by 9. $5 + 2 + 3 + 4 + 4 = 18$, which is divisible by 9.

OPERATIONS WITH FRACTIONS 31

4. (E) $\frac{17}{20} \div \frac{34}{15}$

$$\frac{\cancel{17}^1}{\cancel{20}_4} \cdot \frac{\cancel{15}^3}{\cancel{34}_2} = \frac{3}{8}$$

5. (A) $100 = 99\frac{3}{3}$
$ 62\frac{2}{3} = 62\frac{2}{3}$
$\phantom{(A) 100 62\frac{2}{3} =} \overline{37\frac{1}{3}}$

6. (B) $\frac{12}{5} \div \frac{48}{10} = \frac{\cancel{12}^1}{\cancel{5}_1} \cdot \frac{\cancel{10}^2}{\cancel{48}_4} = \frac{2}{4} = \frac{1}{2}$

7. (B) Use a common denominator of 60.

$\frac{7}{12} = \frac{35}{60}$ $\quad \frac{8}{15} = \frac{32}{60}$ $\quad \frac{11}{20} = \frac{33}{60}$ $\quad \frac{5}{6} = \frac{50}{60}$

$\frac{2}{3} = \frac{40}{60}$

Of these, $\frac{8}{15}$ is the smallest.

8. (A) Use a common denominator of 60.

$\frac{4}{15} = \frac{16}{60}$ $\quad \frac{3}{10} = \frac{18}{60}$ $\quad \frac{3}{20} = \frac{9}{60}$

$\frac{1}{5} = \frac{12}{60}$ $\quad \frac{1}{10} = \frac{6}{60}$

Since $\frac{1}{4} = \frac{15}{60}$, the answer closest to $\frac{1}{4}$ is $\frac{4}{15}$.

9. (A) Multiply every term of the fraction by 12.

$$\frac{30+8}{9+10} = \frac{38}{19} = 2$$

10. (C) $\dfrac{\frac{1}{20}}{\frac{1}{4} + \frac{1}{5}}$

Multiply every term by 20.

$$\frac{1}{5+4} = \frac{1}{9}$$

Verbal Problems Involving Fractions

DIAGNOSTIC TEST

Answers on page 40

Work out each problem in the space provided. Circle the letter before your answer.

1. On Monday evening, Channel 2 scheduled 2 hours of situation comedy, 1 hour of news and 3 hours of movies. What part of the evening's programming was devoted to situation comedy?

   (A) $\frac{1}{3}$ (B) $\frac{2}{3}$ (C) $\frac{1}{2}$ (D) $\frac{1}{6}$ (E) $\frac{2}{5}$

2. What part of a gallon is 2 qt. 1 pt.?

   (A) $\frac{3}{4}$ (B) $\frac{3}{10}$ (C) $\frac{1}{2}$ (D) $\frac{5}{8}$ (E) $\frac{3}{8}$

3. Michelle spent $\frac{1}{2}$ of her summer vacation at camp, $\frac{1}{5}$ of her vacation babysitting and $\frac{1}{4}$ visiting her grandmother. What part of her vacation was left to relax at home?

   (A) $\frac{1}{5}$ (B) $\frac{1}{20}$ (C) $\frac{1}{3}$ (D) $\frac{3}{20}$ (E) $\frac{1}{6}$

4. After doing $\frac{1}{3}$ of the family laundry before breakfast, Mrs. Strauss did $\frac{3}{4}$ of the remainder before lunch. What part of the laundry was left for the afternoon?

   (A) $\frac{1}{2}$ (B) $\frac{1}{4}$ (C) $\frac{2}{3}$ (D) $\frac{1}{5}$ (E) $\frac{1}{6}$

5. Glenn spent $\frac{2}{5}$ of his allowance on a hit record. He then spent $\frac{2}{3}$ of the remainder on a gift. What part of his allowance did he have left?

   (A) $\frac{1}{5}$ (B) $\frac{1}{3}$ (C) $\frac{2}{5}$ (D) $\frac{3}{20}$ (E) $\frac{1}{10}$

6. Barbara's car has a gasoline tank which holds 20 gallons. When her gauge reads $\frac{1}{4}$ full, how many gallons are needed to fill the tank?

   (A) 5   (B) 10   (C) 15   (D) 12   (E) 16

VERBAL PROBLEMS INVOLVING FRACTIONS

7. 42 seniors voted to hold the prom at the Copacabana. This represents $\frac{2}{9}$ of the senior class. How many seniors did not vote for the Copacabana?

(A) 147 (B) 101 (C) 189 (D) 105 (E) 126

8. Steve needs M hours to mow the lawn. After working for X hours, what part of the job remains to be done?

(A) $\frac{M-X}{M}$ (B) $\frac{M-X}{X}$ (C) M - X (D) X - M (E) $\frac{X}{M}$

9. Of D dogs in Mrs. Pace's kennel, $\frac{1}{3}$ are classified as large dogs and $\frac{1}{4}$ of the remainder are classified as medium-sized. How many of the dogs are classified as small?

(A) $\frac{1}{2}D$ (B) $\frac{1}{6}D$ (C) $\frac{5}{6}D$ (D) $\frac{2}{3}D$ (E) $\frac{1}{3}D$

10. A bookshelf contains A autobiographies and B biographies. What part of these books are biographies?

(A) $\frac{B}{A}$ (B) $\frac{B}{A+B}$ (C) $\frac{A}{A+B}$ (D) $\frac{A}{B}$ (E) $\frac{B}{A-B}$

A fraction represents a part of a whole. In dealing with fractional problems, we are usually dealing with a part of a quantity.

> Example: Andrea and Danny ran for president of the Math Club. Andrea got 15 votes, while Danny got the other 10. What part of the votes did Andrea receive?
>
> Solution: Andrea got 15 votes out of 25. That is $\frac{15}{25}$ or $\frac{3}{5}$ of the votes.

Practice 1

Answers on page 40

Work out each problem in the space provided. Circle the letter before your answer.

1. In a class there are 18 boys and 12 girls. What part of the class is girls?

(A) $\frac{2}{3}$ (B) $\frac{3}{5}$ (C) $\frac{2}{5}$ (D) $\frac{1}{15}$ (E) $\frac{3}{2}$

2. A team played 40 games and lost 6. What part of the games played did it win?

(A) $\frac{3}{20}$ (B) $\frac{3}{17}$ (C) $\frac{14}{17}$ (D) $\frac{17}{20}$ (E) $\frac{7}{8}$

3. What part of an hour elapses between 3:45 P.M. and 4:09 P.M.?

(A) $\frac{6}{25}$ (B) $\frac{2}{5}$ (C) $\frac{5}{12}$ (D) $\frac{1}{24}$ (E) 24

VERBAL PROBLEMS INVOLVING FRACTIONS

4. A camp employs 4 men, 6 women, 12 girls, and 8 boys. In the middle of the summer, 3 girls are fired and replaced by women. What part of the staff is then made up of women?

(A) $\frac{1}{5}$ (B) $\frac{2}{9}$ (C) $\frac{1}{3}$ (D) $\frac{3}{10}$ (E) $\frac{1}{2}$

5. There are three times as many seniors as juniors at a high school Junior-Senior dance. What part of the students present are juniors?

(A) $\frac{2}{5}$ (B) $\frac{3}{5}$ (C) $\frac{2}{3}$ (D) $\frac{3}{4}$ (E) $\frac{1}{4}$

6. What part of a yard is 1 ft. 3 in.?

(A) $\frac{5}{12}$ (B) $\frac{1}{3}$ (C) $\frac{1}{2}$ (D) $\frac{5}{8}$ (E) $\frac{4}{9}$

7. Manorville High had a meeting of the Student Senate, which was attended by 10 freshmen, 8 sophomores, 15 juniors, and 7 seniors. What part of the students present at the meeting were sophomores?

(A) $\frac{1}{4}$ (B) $\frac{5}{8}$ (C) $\frac{7}{40}$ (D) $\frac{1}{5}$ (E) $\frac{1}{3}$

8. The Dobkin family budgets its monthly income as follows: $\frac{1}{3}$ for food, $\frac{1}{4}$ for rent, $\frac{1}{10}$ for clothing and $\frac{1}{5}$ for savings. What part is left for other expenses?

(A) $\frac{3}{7}$ (B) $\frac{1}{6}$ (C) $\frac{7}{60}$ (D) $\frac{2}{15}$ (E) $\frac{3}{20}$

Many problems require you to find a fractional part of a fractional part, such as $\frac{3}{4}$ of $\frac{2}{3}$. This involves multiplying the fractions together. $\frac{3}{4}$ of $\frac{2}{3}$ is $\frac{1}{2}$.

Example: $\frac{1}{4}$ of the employees of Mr. Brown's firm earn over $20,000 per year. $\frac{1}{2}$ of the remainder earn between $15,000 and $20,000. What part of the employees earn less than $15,000 per year?

Solution: $\frac{1}{4}$ earn over $20,000. $\frac{1}{2}$ of $\frac{3}{4}$ or $\frac{3}{8}$ earn between $15,000 and $20,000. That accounts for $\frac{1}{4} + \frac{3}{8}$ or $\frac{5}{8}$ of all employees. Therefore the other $\frac{3}{8}$ earn less than $15,000.

Example: A full bottle of alcohol is left open in the school laboratory. If $\frac{1}{3}$ of the alcohol evaporates in the first 12 hours and $\frac{2}{3}$ of the remainder evaporates in the second 12 hours, what part of the bottle is full at the end of 24 hours?

Solution: $\frac{1}{3}$ evaporates during the first 12 hours. $\frac{2}{3}$ of $\frac{2}{3}$ or $\frac{4}{9}$ evaporates during the second 12 hours. This accounts for $\frac{7}{9}$ of the alcohol. Therefore $\frac{2}{9}$ of the bottle is still full.

Practice 2

Answers on page 41

Work out each problem in the space provided. Circle the letter before your answer.

1. Mrs. Natt spent $\frac{2}{3}$ of the family income one year and divided the remainder between 4 different savings banks. If she put $2000 into each bank, what was the amount of her family income that year?

(A) $8000 (B) $16,000 (C) $24,000 (D) $32,000 (E) $6000

2. After selling $\frac{2}{5}$ of the suits in his shop before Christmas, Mr. Gross sold the remainder of the suits at the same price per suit after Christmas for $4500. What was the income from the entire stock?

(A) $3000 (B) $7500 (C) $1800 (D) $2700 (E) $8000

3. Of this year's graduating seniors at South High, $\frac{9}{10}$ will be going to college. Of these, $\frac{4}{5}$ will go to four-year colleges, while the rest will be going to two-year colleges. What part of the class will be going to two-year colleges?

(A) $\frac{9}{50}$ (B) $\frac{1}{5}$ (C) $\frac{4}{5}$ (D) $\frac{36}{50}$ (E) $\frac{4}{25}$

4. Sue and Judy drove from New York to San Francisco, a distance of 3000 miles. They covered $\frac{1}{10}$ of the distance the first day and $\frac{2}{9}$ of the remaining distance the second day. How many miles were left to be driven?

(A) 600 (B) 2000 (C) 2400 (D) 2100 (E) 2700

5. 800 employees work for the Metropolitan Transportation Company. $\frac{1}{4}$ of these are college graduates, while $\frac{5}{6}$ of the remainder are high school graduates. What part of the employees never graduated from high school?

(A) $\frac{1}{6}$ (B) $\frac{1}{8}$ (C) $\frac{7}{8}$ (D) $\frac{1}{12}$ (E) $\frac{3}{4}$

When a fractional part of a number is given and we wish to find the number representing the whole, it is often easiest to translate the words into mathematical symbols and solve the resulting equation.

Example: Norman buys a used car for $2400, which is $\frac{2}{5}$ of the original price. Find the original price.

Solution: $2400 = \frac{2}{5}x$ Multiply by 5.
$12000 = 2x$
$6000 = x$

Example: The gas gauge on Mary's car reads $\frac{1}{8}$ full. She asks the gasoline attendant to fill the tank and finds she needs 21 gallons. What is the capacity of her gas tank?

Solution: $\frac{7}{8}$ of the tank is empty and requires 21 gallons to fill.

$$\frac{7}{8}x = 21 \quad \text{Multiply by 8.}$$
$$7x = 168$$
$$x = 24$$

Practice 3

Answers on page 41

Work out each problem in the space provided. Circle the letter before your answer.

1. Daniel spent $4.50 for a ticket to the movies. This represents $\frac{3}{4}$ of his allowance for the week. What did he have left that week for other expenses?

(A) $6.00 (B) $4.00 (C) $3.39 (D) $1.13 (E) $1.50

2. 350 seniors attended the prom. This represents $\frac{7}{9}$ of the class. How many seniors did not attend the prom?

(A) 50 (B) 100 (C) 110 (D) 120 (E) 450

3. A resolution was passed by a ratio of 5:4. If 900 people voted for the resolution, how many voted against it?

(A) 500 (B) 400 (C) 720 (D) 600 (E) 223

4. Mr. Rich owns $\frac{2}{7}$ of a piece of property. If the value of his share is $14,000, what is the total value of the property?

(A) $70,000 (B) $49,000 (C) $98,000 (D) $10,000 (E) $35,000

5. The Stone family spends $500 per month for rent. This is $\frac{4}{15}$ of their total monthly income. Assuming that salaries remain constant, what is the Stone family income for one year?

(A) $1875 (B) $6000 (C) $60,000 (D) $22,500 (E) $16,000

When problems use letters in place of numbers, the same principles discussed earlier apply. If you are not sure which operations to use, replace the letters with numbers to determine the steps needed in the solution.

Example: It takes Mr. Cohen X days to paint his house. If he works for D days, what part of his house must still be painted?

Solution: He has X - D days of painting left to do out of a total of X days, therefore $\frac{X - D}{X}$ is the correct answer.

VERBAL PROBLEMS INVOLVING FRACTIONS

Example: Sue buys 500 stamps. X of these are 10-cent stamps. $\frac{1}{3}$ of the remainder are 15-cent stamps. How many 15-cent stamps does she buy?

Solution: She buys 500 − X stamps that are not 10-cent stamps. $\frac{1}{3}$ of these are 15-cent stamps. Therefore she buys $\frac{1}{3}(500 - X)$ or $\frac{500 - X}{3}$ 15-cent stamps.

Example: John spent $X on the latest hit record album. This represents $\frac{1}{M}$ of his weekly allowance. What is his weekly allowance?

Solution: Translate the sentence into an algebraic equation.

$$X = \frac{1}{M} \cdot A \qquad \text{Multiply by M.}$$

$$MX = A$$

Practice 4

Answers on page 41

Work out each problem in the space provided. Circle the letter before your answer.

1. A class contains B boys and G girls. What part of the class is boys?

   (A) $\frac{B}{G}$ (B) $\frac{G}{B}$ (C) $\frac{B}{B+G}$ (D) $\frac{B+G}{B}$ (E) $\frac{B}{B-G}$

2. M men agreed to rent a ski lodge for a total of D dollars. By the time they signed the contract, the priced had increased by $100. Find the amount each man had to contribute as his total share.

   (A) $\frac{D}{M}$ (B) $\frac{D}{M} + 100$ (C) $\frac{D + 100}{M}$

   (D) $\frac{M}{D} + 100$ (E) $\frac{M + 100}{D}$

3. Of S students in Bryant High, $\frac{1}{3}$ study French. $\frac{1}{4}$ of the remainder study Italian. How many of the students study Italian?

   (A) $\frac{1}{6}S$ (B) $\frac{1}{4}S$ (C) $\frac{2}{3}S$ (D) $\frac{1}{12}S$ (E) $\frac{3}{7}S$

4. Mr. and Mrs. Feldman took t dollars in travelers checks with them on a trip. During the first week, they spent $\frac{1}{5}$ of their money. During the second week, they spent $\frac{1}{3}$ of the remainder. How much did they have left at the end of the second week?

   (A) $\frac{4t}{15}$ (B) $\frac{t}{15}$ (C) $\frac{7t}{15}$ (D) $\frac{11t}{15}$ (E) $\frac{8t}{15}$

VERBAL PROBLEMS INVOLVING FRACTIONS

5. Frank's gas tank was $\frac{1}{4}$ full. After putting in G gallons of gasoline, the tank was $\frac{7}{8}$ full. What was the capacity of the tank?

(A) $\frac{5G}{8}$ (B) $\frac{8G}{5}$ (C) $\frac{8G}{7}$ (D) $\frac{7G}{8}$ (E) $4G$

Retest

Answers on page 42

Work out each problem in the space provided. Circle the letter before your answer.

1. The All Star Appliance Shop sold 10 refrigerators, 8 ranges, 12 freezers, 12 washing machines, and 8 clothes dryers during January. Freezers made up what part of the appliances sold in January?

(A) $\frac{12}{50}$ (B) $\frac{12}{25}$ (C) $\frac{1}{2}$ (D) $\frac{12}{40}$ (E) $\frac{12}{60}$

2. What part of a day is 4 hours 20 minutes?

(A) $\frac{1}{6}$ (B) $\frac{13}{300}$ (C) $\frac{1}{3}$ (D) $\frac{13}{72}$ (E) $\frac{15}{77}$

3. Mrs. Brown owns X books. $\frac{1}{3}$ of these are novels, $\frac{2}{5}$ of the remainder are poetry and the rest are non-fiction. How many non-fiction books does Mrs. Brown own?

(A) $\frac{4}{15}X$ (B) $\frac{2}{5}X$ (C) $\frac{2}{3}X$ (D) $\frac{3}{5}X$ (E) $\frac{7}{15}X$

4. After typing $\frac{1}{4}$ of a term paper on Friday, Richard completed $\frac{2}{3}$ of the remainder on Saturday. If he wanted to finish the paper that weekend, what part was left to be typed on Sunday?

(A) $\frac{1}{4}$ (B) $\frac{2}{3}$ (C) $\frac{1}{3}$ (D) $\frac{1}{2}$ (E) $\frac{5}{6}$

5. What part of an hour elapses between 6:51 P.M. and 7:27 P.M.?

(A) $\frac{1}{2}$ (B) $\frac{2}{3}$ (C) $\frac{3}{5}$ (D) $\frac{17}{30}$ (E) $\frac{7}{12}$

6. Laurie spent 8 hours reading a novel. If she finished $\frac{2}{5}$ of the book, how many more hours will she need to read the rest of the book?

(A) 20   (B) 12   (C) $3\frac{1}{5}$ (D) 18   (E) 10

7. Mrs. Bach spent $\frac{2}{7}$ of her weekly grocery money on produce. If she spent $28 on produce, what was her total grocery bill that week?

(A) $70   (B) $80   (C) $56   (D) $90   (E) $98

8. After working on a new roof for X hours on Saturday, Mr. Goldman finished the job by working Y hours on Sunday. What part of the total job was done on Sunday?

(A) $\frac{Y}{X+Y}$ (B) $\frac{Y}{X}$ (C) $\frac{X}{X+Y}$ (D) $\frac{Y}{X-Y}$ (E) $\frac{Y}{Y-X}$

VERBAL PROBLEMS INVOLVING FRACTIONS

9. $\frac{1}{2}$ the women in the Spring Garden Club are over 60 years old. $\frac{1}{4}$ of the remainder are under 40. What part of the membership is between 40 and 60 years old?

(A) $\frac{1}{4}$ (B) $\frac{3}{8}$ (C) $\frac{3}{4}$ (D) $\frac{1}{8}$ (E) $\frac{5}{8}$

10. A residential city block contains R one-family homes, S two-family homes, and T apartment houses. What part of the buildings on this block is made up of one or two family houses?

(A) $\dfrac{R}{T} + \dfrac{S}{T}$ (B) $\dfrac{RS}{R+S+T}$ (C) $\dfrac{R+S}{R+S+T}$

(D) $\dfrac{R+S}{RST}$ (E) $R+S$

SOLUTIONS TO PRACTICE EXERCISES

Diagnostic Test

1. (A) There was a total of 6 hours of programming time. $\frac{2}{6} = \frac{1}{3}$

2. (D) Change all measurements to pints. One gallon is 8 pints. 2 qt. 1 pt. = 5 pints = $\frac{5}{8}$ gallon.

3. (B) $\frac{1}{2} + \frac{1}{5} + \frac{1}{4} = \frac{10}{20} + \frac{4}{20} + \frac{5}{20} = \frac{19}{20}$. Therefore, $\frac{1}{20}$ was left to relax.

4. (E) $\frac{3}{4}$ of $\frac{2}{3}$ or $\frac{1}{2}$ of the laundry was done before lunch. Since $\frac{1}{3}$ was done before breakfast, $\frac{1}{3} + \frac{1}{2}$ or $\frac{5}{6}$ was done before the afternoon, leaving $\frac{1}{6}$ for the afternoon.

5. (A) $\frac{2}{3}$ of $\frac{3}{5}$ or $\frac{2}{5}$ of Glenn's allowance was spent on a gift. Since $\frac{2}{5}$ was spent on a hit record, $\frac{2}{5} + \frac{2}{5}$ or $\frac{4}{5}$ was spent, leaving $\frac{1}{5}$.

6. (C) The tank contained $\frac{1}{4} \cdot 20$ or 5 gallons, leaving 15 gallons to fill the tank.

7. (A) $42 = \frac{2}{9}x$ Multiply by 9.
   $378 = 2x$ Divide by 2.
   $189 = x$

   This is the number of seniors. Since 42 seniors voted for the Copacabana, 147 did not.

8. (A) After working for X hours, M − X hours are left out of a total of M hours.

9. (A) $\frac{1}{3}D$ dogs are large. $\frac{1}{4}$ of $\frac{2}{3}D$ or $\frac{1}{6}D$ are medium. The total of these dogs is $\frac{1}{3}D + \frac{1}{6}D$, leaving $\frac{1}{2}D$ small dogs.

10. (B) There are A + B books. B out of A + B are biographies.

Practice 1

1. (C) There are 30 pupils in the class, of which 12 are girls. Therefore, $\frac{12}{30}$ or $\frac{2}{5}$ of the class is made up of girls.

2. (D) The team won 34 games out of 40 or $\frac{34}{40}$ of its games. This reduces to $\frac{17}{20}$.

3. (B) 24 minutes is $\frac{24}{60}$ or $\frac{2}{5}$ of an hour.

4. (D) The number of staff members is still 30. Of these, 9 are now women. Therefore $\frac{9}{30}$ or $\frac{3}{10}$ of the staff are women.

5. (E) Let x = the number of juniors at the dance. 3x = the number of seniors at the dance. Then 4x = the number of students at the dance. x out of these 4x are juniors. That is $\frac{x}{4x}$ or $\frac{1}{4}$ of the students present are juniors.

6. (A) Change all measurements to inches. One yard is 36 inches. 1 ft. 3 in. is 15 inches. $\frac{15}{36} = \frac{5}{12}$

7. (D) There were 40 students at the meeting. $\frac{8}{40} = \frac{1}{5}$

8. (C) $\frac{1}{3} + \frac{1}{4} + \frac{1}{10} + \frac{1}{5} = \frac{20}{60} + \frac{15}{60} + \frac{6}{60} + \frac{12}{60} = \frac{53}{60}$ Therefore, $\frac{7}{60}$ is left for other expenses.

VERBAL PROBLEMS INVOLVING FRACTIONS 41

Practice 2

1. (C) She put $8000 into savings banks.

    $8000 = \frac{1}{3}x$ Multiply by 3.
    $24,000 = x$

2. (B) $4500 = \frac{3}{5}x$ Multiply by $\frac{5}{3}$.
    $7500 = x$

3. (A) Since $\frac{4}{5}$ of $\frac{9}{10}$ will go to four-year colleges, $\frac{1}{5}$ of $\frac{9}{10}$ or $\frac{9}{50}$ will go to two-year colleges.

4. (D) They covered $\frac{1}{10} \cdot 3000$ or 300 miles the first day, leaving 2700 miles still to drive. They covered $\frac{2}{9} \cdot 2700$ or 600 miles the second day, leaving 2100 miles still to drive.

5. (B) $\frac{5}{6}$ of $\frac{3}{4}$ or $\frac{5}{8}$ are high school graduates. Since $\frac{1}{4}$ are college graduates, $\frac{1}{4} + \frac{5}{8}$ or $\frac{7}{8}$ of the employees graduated from high school, leaving $\frac{1}{8}$ who did not.

Practice 3

1. (E) $4.50 = \frac{3}{4}x$ Multiply by 4.
    $18.00 = 3x$ Divide by 3.
    $x = \$6.00$, his allowance for the week. $\$6.00 - \$4.50 = \$1.50$ left for other expenses.

2. (B) $350 = \frac{7}{9}x$ Multiply by 9.
    $3150 = 7x$ Divide by 7.
    $450 = x$

    This is the number of students in the class. If 350 attend the prom, 100 do not.

3. (C) $\frac{5}{9}$ of the voters voted for the resolution.

    $900 = \frac{5}{9}x$ Multiply by 9.
    $8100 = 5x$ Divide by 5.
    $1620 = x$
    $1620 - 900 = 720$ voted against the resolution.

4. (B) $\frac{2}{7}x = 14,000$ Multiply by 7.
    $2x = 98,000$ Divide by 2.
    $x = \$49,000$

5. (D) $\frac{4}{15}x = 500$ Multiply by 15.
    $4x = 7500$ Divide by 4.
    $x = \$1875$ This is their *monthly* income. Multiply by 12 to find yearly income: $22,500.

Practice 4

1. (C) There are $B + G$ students in the class. B out of $B + G$ are boys.

2. (C) The total cost is $D + 100$, which must be divided by the number of men to find each share.

3. (A) $\frac{1}{3}S$ students study French. $\frac{1}{4}$ of $\frac{2}{3}S$ or $\frac{1}{6}S$ study Italian.

4. (E) They spent $\frac{1}{5}t$ the first week. They spent $\frac{1}{3}$ of $\frac{4}{5}t$ or $\frac{4}{15}t$ the second week. During these two weeks they spent a total of $\frac{1}{5}t + \frac{4}{15}t$ or $\frac{7}{15}t$, leaving $\frac{8}{15}t$.

5. (B) The G gallons fill $\frac{7}{8} - \frac{1}{4}$ or $\frac{5}{8}$ of the tank.

    $\frac{5}{8}x = G$ Multiply by $\frac{8}{5}$. $x = \frac{8G}{5}$

Retest

1. (A) There were 50 appliances sold in January; $\frac{12}{50}$ were freezers.

2. (D) Change all measurements to minutes. One day is $60 \cdot 24$ or 1440 minutes. 4 hr. 20 min. = 260 min. $\frac{260}{1440} = \frac{13}{72}$

3. (B) $\frac{1}{3}X$ books are novels. $\frac{2}{5}$ of $\frac{2}{3}X$ or $\frac{4}{15}X$ are poetry. The total of these books is $\frac{1}{3}X + \frac{4}{15}X$ or $\frac{9}{15}X$, leaving $\frac{6}{15}X$ or $\frac{2}{5}X$ books which are non-fiction.

4. (A) $\frac{2}{3}$ of $\frac{3}{4}$ or $\frac{1}{2}$ of the term paper was completed on Saturday. Since $\frac{1}{4}$ was completed on Friday, $\frac{1}{4} + \frac{1}{2}$ or $\frac{3}{4}$ was completed before Sunday, leaving $\frac{1}{4}$ to be typed on Sunday.

5. (C) 36 minutes is $\frac{36}{60}$ or $\frac{3}{5}$ of an hour.

6. (B) $8 = \frac{2}{5}x$ Multiply by 5.
         $40 = 2x$ Divide by 2.
         $20 = x$

This is the total number of hours needed to read the book. Since Laurie already read for 8 hours, she will need 12 more hours to finish the book.

7. (E) $\frac{2}{7}x = 28$ Multiply by 7.
     $2x = 196$ Divide by 2.
     $x = \$98$

8. (A) Mr. Goldman worked a total of $X + Y$ hours. Y out of $X + Y$ was done on Sunday.

9. (B) $\frac{1}{4}$ of $\frac{1}{2}$ or $\frac{1}{8}$ are under 40. Since $\frac{1}{2} + \frac{1}{8}$ or $\frac{5}{8}$ are over 60 or under 40, $\frac{3}{8}$ is between 40 and 60.

10. (C) There is a total of $R + S + T$ buildings on the block. $R + S$ out of $R + S + T$ are one or two family houses.

Variation

DIAGNOSTIC TEST

Answers on page 52

Work out each problem in the space provided. Circle the letter before your answer.

1. Solve for x: $\dfrac{2x}{3} = \dfrac{x+5}{4}$

   (A) 2 (B) 3 (C) 4 (D) $4\frac{1}{2}$ (E) 5

2. Solve for x if a = 7, b = 8, c = 5: $\dfrac{a-3}{x} = \dfrac{b+2}{4c}$

   (A) 4 (B) 5 (C) 6 (D) 7 (E) 8

3. A map is drawn using a scale of 2 inches = 25 miles. How far apart in miles are two cities which are $5\frac{2}{5}$ inches apart on the map?

   (A) 60 (B) 65 (C) $67\frac{1}{2}$ (D) 69 (E) 70

4. How many apples can be bought for c cents if n apples cost d cents?

   (A) $\dfrac{nc}{d}$ (B) $\dfrac{nd}{c}$ (C) $\dfrac{cd}{n}$ (D) $\dfrac{d}{c}$ (E) nc

5. Ms. Dehn drove 7000 miles during the first 5 months of the year. At this rate, how many miles will she drive in a full year?

   (A) 16,000 (B) 16,800 (C) 14,800 (D) 15,000 (E) 16,400

6. A gear having 20 teeth turns at 30 revolutions per minute and is meshed with another gear having 25 teeth. At how many revolutions per minute is the second gear turning?

   (A) 35 (B) $37\frac{1}{2}$ (C) $22\frac{1}{2}$ (D) 30 (E) 24

7. A boy weighing 90 pounds sits 3 feet from the fulcrum of a seesaw. His younger brother weighs 50 pounds. How far on the other side of the fulcrum should he sit to balance the seesaw?

(A) $5\frac{3}{4}$ ft. (B) $5\frac{2}{5}$ ft. (C) $1\frac{2}{3}$ ft. (D) $1\frac{1}{3}$ ft. (E) $4\frac{1}{2}$ ft.

8. Alan has enough dog food to last his two dogs for three weeks. If a neighbor asks him to feed her dog as well, how long will the dog food last, assuming that all three dogs eat the same amount?

(A) 10 days (B) 12 days (C) 14 days (D) 16 days (E) 18 days

9. A newspaper can be printed by m machines in h hours. If 2 of the machines are not working, how many hours will it take to print the paper?

(A) $\frac{mh - 2h}{m}$ (B) $\frac{m - 2}{mh}$ (C) $\frac{mh + 2h}{m}$

(D) $\frac{mh}{m - 2}$ (E) $\frac{mh}{m + 2}$

10. An army platoon has enough rations to last 20 men for 6 days. If 4 more men join the group, for how many fewer days will the rations last?

(A) 5 (B) 2 (C) 1 (D) 1.8 (E) 4

1. RATIO AND PROPORTION

A ratio is a comparison between two quantities. In making this comparison, both quantities must be expressed in terms of the same units.

Example: Express the ratio of 1 hour to 1 day.

Solution: A day contains 24 hours. The ratio is $\frac{1}{24}$, which can also be written 1 : 24.

Example: Find the ratio of the shaded portion to the unshaded portion.

Solution: There are 5 squares shaded out of 9. The ratio of the shaded portion to unshaded portion is $\frac{5}{4}$.

A proportion is a statement of equality between two ratios. The denominator of the first fraction and the numerator of the second are called the means of the proportion. The numerator of the first fraction and the denominator of the second are called the extremes. In solving a proportion, we use the theorem that states the product of the means is equal to the product of the extremes. We refer to this as *cross multiplying*.

Example: Solve for x: $\dfrac{x+3}{5} = \dfrac{8-x}{6}$

Solution: Cross multiply. $6x + 18 = 40 - 5x$
$11x = 22$
$x = 2$

Example: Solve for x: $4:x = 9:18$

Solution: Rewrite in fraction form. $\dfrac{4}{x} = \dfrac{9}{18}$

Cross multiply. $9x = 72$
$x = 8$

If you observe that the second fraction is equal to $\frac{1}{2}$, then the first must also be equal to $\frac{1}{2}$. Therefore the missing denominator must be 8. Observation often saves valuable time.

Practice 1

Answers on page 53

Work out each problem in the space provided. Circle the letter before your answer.

1. Find the ratio of 1 ft. 4 in. to 1 yd.

(A) 1:3   (B) 2:9   (C) 4:9   (D) 3:5   (E) 5:12

2. A team won 25 games in a 40 game season. Find the ratio of games won to games lost.

(A) $\frac{5}{8}$ (B) $\frac{3}{8}$ (C) $\frac{3}{5}$ (D) $\frac{5}{3}$ (E) $\frac{3}{2}$

3. In the proportion $a:b = c:d$, solve for d in terms of a, b and c.

(A) $\dfrac{ac}{b}$ (B) $\dfrac{bc}{a}$ (C) $\dfrac{ab}{c}$ (D) $\dfrac{a}{bc}$ (E) $\dfrac{bc}{d}$

4. Solve for x: $\dfrac{x+1}{8} = \dfrac{28}{32}$

(A) $6\frac{1}{2}$ (B) 5   (C) 4   (D) 7   (E) 6

46 VARIATION

5. Solve for y: $\dfrac{2y}{9} = \dfrac{y-1}{3}$

(A) 3   (B) $\frac{1}{3}$ (C) $\frac{9}{15}$ (D) $\frac{9}{4}$ (E) $\frac{4}{9}$

2. DIRECT VARIATION

Two quantities are said to vary directly if they change in the same direction. As the first increases, the second does also. As the first decreases, the second does also.

For example, the distance I travel at a constant rate varies directly as the time spent traveling. The number of pounds of apples I buy varies directly as the amount of money I spend. The number of pounds of butter I use in a cookie recipe varies directly as the number of cups of sugar I use.

Whenever two quantities vary directly, a problem can be solved using a proportion. We must be very careful to compare quantities in the same order and in terms of the same units in both fractions. If we compare miles with hours in the first fraction, we must compare miles with hours in the second fraction.

You must always be sure that as one quantity increases or decreases, the other changes in the same direction before you try to solve using a proportion.

Example: If 4 bottles of milk cost $2, how many bottles of milk can I buy for $8?

Solution: The more milk I buy the more it will cost. This is *direct*. We are comparing the number of bottles with cost.

$$\frac{4}{2} = \frac{x}{8}$$

If we cross multiply, we get 2x = 32 or x = 16.

A shortcut in the above example would be to observe what change takes place in the denominator and apply the same change to the numerator. The denominator of the left fraction was multiplied by 4 to give the denominator of the right fraction. Therefore we multiply the numerator by 4 as well to maintain the equality. This method often means a proportion can be solved at sight with no written computation at all, saving valuable time.

Example: If b boys can deliver n newspapers in one hour, how many newspapers can c boys deliver in the same time?

Solution: The more boys, the more papers will be delivered. This is *direct*. We are comparing the number of boys with the number of newspapers.

$$\frac{b}{n} = \frac{c}{x} \quad \text{Cross multiply and solve for x.}$$

$$bx = cn$$

$$x = \frac{cn}{b}$$

Practice 2

Answers on page 53

Work out each problem in the space provided. Circle the letter before your answer.

1. Find the cost, in cents, of 8 books if 3 books of the same kind cost D dollars.

   (A) $\frac{8D}{3}$ (B) $\frac{3}{800D}$ (C) $\frac{3}{8D}$ (D) $\frac{800D}{3}$ (E) $\frac{108D}{3}$

2. On a map ½ inch = 10 miles. How many miles apart are two towns which are 2¼ inches apart on the map?

   (A) 11¼ (B) 45 (C) 22½ (D) 40½ (E) 42

3. The toll on the Intercoastal Thruway is 8¢ for every 5 miles traveled. What is the toll for a trip of 115 miles on this road?

   (A) $9.20 (B) $1.70 (C) $1.84 (D) $1.64 (E) $1.76

4. Mark's car uses 20 gallons of gas to drive 425 miles. At this rate, how many gallons of gas will he need approximately for a trip of 1000 miles?

   (A) 44 (B) 45 (C) 46 (D) 47 (E) 49

5. If r planes can carry p passengers, how many planes are needed to carry m passengers?

   (A) $\frac{rm}{p}$ (B) $\frac{rp}{m}$ (C) $\frac{p}{rm}$ (D) $\frac{pm}{r}$ (E) $\frac{m}{rp}$

3. INVERSE VARIATION

Two quantities are said to vary inversely if they change in opposite directions. As the first increases, the second decreases. As the first decreases, the second increases.

48   VARIATION

Whenever two quantities vary inversely, their product remains constant. Instead of dividing one quantity by the other and setting their quotients equal as we did in direct variation, we multiply one quantity by the other and set the products equal.

There are several situations which are good examples of inverse variation.

A) The number of teeth in a meshed gear varies inversely as the number of revolutions it makes per minute. The more teeth a gear has, the fewer revolutions it will make per minute. The less teeth it has, the more revolutions it will make per minute. The product of the number of teeth and the revolutions per minute remains constant.

B) The distance a weight is placed from the fulcrum of a balanced lever varies inversely as its weight. The heavier the object, the shorter must be its distance from the fulcrum. The lighter the object, the greater must be the distance. The product of the weight of the object and its distance from the fulcrum remains constant.

C) When two pulleys are connected by a belt, the diameter of a pulley varies inversely as the number of revolutions per minute. The larger the diameter, the smaller the number of revolutions per minute. The smaller the diameter, the greater the number of revolutions per minute. The product of the diameter of a pulley and the number of revolutions per minute remains constant.

D) The number of people hired to work on a job varies inversely as the time needed to complete the job. The more people working, the less time it will take. The fewer people working, the longer it will take. The product of the number of people and the time worked remains constant.

E) How long food, or any commodity, lasts varies inversely as the number of people who consume it. The more people, the less time it will last. The fewer people, the longer it will last. The product of the number of people and the time it will last remains constant.

Example: If 3 men can paint a house in 2 days, how long will it take 2 men to do the same job?

Solution: The fewer men, the more days. This is *inverse*.

$$3 \cdot 2 = 2 \cdot x$$
$$6 = 2x$$
$$x = 3 \text{ days}$$

Practice 3

Answers on page 54

Work out each problem in the space provided. Circle the letter before your answer.

1. A field can be plowed by 8 machines in 6 hours. If 3 machines are broken and cannot be used, how many hours will it take to plow the field?

(A) 12   (B) $9\frac{3}{5}$ (C) $3\frac{3}{4}$ (D) 4   (E) 16

2. Camp Starlight has enough milk to feed 90 children for 4 days. If 10 of the children do not drink milk, how many days will the supply last?

(A) 5   (B) 6   (C) $4\frac{1}{2}$ (D) $4\frac{1}{8}$ (E) $5\frac{1}{3}$

3. A pulley revolving at 200 revolutions per minute has a diameter of 15 inches. It is belted to a second pulley which revolves at 150 revolutions per minute. Find the diameter, in inches, of the second pulley.

(A) 11.2   (B) 20   (C) 18   (D) 16.4   (E) 2

4. Two boys weighing 60 pounds and 80 pounds balance a seesaw. How many feet from the fulcrum must the heavier boy sit if the lighter boy is 8 feet from the fulcrum?

(A) 10   (B) $10\frac{2}{3}$ (C) 9   (D) $7\frac{1}{2}$ (E) 6

5. A gear with 20 teeth revolving at 200 revolutions per minute is meshed with a second gear turning at 250 revolutions per minute. How many teeth does this gear have?

(A) 16   (B) 25   (C) 15   (D) 10   (E) 24

In solving variation problems, you must decide whether the two quantities involved change in the same direction, in which case it is direct variation and should be solved by means of proportions. If the quantities change in opposite directions, it is inverse variation, solved by means of constant products. In the following exercises, decide carefully whether each is an example of direct or inverse variation.

Practice 4

Answers on page 54

Work out each problem in the space provided. Circle the letter before your answer.

1. A farmer has enough chicken feed to last 30 chickens for 4 days. If 10 more chickens are added, how many days will the feed last?

(A) 3   (B) $1\frac{1}{3}$ (C) 12   (D) $2\frac{2}{3}$ (E) $5\frac{1}{3}$

2. At c cents per pack, what is the cost of p cartons of cigarettes if there are 10 packs in a carton?

(A) 10cp   (B) $\frac{cp}{10}$ (C) $\frac{10}{cp}$ (D) $\frac{10p}{c}$ (E) $\frac{10c}{p}$

3. If m boys can put up a fence in d days, how many days will it take to put up the fence if two of the boys cannot participate?

(A) $\frac{d}{-2}$ (B) $\frac{d(m-2)}{m}$ (C) $\frac{md}{m-2}$ (D) $\frac{m-2}{md}$ (E) $\frac{m(m-2)}{d}$

50 VARIATION

4. A recipe calls for $\frac{3}{4}$ lb. of butter and 18 oz. of sugar. If only 10 oz. of butter are available, how many ounces of sugar should be used?

(A) $13\frac{1}{2}$ (B) 23 (C) 24 (D) 14 (E) 15

5. If 3 kilometers are equal to 1.8 miles, how many kilometers are equal to 100 miles?

(A) 60 (B) $166\frac{2}{3}$ (C) 540 (D) $150\frac{1}{2}$ (E) 160.4

Retest

Answers on page 55

Work out each problem in the space provided. Circle the letter before your answer.

1. Solve for x: $\dfrac{3x}{8} = \dfrac{x+7}{12}$

(A) $\frac{7}{28}$ (B) 2 (C) 4 (D) $2\frac{3}{4}$ (E) 1

2. Solve for x if a = 5, b = 8 and c = 3: $\dfrac{a-3}{x} = \dfrac{b+2}{5c}$

(A) 5 (B) 20 (C) 2 (D) 3 (E) 6

3. A map is drawn to a scale of $\frac{1}{2}$ inch = 20 miles. How many miles apart are two cities which are $3\frac{1}{4}$ inches apart on the map?

(A) 70 (B) 130 (C) 65 (D) $32\frac{1}{2}$ (E) 35

4. Mr. Weiss earned $12,000 during the first 5 months of the year. If his salary continues at the same rate, what will his annual income be that year?

(A) $60,000 (B) $28,000 (C) $27,000 (D) $30,000 (E) $28,800

5. How many pencils can be bought for D dollars if n pencils cost c cents?

(A) $\dfrac{nD}{c}$ (B) $\dfrac{nD}{100c}$ (C) $\dfrac{100D}{nc}$ (D) $\dfrac{100nD}{c}$ (E) $\dfrac{nc}{100D}$

6. Ten boys agree to paint the gym in 5 days. If 5 more boys join in before the work begins, how many days should the painting take?

(A) $3\frac{1}{3}$ (B) $3\frac{1}{2}$ (C) 10 (D) $2\frac{1}{2}$ (E) $2\frac{3}{4}$

7. A weight of 120 pounds is placed 5 feet from the fulcrum of a lever. How far from the fulcrum should a 100 pound weight be placed in order to balance the lever?

(A) 6 ft. (B) $4\frac{1}{6}$ ft. (C) $5\frac{1}{2}$ ft. (D) $6\frac{1}{2}$ ft. (E) $6\frac{2}{3}$ ft.

8. A photograph negative measures $1\frac{7}{8}$ inches by $2\frac{1}{2}$ inches. The printed picture is to have its longer dimension 4 inches. How long should the shorter dimension be?

(A) $2\frac{3}{8}''$ (B) $2\frac{1}{2}''$ (C) $3''$ (D) $3\frac{1}{8}''$ (E) $3\frac{3}{8}''$

9. A gear with 60 teeth is meshed to a gear with 40 teeth. If the larger gear revolves at 20 revolutions per minute, how many revolutions does the smaller gear make in a minute?

(A) $13\frac{1}{3}$ (B) 3   (C) 300   (D) 120   (E) 30

10. How many gallons of paint must be purchased to paint a room containing 820 square feet of wall space, if one gallon covers 150 square feet?

(A) 4   (B) 5   (C) 6   (D) 7   (E) 8

52 VARIATION

SOLUTIONS TO PRACTICE EXERCISES

Diagnostic Test

1. (B) $2x(4) = 3(x + 5)$
   $8x = 3x + 15$
   $5x = 15$
   $x = 3$

2. (E) $\dfrac{4}{x} = \dfrac{10}{20}$ Cross multiply.
   $80 = 10x$
   $x = 8$

3. (C) We compare inches to miles.
   $\dfrac{2}{25} = \dfrac{5\frac{2}{5}}{x}$ Cross multiply.
   $2x = 135$
   $x = 67\frac{1}{2}$

4. (A) We compare apples to cents.
   $\dfrac{x}{c} = \dfrac{n}{d}$ Cross multiply.
   $dx = nc$
   $x = \dfrac{nc}{d}$

5. (B) We compare miles to months.
   $\dfrac{5}{7000} = \dfrac{12}{x}$
   $5x = 84{,}000$
   $x = 16{,}800$

6. (E) Number of teeth times speed remains constant.
   $20 \cdot 30 = x \cdot 25$
   $600 = 25x$
   $x = 24$

7. (B) Weight times distance from the fulcrum remains constant.
   $90 \cdot 3 = 50 \cdot x$
   $270 = 50x$
   $x = 5\frac{2}{5}$ ft.

8. (C) The more dogs, the fewer days. This is inverse variation.
   $2 \cdot 3 = 3 \cdot x$
   $6 = 3x$
   $x = 2$ weeks $= 14$ days

9. (D) Number of machines times hours needed remains constant.
   $m \cdot h = (m - 2) \cdot x$
   $x = \dfrac{mh}{m - 2}$

10. (C) The more men, the fewer days. This is inverse variation.
    $20 \cdot 6 = 24 \cdot x$
    $120 = 24x$
    $x = 5$

    The rations will last 1 day less.

Practice 1

1. (C) 1 ft. 4 in. = 16 in.
   1 yd. = 36 in.
   $\frac{16}{36} = \frac{4}{9}$

2. (D) The team won 25 games and lost 15.
   $\frac{25}{15} = \frac{5}{3}$

3. (B) $\frac{a}{b} = \frac{c}{d}$ Cross multiply.
   ad = bc Divide by a.
   $d = \frac{bc}{a}$

4. (E) 32(x + 1) = 28(8)
   32x + 32 = 224
   32x = 192
   x = 6

5. (A) 9(y − 1) = 2y(3)
   9y − 9 = 6y
   3y = 9
   y = 3

Practice 2

1. (D) We compare books with cents. D dollars is equivalent to 100D cents.
   $\frac{3}{100D} = \frac{8}{x}$
   3x = 800D
   $x = \frac{800D}{3}$

2. (B) We compare inches to miles.
   $\frac{\frac{1}{2}}{10} = \frac{2\frac{1}{4}}{x}$ Cross multiply.
   $\frac{1}{2}x = 22\frac{1}{2}$ Multiply by 2.
   x = 45

3. (C) We compare cents to miles.
   $\frac{8}{5} = \frac{x}{115}$ Cross multiply.
   5x = 920
   x = $1.84

4. (D) We compare gallons to miles.
   $\frac{20}{425} = \frac{x}{1000}$ Cross multiply.
   425x = 20,000 To avoid large numbers, divide by 25.
   17x = 800
   $x = 47\frac{1}{17}$

5. (A) We compare planes to passengers.
   $\frac{r}{p} = \frac{x}{m}$ Cross multiply.
   px = rm Divide by p.
   $x = \frac{rm}{p}$

54   VARIATION

Practice 3

1. **(B)** Number of machines times hours needed remains constant.

$$8 \cdot 6 = 5 \cdot x$$
$$5x = 48$$
$$x = 9\tfrac{3}{5}$$

2. **(C)** Number of children times days remains constant.

$$90 \cdot 4 = 80 \cdot x$$
$$80x = 360$$
$$x = 4\tfrac{1}{2}$$

3. **(B)** Diameter times speed remains constant.

$$15 \cdot 200 = x \cdot 150$$
$$3000 = 150x$$
$$x = 20$$

4. **(E)** Weight times distance from fulcrum remains constant.

$$80 \cdot x = 60 \cdot 8$$
$$80x = 480$$
$$x = 6$$

5. **(A)** Number of teeth times speed remains constant.

$$20 \cdot 200 = x \cdot 250$$
$$250x = 4000$$
$$x = 16$$

Practice 4

1. **(A)** The more chickens, the fewer days. This is *inverse*.

$$30 \cdot 4 = 40 \cdot x$$
$$40x = 120$$
$$x = 3$$

2. **(A)** The more cartons, the more cents. This is *direct*. We compare cents with packs. In p cartons there will be 10p packs.

$$\frac{c}{1} = \frac{x}{10p}$$
$$x = 10cp$$

3. **(C)** The more boys, the fewer days. This is *inverse*.

$$m \cdot d = (m - 2) \cdot x$$
$$\frac{md}{m - 2} = x$$

4. **(E)** The more butter, the more sugar. This is *direct*. Change $\tfrac{3}{4}$ lb. to 12 oz.

$$\frac{12}{18} = \frac{10}{x}$$
$$12x = 180$$
$$x = 15$$

5. **(B)** The more kilometers, the more miles. This is *direct*.

$$\frac{3}{1.8} = \frac{x}{100}$$
$$1.8x = 300$$
$$18x = 3000$$
$$x = 166\tfrac{2}{3}$$

VARIATION

Retest

1. (B) $3x(12) = 8(x + 7)$
   $36x = 8x + 56$
   $28x = 56$
   $x = 2$

2. (D) $\dfrac{2}{x} = \dfrac{10}{15}$ Cross multiply.
   $30 = 10x$
   $x = 3$

3. (B) We compare inches to miles.
   $\dfrac{\frac{1}{2}}{20} = \dfrac{3\frac{1}{4}}{x}$ Cross multiply.
   $\frac{1}{2}x = 65$ Multiply by 2.
   $x = 130$

4. (E) We compare dollars to months.
   $\dfrac{12{,}000}{5} = \dfrac{x}{12}$ Cross multiply.
   $144{,}000 = 5x$
   $x = \$28{,}800$

5. (D) We compare pencils to dollars. The cost of n pencils is $\dfrac{c}{100}$ dollars.
   $\dfrac{x}{D} = \dfrac{n}{\frac{c}{100}}$ Cross multiply.
   $\dfrac{cx}{100} = nD$ Multiply by $\dfrac{100}{c}$.
   $x = \dfrac{100nD}{c}$

6. (A) The more boys, the fewer days. This is *inverse*.
   $10 \cdot 5 = 15 \cdot x$
   $50 = 15x$
   $x = 3\frac{1}{3}$

7. (A) Weight times distance from the fulcrum remains constant.
   $120 \cdot 5 = 100 \cdot x$
   $600 = 100x$
   $x = 6$ ft.

8. (C) $\dfrac{2\frac{1}{2}}{4} = \dfrac{1\frac{7}{8}}{x}$ Cross multiply.
   $\frac{5}{2}x = \frac{15}{2}$ Multiply by 2.
   $5x = 15$
   $x = 3''$

9. (E) Number of teeth times speed remains constant.
   $60 \cdot 20 = 40 \cdot x$
   $1200 = 40x$
   $x = 30$

10. (C) We compare gallons to square feet.
    $\dfrac{x}{820} = \dfrac{1}{150}$ Cross multiply.
    $150x = 820$
    $x = 5.47$, which means 6 gallons must be purchased.

Percent

DIAGNOSTIC TEST

Answers on page 67

Work out each problem in the space provided. Circle the letter before your answer.

1. Write as a fraction: 4.5%

   (A) $\frac{9}{2}$ (B) $\frac{9}{20}$ (C) $\frac{9}{200}$ (D) $\frac{9}{2000}$ (E) $\frac{4.5}{10}$

2. Write $\frac{2}{5}$% as a decimal.

   (A) .40 (B) .04 (C) 40.0 (D) .004 (E) 4.00

3. What is $62\frac{1}{2}$% of 80?

   (A) 5000 (B) 500 (C) 50 (D) 5 (E) .5

4. Find 6% of b.

   (A) .6b (B) .06b (C) $\frac{b}{6}$ (D) $\frac{b}{.06}$ (E) $\frac{100b}{6}$

5. 80 is 40% of what number?

   (A) 3200 (B) 320 (C) 32 (D) 200 (E) 20

6. c is $83\frac{1}{3}$% of what number?

   (A) $\frac{5c}{6}$ (B) $\frac{6c}{5}$ (C) $\frac{7c}{8}$ (D) $\frac{8c}{7}$ (E) $\frac{2c}{3}$

7. How many sixteenths are there in $87\frac{1}{2}$%?

   (A) 7 (B) 8 (C) 10 (D) 12 (E) 14

8. What percent of 40 is 16?

(A) $2\frac{1}{2}$ (B) 25   (C) 30   (D) 40   (E) 45

9. Find 112% of 80.

(A) 92   (B) 89.6   (C) 88   (D) 70.5   (E) 91

10. What percent of 60 is 72?

(A) 105   (B) 125   (C) 120   (D) $83\frac{1}{3}$ (E) 110

1. FRACTIONAL AND DECIMAL EQUIVALENTS OF PERCENTS

Percent means "out of 100." If you understand this concept, it then becomes very easy to change a percent to an equivalent decimal or fraction.

Example: 5% means 5 out of 100 or $\frac{5}{100}$, which is equal to .05

3.4% means 3.4 out of 100 or $\frac{3.4}{100}$, which is equivalent to $\frac{34}{1000}$ or .034

c% means c out of 100 or $\frac{c}{100}$, which is equivalent to $\frac{1}{100} \cdot c$ or .01c

$\frac{1}{4}$% means $\frac{1}{4}$ out of 100 or $\frac{\frac{1}{4}}{100}$, which is equivalent to $\frac{1}{100} \cdot .25$ or .0025

To change a percent to a decimal, therefore, we must move the decimal point two places to the *left*, as we are dividing by 100.

Example: 62% = .62
.4% = .004
3.2% = .032

To change a decimal to a percent, we must reverse the above steps. We multiply by 100, which has the effect of moving the decimal point two places to the *right*, and insert the percent sign.

58   PERCENT

Example: .27 = 27%
.012 = 1.2%
.003 = .3%

To change a percent to a fraction, we remove the percent sign and divide by 100. This has the effect of putting the percent over 100 and then reducing the resulting fraction.

Example: $25\% = \dfrac{25}{100} = \dfrac{1}{4}$

$70\% = \dfrac{70}{100} = \dfrac{7}{10}$

$.5\% = \dfrac{.5}{100} = \dfrac{5}{1000} = \dfrac{1}{200}$

To change a fraction to a percent, we must reverse the above steps. We multiply by 100 and insert the percent sign.

Example: $\dfrac{4}{5} = \dfrac{4}{\cancel{5}} \cdot \cancel{100}^{20}\% = 80\%$

$\dfrac{3}{8} = \dfrac{3}{\underset{2}{\cancel{8}}} \cdot \cancel{100}^{25}\% = \dfrac{75}{2}\% = 37\dfrac{1}{2}\%$

Some fractions do not convert easily, as the denominator does not divide into 100. Such fractions must be changed to decimals first by dividing the denominator into the numerator. Then convert the decimal to a percent as explained on the previous page. Divide to 2 places only, unless it clearly comes out even in one or two additional places.

Example: $\dfrac{8}{17} = 17\overline{)8.00} = 47\dfrac{1}{17}\%$

```
      .47
  17)8.00
     6 8
     1 20
     1 19
        1
```

$\dfrac{4}{125} = 125\overline{)4.000} = 3.2\%$

```
      .032
 125)4.000
     3 75
       250
       250
```

Certain fractional and decimal equivalents of common percents occur frequently enough so that they should be memorized. Learning the values in the following table will make your work with percent problems much easier.

PERCENT	DECIMAL	FRACTION
50%	.5	$\frac{1}{2}$
25%	.25	$\frac{1}{4}$
75%	.75	$\frac{3}{4}$
10%	.1	$\frac{1}{10}$
30%	.3	$\frac{3}{10}$
70%	.7	$\frac{7}{10}$
90%	.9	$\frac{9}{10}$
$33\frac{1}{3}$%	$.33\frac{1}{3}$	$\frac{1}{3}$
$66\frac{2}{3}$%	$.66\frac{2}{3}$	$\frac{2}{3}$
$16\frac{2}{3}$%	$.16\frac{2}{3}$	$\frac{1}{6}$
$83\frac{1}{3}$%	$.83\frac{1}{3}$	$\frac{5}{6}$
20%	.2	$\frac{1}{5}$
40%	.4	$\frac{2}{5}$
60%	.6	$\frac{3}{5}$
80%	.8	$\frac{4}{5}$
$12\frac{1}{2}$%	.125	$\frac{1}{8}$
$37\frac{1}{2}$%	.375	$\frac{3}{8}$
$62\frac{1}{2}$%	.625	$\frac{5}{8}$
$87\frac{1}{2}$%	.875	$\frac{7}{8}$

Practice 1

Answers on page 67

Work out each problem in the space provided. Circle the letter before your answer.

1. $3\frac{1}{2}$% may be written as a decimal as

(A) 3.5   (B) .35   (C) .035   (D) .0035   (E) 3.05

2. Write as a fraction in lowest terms: 85%.

(A) $\frac{13}{20}$ (B) $\frac{17}{20}$ (C) $\frac{17}{10}$ (D) $\frac{19}{20}$ (E) $\frac{17}{2}$

3. Write 4.6 as a percent.

(A) 4.6%   (B) .46%   (C) .046%   (D) 46%   (E) 460%

4. Write $\frac{5}{12}$ as an equivalent percent.

(A) 41%   (B) 41.6%   (C) $41\frac{2}{3}$%   (D) 4.1%   (E) $.41\frac{2}{3}$%

60 PERCENT

5. Write $\frac{1}{2}$% as a decimal.

(A) .5   (B) .005   (C) 5.0   (D) 50.0   (E) .05

2. FINDING A PERCENT OF A NUMBER

Most percentage problems can be solved by using the proportion

$$\frac{\%}{100} = \frac{\text{part}}{\text{whole}}.$$

Although this method will work, it often yields unnecessarily large numbers which make for difficult computation. As we look at different types of percent problems, we will compare methods of solution. In finding a percent of a number, it is usually easier to change the percent to an equivalent decimal or fraction and multiply by the given number.

Example: Find 32% of 84.

Proportion Method

$$\frac{32}{100} = \frac{x}{84}$$

$$100x = 2688$$

$$x = 26.88$$

Decimal Method

Change 32% to .32 and multiply.

```
    84
   .32
   ───
   1 68
  25 2
   ────
  26.88
```

Example: Find $12\frac{1}{2}$% of 112.

Proportion Method

$$\frac{12\frac{1}{2}}{100} = \frac{x}{112}$$

$$100x = 1400$$

$$x = 14$$

Decimal Method

```
    112
   .125
   ────
    560
   2 24
  11 2
   ─────
  14.000
```

Fraction Method

Change $12\frac{1}{2}$% to $\frac{1}{8}$

$$\frac{1}{\cancel{8}} \cdot \cancel{112}^{14} = 14$$

Which method do you think is the easiest? When the fractional equivalent of the required percent is among those given in the previous chart, the fraction method is by far the least time-consuming. It really pays to memorize those fractional equivalents.

Practice 2

Answers on page 67

Work out each problem in the space provided. Circle the letter before your answer.

1. What is 40% of 40?
   (A) .16   (B) 1.6   (C) 16   (D) 160   (E) 1600

2. What is 42% of 67?
   (A) 2814   (B) 281.4   (C) 2.814   (D) .2814   (E) 28.14

3. Find $16\frac{2}{3}$% of 120.
   (A) 20   (B) 2   (C) 200   (D) 16   (E) 32

4. What is $\frac{1}{5}$% of 40?
   (A) 8   (B) .8   (C) .08   (D) .008   (E) .0008

5. Find r% of s.
   (A) $\frac{100s}{r}$ (B) $\frac{rs}{100}$ (C) $\frac{100r}{s}$ (D) $\frac{r}{100s}$ (E) $\frac{s}{100r}$

3. FINDING A NUMBER WHEN A PERCENT OF IT IS GIVEN

This type of problem may be solved using the proportion method, although this may again result in the unnecessary use of time. It is often easiest to translate the words of such a problem into an algebraic statement, using decimal or fractional equivalents for the percents involved. Then it will become evident that we divide the given number by the given percent to solve.

Example: 7 is 5% of what number?

Proportion Method

$$\frac{5}{100} = \frac{7}{x}$$

$$5x = 700$$

$$x = 140$$

Equation Method

$$7 = .05x$$

$$700 = 5x$$

$$140 = x$$

Example: 40 is $66\frac{2}{3}$% of what number?

62 PERCENT

Proportion Method   *Equation Method*

$$\frac{66\frac{2}{3}}{100} = \frac{40}{x} \qquad 40 = \frac{2}{3}x$$

$$66\frac{2}{3}x = 4000 \qquad 120 = 2x$$

$$\frac{200}{3}x = 4000 \qquad 60 = x$$

$$200x = 12000$$

$$2x = 120$$

$$x = 60$$

Just think of the amount of time you will save and the extra problems you will get to do if you know that $66\frac{2}{3}\%$ is $\frac{2}{3}$ and use the equation method. Are you convinced that the common fraction equivalents in the previously given chart should be memorized?

Practice 3

Answers on page 68

Work out each problem in the space provided. Circle the letter before your answer.

1. 72 is 12% of what number?

   (A) 6   (B) 60   (C) 600   (D) 86.4   (E) 8.64

2. 80 is $12\frac{1}{2}\%$ of what number?

   (A) 10   (B) 100   (C) 64   (D) 640   (E) 6400

3. $37\frac{1}{2}\%$ of what number is 27?

   (A) 72   (B) $10\frac{1}{8}$ (C) 90   (D) 101.25   (E) 216

4. m is p% of what number?

   (A) $\dfrac{mp}{100}$ (B) $\dfrac{100p}{m}$ (C) $\dfrac{m}{100p}$ (D) $\dfrac{p}{100m}$ (E) $\dfrac{100m}{p}$

5. 50% of what number is r?

   (A) $\frac{1}{2}r$ (B) 5r   (C) 10r   (D) 2r   (E) 100r

4. TO FIND WHAT PERCENT ONE NUMBER IS OF ANOTHER

This type of problem may also be solved using the proportion method. However, this may again result in the use of an unnecessary amount of

PERCENT 63

time. It is often easier to put the part over the whole, reduce the resulting fraction and multiply by 100.

Example: 30 is what percent of 1500?

Proportion Method

$$\frac{x}{100} = \frac{30}{1500}$$

$$1500x = 3000$$

$$x = 2\%$$

Fraction Method

$$\frac{30}{1500} = \frac{3}{150} = \frac{1}{50} \cdot 100 = 2\%$$

Example: 12 is what percent of 72?

Proportion Method

$$\frac{x}{100} = \frac{12}{72}$$

$$72x = 1200$$

Time consuming long division is needed to find $x = 16\frac{2}{3}\%$

Fraction Method

$$\frac{12}{72} = \frac{1}{6} = 16\frac{2}{3}\%$$

If you have memorized the fractional equivalents of common percents, this method requires only a few seconds.

Example: What percent of 72 is 16?

Proportion Method

$$\frac{x}{100} = \frac{16}{72}$$

$$72x = 1600$$

$$x = 22\frac{2}{9}\%$$

Fraction Method

$$\frac{16}{72} = \frac{2}{9} \cdot 100 = \frac{200}{9} = 22\frac{2}{9}\%$$

Practice 4

Answers on page 68

Work out each problem in the space provided. Circle the letter before your answer.

1. 4 is what percent of 80?

   (A) 20   (B) 2   (C) 5   (D) .5   (E) 40

2. $\frac{1}{2}$ of 6 is what percent of $\frac{1}{4}$ of 60?

   (A) 5   (B) 20   (C) 10   (D) 25   (E) 15

3. What percent of 96 is 12?

   (A) $16\frac{2}{3}$ (B) $8\frac{1}{3}$ (C) $37\frac{1}{2}$ (D) 8   (E) $12\frac{1}{2}$

64 PERCENT

4. What percent of 48 is 48?

(A) 1   (B) 10   (C) 100   (D) 48   (E) 0

5. What percent of y is x?

(A) $\dfrac{x}{y}$ (B) $\dfrac{x}{100y}$ (C) $\dfrac{xy}{100}$ (D) $\dfrac{100x}{y}$ (E) $\dfrac{100y}{x}$

5. PERCENTS GREATER THAN 100

When the percentage involved in a problem is greater than 100, the same methods apply. Remember that 100% = 1, 200% = 2, 300% = 3 and so forth. Therefore 150% will be equal to 100% + 50% or $1\frac{1}{2}$. Let us look at one example of each previously discussed problem, using percents greater than 100.

Example: Find 175% of 60

Proportion Method

$$\dfrac{175}{100} = \dfrac{x}{60}$$

$$100x = 10500$$

$$x = 105$$

Decimal Method

$$\begin{array}{r} 60 \\ \underline{1.75} \\ 300 \\ 4200 \\ \underline{6000} \\ 105.00 \end{array}$$

Fraction Method

$1\frac{3}{4} \cdot 60$

$\dfrac{7}{4} \cdot \overset{15}{\cancel{60}} = 105$

Example: 80 is 125% of what number?

Proportion Method

$$\dfrac{125}{100} = \dfrac{80}{x}$$

$$125x = 8000$$

$$x = 64$$

Decimal Method

$$80 = 1.25x$$

$$8000 = 125x$$

$$x = 64$$

Fraction Method

$$80 = 1\frac{1}{4}x$$

$$80 = \tfrac{5}{4}x$$

$$320 = 5x$$

$$x = 64$$

Example: 40 is what percent of 30?

Proportion Method

$$\dfrac{x}{100} = \dfrac{40}{30}$$

$$30x = 4000$$

$$x = 133\tfrac{1}{3}\%$$

Fraction Method

$$\dfrac{40}{30} = \dfrac{4}{3} = 1\tfrac{1}{3} = 133\tfrac{1}{3}\%$$

Practice 5

Answers on page 68

Work out each problem in the space provided. Circle the letter before your answer.

1. 36 is 150% of what number?
   (A) 24 (B) 54 (C) 26 (D) 12 (E) 48

2. What is 300% of 6?
   (A) 2 (B) 3 (C) 12 (D) 18 (E) 24

3. What percent of 90 is 120?
   (A) 75 (B) $133\frac{1}{3}$ (C) 125 (D) 120 (E) $1\frac{1}{3}$

4. 500 is 200% of what number?
   (A) 250 (B) 1000 (C) 100 (D) 750 (E) 300

5. To multiply a number by $137\frac{1}{2}$%, the number should be multiplied by
   (A) 137.5 (B) 13750 (C) 1.375 (D) 13.75 (E) .1375

Retest

Answers on page 68

Work out each problem in the space provided. Circle the letter before your answer.

1. Write as a fraction in lowest terms: .25%.
   (A) $\frac{1}{4}$ (B) $\frac{1}{40}$ (C) $\frac{1}{400}$ (D) $\frac{1}{4000}$ (E) $\frac{1}{25}$

2. Write $\frac{3}{4}$% as a decimal.
   (A) .75 (B) 75.0 (C) .075 (D) .0075 (E) 7.5

3. Find 12% of 80.
   (A) 10 (B) .96 (C) .096 (D) 960 (E) 9.6

4. 18 is 20% of what number?
   (A) 3.6 (B) 90 (C) 72 (D) 21.6 (E) 108

5. What is b% of 6?
   (A) $\frac{3b}{50}$ (B) $\frac{3}{50b}$ (C) $\frac{50b}{3}$ (D) $\frac{50}{3b}$ (E) $\frac{b}{150}$

66 PERCENT

6. m is $62\frac{1}{2}\%$ of what number?

(A) $\dfrac{5m}{8}$ (B) $\dfrac{8m}{5}$ (C) 8m   (D) $\dfrac{5}{8m}$ (E) $\dfrac{8}{5m}$

7. What percent of 12 is 2?

(A) 600   (B) $12\frac{1}{2}$ (C) $16\frac{2}{3}$ (D) $6\frac{2}{3}$ (E) 6

8. What is 140% of 70?

(A) 9800   (B) 980   (C) .98   (D) 9.8   (E) 98

9. How many fifths are there in 280%?

(A) 28   (B) 1.4   (C) 14   (D) 56   (E) 2.8

10. What percent of 12 is 16?

(A) $133\frac{1}{3}$ (B) 125   (C) 75   (D) 80   (E) $1\frac{1}{4}$

SOLUTIONS TO PRACTICE EXERCISES

DIAGNOSTIC TEST

1. (C) $4.5\% = \dfrac{4.5}{100} = \dfrac{45}{1000} = \dfrac{9}{200}$

2. (D) $\dfrac{2}{5}\% = .4\% = .004$

3. (C) $62\dfrac{1}{2}\% = \dfrac{5}{8}$ $\dfrac{5}{\cancel{8}} \cdot \cancel{80}^{10} = 50$

4. (B) $6\% = .06$ $.06 \cdot b = .06b$

5. (D) $80 = .40x$ Divide by .40 $200 = x$

6. (B) $83\dfrac{1}{3}\% = \dfrac{5}{6}$

   $c = \dfrac{5}{6}x$ Multiply by 6.

   $6c = 5x$ Divide by 5.

   $\dfrac{6c}{5} = x$

7. (E) $87\dfrac{1}{2}\% = \dfrac{7}{8} = \dfrac{14}{16}$

8. (D) $\dfrac{16}{40} = \dfrac{2}{5} = 40\%$

9. (B) $112\% = 1.12$

    $1.12 \cdot 80 = 89.6$

10. (C) $\dfrac{72}{60} = \dfrac{6}{5} = 120\%$

Practice 1

1. (C) $3\dfrac{1}{2}\% = 3.5\% = .035$ To change a percent to a decimal, move the decimal point two places to the *left*.

2. (B) $85\% = \dfrac{85}{100} = \dfrac{17}{20}$

3. (E) To change a decimal to a percent, move the decimal point two places to the *right*.

4. (C) $\dfrac{5}{\cancel{12}_{3}} \cdot \cancel{100}^{25} = \dfrac{125}{3} = 41\dfrac{2}{3}\%$ To change a fraction to a percent, multiply by 100.

Practice 2

1. (C) $40\% = \dfrac{2}{5}$ $\dfrac{2}{\cancel{5}} \cdot \cancel{40}^{8} = 16$

2. (E)   67
         .42
         ‾‾‾
         1 34
        26 80
        ‾‾‾‾‾
        28.14

3. (A) $16\dfrac{2}{3}\% = \dfrac{1}{6}$ $\dfrac{1}{\cancel{6}} \cdot \cancel{120}^{20} = 20$

4. (C) $\dfrac{1}{5}\% = .2\% = .002$ 40
                                         .002
                                         ‾‾‾‾
                                         .0800

5. (B) $r\% = \dfrac{r}{100}$ $\dfrac{r}{100} \cdot s = \dfrac{rs}{100}$

Practice 3

1. (C) $72 = .12x$
   $7200 = 12x$
   $x = 600$

2. (D) $80 = \frac{1}{8}x$
   $640 = x$

3. (A) $\frac{3}{8}x = 27$
   $3x = 216$
   $x = 72$

4. (E) $m = \frac{p}{100} \cdot x$
   $100m = px$
   $\frac{100m}{p} = x$

5. (D) $\frac{1}{2}x = r$
   $x = 2r$

Practice 4

1. (C) $\frac{4}{80} = \frac{1}{20} \cdot \overset{5}{100} = 5\%$

2. (B) $\frac{1}{2}$ of $6 = 3$ $\frac{1}{4}$ of $60 = 15$
   $\frac{3}{15} = \frac{1}{5} = 20\%$

3. (E) $\frac{12}{96} = \frac{1}{8} = 12\frac{1}{2}\%$

4. (C) $\frac{48}{48} = 1 = 100\%$

5. (D) $\frac{x}{y} \cdot 100 = \frac{100x}{y}$

Practice 5

1. (A) $36 = 1\frac{1}{2}x$
   $36 = \frac{3}{2}x$
   $72 = 3x$
   $x = 24$

2. (D) $300\% = 3$
   $6 \cdot 3 = 18$

3. (B) $\frac{120}{90} = \frac{4}{3} = 133\frac{1}{3}\%$

4. (A) $500 = 2x$
   $250 = x$

5. (C) $137.5\% = 1.375$

Retest

1. (C) $.25\% = \frac{.25}{100} = \frac{25}{10,000} = \frac{1}{400}$

2. (D) $\frac{3}{4}\% = .75\% = .0075$

3. (E) $12\% = .12$ $.12 \cdot 80 = 9.6$

4. (B) $18 = .20x$ Divide by $.20$.
   $90 = x$

5. (A) $b\% = \frac{b}{100}$ $\frac{b}{\underset{50}{\cancel{100}}} \cdot \cancel{6}^{3} = \frac{3b}{50}$

Retest

6. (B) $62\frac{1}{2}\% = \frac{5}{8}$

   $m = \frac{5}{8}x$ Multiply by 8.

   $8m = 5x$ Divide by 5.

   $\frac{8m}{5} = x$

7. (C) $\frac{2}{12} = \frac{1}{6} = 16\frac{2}{3}\%$

8. (E) $140\% = 1.40$

   $1.40 \cdot 70 = 98$

9. (C) $280\% = \frac{280}{100} = \frac{28}{10} = \frac{14}{5}$

10. (A) $\frac{16}{12} = \frac{4}{3} = 133\frac{1}{3}\%$

Verbal Problems Involving Percent

DIAGNOSTIC TEST

Answers on page 80

Work out each problem in the space provided. Circle the letter before your answer.

1. A book dealer bought 100 books for $1250. If she sold 30% of these at $10 each and the rest at $15 each, what was her total profit?

(A) $350   (B) $1350   (C) $300   (D) $1050   (E) $100

2. The Fishman family income for one month is $2000. If 25% is spent for lodging, 35% for food, 5% for clothing and 10% for savings, how many dollars are left for other expenses?

(A) $1500   (B) $400   (C) $500   (D) $1600   (E) $600

3. The enrollment of Kennedy High School dropped from 1200 to 1000 over a three-year period. What was the percent of decrease during this time?

(A) 20   (B) $16\frac{2}{3}$ (C) 25   (D) 200   (E) 2

4. A baseball team won 50 of the first 92 games played in a season. If the season consists of 152 games, how many more games must the team win to finish the season winning $62\frac{1}{2}\%$ of games played?

(A) 37   (B) 45   (C) 40   (D) 95   (E) 19

5. The Strauss Insurance Company laid off 20% of its employees one year and then increased its staff by $12\frac{1}{2}\%$ the following year. If the firm originally employed 120 workers, what was the net change in staff over the two-year period?

(A) decrease of 12   (B) increase of 15
(C) decrease of 9   (D) decrease of 24
(E) increase of 12

6. How much money is saved by buying an article priced at $80 with a 40% discount, rather than buying an article marked at $90 with discounts of 35% and 10%?

(A) $4.65   (B) $1.50   (C) $10.50   (D) $3.15   (E) $4.25

7. In Central City, a property owner pays school taxes at the rate of 2% of the first $1500 of assessed valuation, 3% of the next $2000, 5% of the next $3000 and 6% of the remainder. How much must Mr. Williams pay in school taxes each year if his home is assessed at $8000?

(A) $300   (B) $230   (C) $600   (D) $330   (E) $195

8. Jeffrey delivers newspapers for a salary of $20 per week plus a 4% commission on all sales. One week his sales amounted to $48. What was his income that week?

(A) $19.20   (B) $21.92   (C) $1.92   (D) $39.20   (E) $32

9. At Baker High, 3 out of every 4 graduates go on to college. Of these, 2 out of every 3 graduate from college. What percent of students graduating from Baker High will graduate from college?

(A) $66\frac{2}{3}$ (B) 75   (C) 50   (D) $33\frac{1}{3}$ (E) 25

10. The basic sticker price on Mr. Feldman's new car was $3200. The options he desired cost an additional $1800. What percent of the total price was made up of options?

(A) $56\frac{1}{4}$ (B) 36   (C) 64   (D) 18   (E) 9

Certain types of business situations are excellent applications of percent. Study the following examples carefully, as these are problems you will encounter in everyday life as well as on these examinations.

1. PERCENT OF INCREASE OR DECREASE

The percent of increase or decrease is found by putting the amount of increase or decrease over the original amount and changing this fraction to a percent by multiplying by 100.

Example: The number of automobiles sold by the Cadcoln Dealership increased from 300 one year to 400 the following year. What was the percent of increase?

Solution: There was an increase of 100, which must be compared to the original 300.

$\frac{100}{300} = \frac{1}{3} = 33\frac{1}{3}\%$

Example: The Sunset School dismisses 20% of its staff of 150 due to budgetary problems. By what percent must it now increase its staff to return to the previous level?

72 VERBAL PROBLEMS INVOLVING PERCENT

Solution: $20\% = \frac{1}{5}$ $\frac{1}{5} \cdot 150 = 30$
The school now has 150 − 30 or 120 employees. To increase by 30, the percent of increase is $\frac{30}{120} = \frac{1}{4}$ or 25%.

Practice 1

Answers on page 81

Work out each problem in the space provided. Circle the letter before your answer.

1. Mrs. Morris receives a salary raise from $25,000 to $27,500. Find the percent of increase.

(A) 9   (B) 10   (C) 90   (D) 15   (E) $12\frac{1}{2}$

2. The population of Stormville has increased from 80,000 to 100,000 in the last twenty years. Find the percent of increase.

(A) 20   (B) 25   (C) 80   (D) 60   (E) 10

3. The value of Super Company Stock dropped from $25 a share to $21 a share. Find the percent of decrease.

(A) 4   (B) 8   (C) 12   (D) 16   (E) 20

4. The Rubins bought their home for $30,000 and sold it for $60,000. What was the percent of increase?

(A) 100   (B) 50   (C) 200   (D) 300   (E) 150

5. During the pre-holiday rush, Martin's Department Store increased its sales staff from 150 to 200 persons. By what percent must it now decrease its sales staff to return to the usual number of salespersons?

(A) 25   (B) $33\frac{1}{3}$ (C) 20   (D) 40   (E) 75

2. DISCOUNT

A discount is usually expressed as a percent of the marked price, which will be deducted from the marked price to determine the sale price. If an article is sold at a 20% discount, the buyer pays 80% of the marked price. Instead of first finding the amount of discount by finding 20% of the marked price and subtracting to find the sale price, it is shorter and easier to find 80% of the marked price directly.

Example: A store offers a 25% discount on all appliances for paying cash. How much will a microwave oven marked at $400 cost if payment is made in cash?

Solution: We can find 25% or $\frac{1}{4}$ of $400, which is $100 and then subtract $100 from $400 to get a cash price of $300. The danger in this method is that the amount of discount, $100, is sure to be among the multiple-choice answers, as students often look for the first answer they get without bothering to finish the problem. It is safer, and easier, to realize that a 25% discount means 75% must be paid. 75% = $\frac{3}{4}$ and $\frac{3}{4}$ of $400 is $300.

Some problems deal with successive discounts. In such cases, the first discount is figured on the marked price, while the second discount is figured on the intermediate price.

Example: Johnson's Hardware Store is having a moving sale in which everything in the store is being marked down 20% with an additional 5% discount for paying cash. What will be the net cost of a toaster, paid with cash, marked at $25?

Solution: The first discount is 20% or $\frac{1}{5}$. We then pay $\frac{4}{5}$ of $25 or $20. An additional 5% is given off this amount. $\frac{5}{100} = \frac{1}{20}$ off. $\frac{19}{20} \cdot 20 = \$19$. The net price is $19.

Practice 2

Answers on page 81

Work out each problem in the space provided. Circle the letter before your answer.

1. How much is saved by buying a freezer marked at $600 with a discount of 20% rather than one marked at $600 with discounts of 10% and 10%?

(A) $6   (B) $8   (C) $10   (D) $12   (E) $20

2. Mr. Kaplan builds a home at a cost of $60,000. After pricing the home for sale by adding 25% of his expenses, he offers a discount of 20% to encourage sales. What did he make on the house?

(A) $15,000   (B) $1500   (C) $0
(D) $5000   (E) $1200

3. Christmas cards are sold after Christmas for 90 cents a box instead of $1.20 a box. The rate of discount is

(A) 20%   (B) 25%   (C) 30%   (D) $33\frac{1}{3}$%   (E) 40%

4. A television set listed at $160 is offered at a $12\frac{1}{2}$% discount during a storewide sale. If an additional 3% is allowed on the net price for payment in cash, how much can Josh save by buying this set during the sale for cash?

(A) $24.36   (B) $24.80   (C) $17.20   (D) $24.20   (E) $23.20

74   VERBAL PROBLEMS INVOLVING PERCENT

5. Pam pays $6 for a sweater after receiving a discount of 25%. What was the marked price of the sweater?

(A) $9   (B) $12   (C) $7   (D) $7.50   (E) $8

3. COMMISSION

In order to inspire sales, many companies pay their salespeople a percentage of the money the salespeople bring in. This is called a commission.

Example: Mr. Silver sells shoes at the Emporium, where he is paid $100 per week plus a 5% commission on all his sales. How much does he earn in a week in which his sales amount to $1840?

Solution: Find 5% of $1840 and add this amount to $100.

$$\begin{array}{r} 1840 \\ \underline{.05} \end{array}$$

$92.00 + $100 = $192

Example: Audrey sells telephone order merchandise for a cosmetics company. She keeps 12% of all money collected. One month she was able to keep $108. How much did she forward to the cosmetics company?

Solution: We must first find the total amount of her sales by asking: 108 is 12% of what number?

$$108 = .12x$$
$$10800 = 12x$$
$$900 = x$$

If Audrey collected $900 and kept $108, she sent the company $792.

Practice 3   Answers on page 82

Work out each problem in the space provided. Circle the letter before your answer.

1. Janice receives a 6% commission for selling newspaper advertisements. If she sells 15 ads for $50 each, how much does she earn?

(A) $30   (B) $40   (C) $45   (D) $18   (E) $450

2. Michael sells appliances and receives a salary of $125 per week plus a 5% commission on all sales over $750. How much does he earn in a week in which his sales amount to $2130?

(A) $69   (B) $294   (C) $106.50
(D) $194   (E) $162.50

VERBAL PROBLEMS INVOLVING PERCENT

3. Mr. Rosen receives a salary of $100 per month plus a commission of 3% of his sales. What was the amount of his sales in a month in which he earned a total salary of $802?

(A) $23,500 (B) $23,400 (C) $7800 (D) $7900 (E) $7700

4. Bobby sent $27 to the newspaper dealer for whom he delivers papers, after deducting his 10% commission. How many papers did he deliver if they sell for 20 cents each?

(A) 150 (B) 135 (C) 600 (D) 160 (E) 540

5. Mrs. Mitherz wishes to sell her home. She must pay the real estate agent who makes the sale 8% of the selling price. At what price must she sell her home if she wishes to net $73,600?

(A) $79,488 (B) $75,000 (C) $80,000 (D) $82,400 (E) $84,322

4. PROFIT AND LOSS

When a merchant purchases an article he adds a percent of this cost to what he paid to arrive at a selling price. This amount is called his profit.

Example: A radio sells for $40, giving the dealer a 25% profit. What was his cost?

Solution: If the dealer gets back all of his cost plus an extra 25%, then the $40 sales price represents 125% of his cost.

$1.25x = 40$
$125x = 4000$
$x = \$32$

Example: Joan's Boutique usually sells a handbag for $80 which yields a $33\frac{1}{3}\%$ profit. During a special sale, the profit is cut to 10%. What is the sale price of the handbag?

Solution: $80 represents $133\frac{1}{3}\%$ or $\frac{4}{3}$ of the cost.

$\frac{4}{3}x = 80$
$4x = 240$
$x = 60$

If the cost was $60 and the dealer wishes to add 10% for profit, he must add 10% of $60 or $6, making the sale price $66.

If a merchant sells an article for less than his cost, he takes a loss. A loss is figured as a percent of his cost in the same manner we figured a profit in the previous examples.

VERBAL PROBLEMS INVOLVING PERCENT

Practice 4

Answers on page 82

Work out each problem in the space provided. Circle the letter before your answer.

1. Steve buys a ticket to the opera. At the last moment, he finds he cannot go and sells the ticket to Judy for $10, which was a loss of $16\frac{2}{3}\%$. What was the original price of the ticket?

(A) $8.33   (B) $16.66   (C) $12   (D) $11.66   (E) $15

2. Alice bought a bicycle for $120. After using it for only a short time, she sold it to a bike store at a 20% loss. How much money did the bike store give Alice?

(A) $24   (B) $96   (C) $144   (D) $100   (E) $108

3. Julie's Dress Shop sold a gown for $150, thereby making a 25% profit. What was the cost of the gown to the dress shop?

(A) $120   (B) $112.50   (C) $117.50   (D) $187.50   (E) $125

4. If a music store sells a clarinet at a profit of 20% based on the selling price, what percent is made on the cost?

(A) 20   (B) 40   (C) 25
(D) 80   (E) none of these

5. Radio House paid $60 for a tape player. At what price should it be offered for sale, if the store offers customers a 10% discount, but still wants to make a profit of 20% of the cost?

(A) $64.80   (B) $72   (C) $79.20   (D) $80   (E) $84.20

5. TAXES

Taxes are a percent of money spent, money earned, or value.

> Example: Broome County has a 4% sales tax on appliances. How much will Mrs. Steinberg have to pay for a new dryer marked at $240?
>
> Solution: Find 4% of $240 to figure the tax and add this amount to $240. This can be done in one step by finding 104% of $240.
>
> $$\begin{array}{r} 240 \\ \underline{1.04} \\ 960 \\ \underline{24000} \\ \$249.60 \end{array}$$

VERBAL PROBLEMS INVOLVING PERCENT   77

Example: The Social Security tax is $7\frac{1}{4}$%. How much must Mrs. Grossman pay in a year, if her salary is $2000 per month?

Solution: Her annual salary is 12(2000) or $24,000. Find $7\frac{1}{4}$% of $24,000.

$7\frac{1}{4}$% = 7.25% = .0725

```
    24,000
     .0725
   12 0000
   48 0000
 1680 0000
$1740.0000
```

Practice 5

Answers on page 83

Work out each problem in the space provided. Circle the letter before your answer.

1. In Manorville, the current rate for school taxes is 7.5% of property value. Find the tax on a house assessed at $20,000.

(A) $150   (B) $1500   (C) $15,000   (D) $1250   (E) $105

2. The income tax in a certain state is figured at 2% of the first $1000, 3% of the next $2000, 4% of the next $3000 and 5% thereafter. Find the tax on an income of $25,000.

(A) $1150   (B) $1015   (C) $295   (D) $280   (E) $187

3. The sales tax in Nassau County is 7%. If Mrs. Gutman paid a total of $53.50 for new curtains, what was the marked price of the curtains?

(A) $49.75   (B) $49   (C) $57.25   (D) $50   (E) $45.86

4. Eric pays r% tax on an article marked at s dollars. How many dollars tax does he pay?

(A) $\dfrac{s}{100r}$ (B) rs   (C) $\dfrac{100s}{r}$ (D) 100rs   (E) $\dfrac{rs}{100}$

5. The sales tax on luxury items is 8%. If Mrs. Behr purchases a mink coat marked at $4000, what will be the total price for the coat including tax?

(A) $320   (B) $4032   (C) $4320   (D) $4500   (E) $500

VERBAL PROBLEMS INVOLVING PERCENT

Retest

Answers on page 83

Work out each problem in the space provided. Circle the letter before your answer.

1. A TV sells for $121. What was the cost if the profit is 10% of the cost?

(A) $110   (B) $108.90   (C) $120   (D) $116   (E) $111.11

2. Green's Sport Shop offers its salespeople an annual salary of $10,000 plus a 6% commission on all sales above $20,000. Every employee receives a Christmas bonus of $500. What are Mr. Cahn's total earnings in a year in which his sales amounted to $160,000?

(A) $18,900   (B) $18,400   (C) $19,600   (D) $20,100   (E) $8900

3. A car dealer purchased 40 new cars at $6500 each. He sold 40% of them at $8000 each and the rest at $9000 each. What was his total profit?

(A) $24,000   (B) $60,000   (C) $84,000
(D) $344,000   (E) $260,000

4. Mr. Adams' income rose from $20,000 one year to $23,000 the following year. What was the percent of increase?

(A) 3%   (B) 12%   (C) 15%   (D) 13%   (E) 87%

5. The enrollment at Walden School is 1400. If 20% of the students study French, 25% study Spanish, 10% study Italian, 15% study German, and the rest study no language, how many students do not study language, assuming each student may study only one language?

(A) 30   (B) 42   (C) 560   (D) 280   (E) 420

6. How much money is saved by buying a car priced at $6000 with a single discount of 15% rather than buying the same car with discounts of 10% and 5%?

(A) $51.30   (B) $30   (C) $780   (D) $87   (E) $900

7. At the Acme Cement Company, employees contribute to a welfare fund at the rate of 4% of the first $1000 earned, 3% of the next $1000, 2% of the next $1000 and 1% of any additional income. What will Mr. Morris contribute in a year in which he earns $20,000?

(A) $290   (B) $200   (C) $90   (D) $260   (E) $240

8. A salesman receives a commission of c% on a sale of D dollars. Find his commission.

(A) cD (B) $\dfrac{cD}{100}$ (C) 100cD (D) $\dfrac{c}{100D}$ (E) $\dfrac{100c}{D}$

9. John buys a tape player for $54 after receiving a discount of 10%. What was the marked price?

(A) $48.60 (B) $59.40 (C) $60 (D) $61.40 (E) $64

10. What single discount is equivalent to two successive discounts of 15% and 10%?

(A) 25% (B) 24.5% (C) 24% (D) 23.5% (E) 23%

SOLUTIONS TO PRACTICE EXERCISES

Diagnostic Test

1. (E) $30\% = \frac{3}{10}$
   $\frac{3}{10} \cdot 100 = 30$ books at $10 each
   $\phantom{\frac{3}{10} \cdot 100} = \$300$ in sales
   $100 - 30 = 70$ books at $15 each
   $ = \$1050$ in sales
   Total sales $\$300 + \$1050 = \$1350$
   Total profit $\$1350 - \$1250 = \$100$

2. (C) $25\% + 35\% + 5\% + 10\% = 75\%$
   $100\% - 75\% = 25\%$ for other expenses
   $25\% = \frac{1}{4}$ $\frac{1}{4} \cdot \$2000 = \$500$

3. (B) Amount of decrease = 200
   Percent of decrease $= \frac{200}{1200} = \frac{1}{6} = 16\frac{2}{3}\%$

4. (B) $62\frac{1}{2}\% = \frac{5}{8}$
   $\frac{5}{8} \cdot 152 = 95$ total wins needed
   $95 - 50 = 45$ wins still needed

5. (A) $20\% = \frac{1}{5}$
   $\frac{1}{5} \cdot 120 = 24$ employees laid off
   New number of employees $= 96$
   $12\frac{1}{2}\% = \frac{1}{8}$
   $\frac{1}{8} \cdot 96 = 12$ employees added to staff
   Therefore final number of employees is 108. Net change is $120 - 108 =$ decrease of 12.

6. (A) $40\% = \frac{2}{5}$ $\frac{2}{5} \cdot 80 = \$32$ off
   $\phantom{(A) 40\% = \frac{2}{5}}$ $\$48$ net price
   $35\% = \frac{7}{20}$ $\frac{7}{20} \cdot 90 = \$31.50$ off
   $\phantom{35\% = \frac{7}{20}}$ $\$58.50$ first net price
   $10\% = \frac{1}{10}$ $\frac{1}{10} \cdot 58.50 = \$5.85$ off
   $\phantom{10\% = \frac{1}{10}}$ $\$52.65$ net price
   $\$52.65 - \$48 = \$4.65$ was saved.

7. (D) 2% of $1500 = \$30$
   3% of $2000 = \$60$
   5% of $3000 = \$150$
   6% of ($\$8000 - \$6500$)
   $ = 6\%$ of $\$1500 = \$90$
   Total tax $= \$330$

8. (B) He earns 4% of $48.
   $$\begin{array}{r} 48 \\ \underline{.04} \\ \$1.92 \end{array}$$
   Add this to his basic salary of $20: $21.92.

9. (C) $\frac{\cancel{2}}{\cancel{3}} \cdot \frac{\cancel{3}}{\underset{2}{\cancel{4}}} = \frac{1}{2} = 50\%$ of the students will graduate from college.

10. (B) Total price is $5000.
    Percent of total that was options $= \frac{1800}{5000}$
    $= \frac{9}{25} = 36\%$

Practice 1

1. **(B)** Amount of increase = $2500

    Percent of increase = $\dfrac{\text{amount of increase}}{\text{original}}$

    $\dfrac{2500}{25{,}000} = \dfrac{1}{10} = 10\%$

2. **(B)** Amount of increase = 20,000

    Percent of increase = $\dfrac{20{,}000}{80{,}000} = \dfrac{1}{4} = 25\%$

3. **(D)** Amount of decrease = $4

    Percent of decrease = $\dfrac{4}{25} = \dfrac{16}{100} = 16\%$

4. **(A)** Amount of increase $30,000

    Percent of increase = $\dfrac{30{,}000}{30{,}000} = 1 = 100\%$

5. **(A)** Amount of decrease = 50

    Percent of decrease = $\dfrac{50}{200} = \dfrac{1}{4} = 25\%$

Practice 2

1. **(A)** $20\% = \dfrac{1}{5}$ $\dfrac{1}{5} \cdot 600 = \$120$ off

                           $480 net price

    $10\% = \dfrac{1}{10}$ $\dfrac{1}{10} \cdot 600 = \$60$ off

                           $540 first net price

    $\dfrac{1}{10} \cdot 540 = \$54$ off

                           $486 net price

    Therefore, $6 is saved.

2. **(C)** $25\% = \dfrac{1}{4}$
    $\dfrac{1}{4} \cdot 60{,}000 = \$15{,}000$ added to cost
    Original sale price = $75,000
    $20\% = \dfrac{1}{5}$ $\dfrac{1}{5} \cdot 75{,}000 = \%15{,}000$ discount
    Final sale price $60,000
    Therefore he made nothing on the sale.

3. **(B)** Discount = 30 cents. Rate of discount is figured on the original price.
    $\dfrac{30}{120} = \dfrac{1}{4} = 25\%$

4. **(D)** $12\tfrac{1}{2}\% = \dfrac{1}{8}$ $\dfrac{1}{8} \cdot 160 = \$20$ discount
    New sale price = $140
    $3\% = \dfrac{3}{100}$ $\dfrac{3}{100} \cdot 140 = \dfrac{420}{100}$
           = $4.20 second discount
    $135.80 final sale price
    Therefore, $160 − $135.80 or $24.20 was saved.

5. **(E)** $6 is 75% of the marked price.
    $6 = \dfrac{3}{4} x$
    $24 = 3x$
    $x = \$8$

VERBAL PROBLEMS INVOLVING PERCENT

Practice 3

1. (C) She sells 15 ads at $50 each for a total of $750. She earns 6% of this amount.

$$\begin{array}{r} 750 \\ \underline{.06} \\ \$45.00 \end{array}$$

2. (D) He earns 5% of ($2130 − $750).

$$\begin{array}{r} 1380 \\ \underline{.05} \\ \$69.00 \end{array}$$

   Add this to his basic salary of $125: $194.

3. (B) If his basic salary was $100, his commission amounted to $702. 702 is 3% of what?

$$702 = .03x$$
$$70{,}200 = 3x$$
$$\$23{,}400 = x$$

4. (A) $27 is 90% of what he collected.

$$27 = .90x$$
$$270 = 9x$$
$$x = \$30$$

   If each paper sells for 20 cents, he sold $\frac{30.00}{.20}$ or 150 papers.

5. (C) $73,600 is 92% of the selling price.

$$73{,}600 = .92x$$
$$7{,}360{,}000 = 92x$$
$$\$80{,}000 = x$$

Practice 4

1. (C) $16\frac{2}{3}\% = \frac{1}{6}$ $10 is $\frac{5}{6}$ of the original price.

$$10 = \tfrac{5}{6}x$$
$$60 = 5x$$
$$x = 12$$

2. (B) The store gave Alice 80% of the price she paid.

$$80\% = \tfrac{4}{5} \quad \tfrac{4}{5} \cdot 120 = \$96$$

3. (A) $150 is 125% of the cost.

$$150 = 1.25x$$
$$15{,}000 = 125x$$
$$x = \$120$$

4. (C) Work with an easy number such as $100 for the selling price. $20\% = \tfrac{1}{5}$ $\tfrac{1}{5} \cdot 100 = \$20$ profit, thereby making the cost $80. $\tfrac{20}{80} = \tfrac{1}{4} = 25\%$

5. (D) The dealer wishes to make 20% or $\tfrac{1}{5}$ of $60, which is $12 profit. The dealer wishes to clear $60 + $12 or $72. $72 will be 90% of the marked price.

$$72 = .90x$$
$$720 = 9x$$
$$x = \$80$$

Practice 5

1. (B) $\quad$ 20,000
   $\quad\quad\quad\times$ .075
   $\quad\quad$ ─────
   $\quad\quad$ 10 0000
   $\quad\quad$ 140 000
   $\quad\quad$ ─────
   $\quad\quad$ 1500.000

2. (A) 2% of $1000 = $20
   3% of $2000 = $60
   4% of $3000 = $120
   5% of ($25,000 − $6,000)
   $\quad$ = 5% of $19,000 = $950
   Total tax = $1150

3. (D) $53.50 is 107% of the marked price
   $\quad\quad$ 53.50 = 1.07x
   $\quad\quad$ 5350 = 107x
   $\quad\quad\quad$ x = $50

4. (E) $r\% = \dfrac{r}{100}$ $\quad\quad \dfrac{r}{100} \cdot s = \dfrac{rs}{100}$

5. (C) $\quad$ 4000
   $\quad\quad\quad\times$ .08
   $\quad\quad$ ─────
   $\quad\quad$ 320.00 tax $\quad\quad$ Total price $4320

Retest

1. (A) $121 is 110% of the cost.
   $\quad\quad$ 121 = 1.10x
   $\quad\quad$ 1210 = 11x
   $\quad\quad\quad$ x = $110

2. (A) He earns 6% of ($160,000 − $20,000).
   $\quad\quad$ 140,000
   $\quad\quad\quad\times$ .06
   $\quad\quad$ ─────
   $\quad\quad$ $8400.00

   Add this to his basic salary of $10,000 and his Christmas bonus of $500: $18,900.

3. (C) $40\% = \tfrac{2}{5}$ $\quad \tfrac{2}{5} \cdot 40 = 16$ cars at $8000
   each = $128,000 in sales
   40 − 16 = 24 cars at $9000 each
   $\quad$ = $216,000 in sales
   Total sales $128,000 + $216,000
   $\quad$ = $344,000
   Total expense $6500 · 40 = $260,000
   Total profit $344,000 − $260,000
   $\quad$ = $84,000

4. (C) Amount of increase = $3000
   $\quad$ Percent of increase = $\dfrac{3000}{20,000}$
   $\quad\quad\quad\quad\quad = \dfrac{3}{20} = 15\%$

5. (E) 20% + 25% + 10% + 15% = 70%
   100% − 70% = 30% study no language
   $30\% = \tfrac{3}{10}$ $\quad \tfrac{3}{10} \cdot 1400 = 420$

6. (B) $15\% = \tfrac{3}{20}$ $\quad \tfrac{3}{20} \cdot \$6000 = \$900$ off
   $\quad\quad\quad\quad\quad\quad\quad\quad$ $5100 net price
   $10\% = \tfrac{1}{10}$ $\quad \tfrac{1}{10} \cdot \$6000 = \$600$ off
   $\quad\quad\quad\quad\quad\quad\quad\quad$ $5400 first net price
   $5\% = \tfrac{1}{20}$ $\quad \tfrac{1}{20} \cdot 5400 = \$270$ off
   $\quad\quad\quad\quad\quad\quad\quad\quad$ $5130 net price
   $5130 − $5100 = $30 was saved.

7. (D) 4% of $1000 = $40
   3% of $1000 = $30
   2% of $1000 = $20
   1% of $17,000 = $170
   Total contribution = $260

84 VERBAL PROBLEMS INVOLVING PERCENT

8. (B) $c\% = \dfrac{c}{100}$ $\dfrac{c}{100} \cdot D = \dfrac{cD}{100}$

9. (C) $54 is 90% of the marked price.

$$54 = \tfrac{9}{10} x$$
$$540 = 9x$$
$$x = \$60$$

10. (D) Work with an easy number such as $100.
$15\% = \tfrac{3}{20}$ $\tfrac{3}{20} \cdot \$100 = \$15$ off
$\qquad\qquad\qquad\quad$ $85 first net price
$10\% = \tfrac{1}{10}$ $\tfrac{1}{10} \cdot \$85 = \$8.50$ off
$\qquad\qquad\qquad\quad$ $76.50 net price
$100 − $76.50 = $23.50 total discount
$\dfrac{23.50}{100} = 23.5\%$

Averages

DIAGNOSTIC TEST

Answers on page 92

Work out each problem in the space provided. Circle the letter before your answer.

1. Find the average of the first ten positive even integers.

(A) 9   (B) 10   (C) 11   (D) 12   (E) $5\frac{1}{2}$

2. What is the average of x − 4, x and x + 4?

(A) 3x   (B) x   (C) x − 1   (D) x + 1   (E) $\frac{3x-8}{3}$

3. Find the average of $\sqrt{.09}$, .4 and $\frac{1}{2}$.

(A) .31   (B) .35   (C) .04   (D) .4   (E) .45

4. Valerie received test grades of 93 and 88 on her first two French tests. What grade must she get on the third test to have an average of 92?

(A) 95   (B) 100   (C) 94   (D) 96   (E) 92

5. The average of W and another number is A. Find the other number.

(A) A − W   (B) A + W   (C) $\frac{1}{2}$(A − W)   (D) $\frac{1}{2}$(A + W)
(E) 2A − W

6. The weight of three packages are 4 lb. 10 oz., 6 lb. 13 oz. and 3 lb. 6 oz. Find the average weight of these packages.

(A) 4 lb. 43 oz.   (B) 4 lb. $7\frac{1}{2}$ oz.   (C) 4 lb. 15 oz.
(D) 4 lb. 6 oz.   (E) 4 lb. 12 oz.

7. If Barbara drove for 4 hours at 50 miles per hour and then for 2 more hours at 60 miles per hour, what was her average rate, in miles per hour, for the entire trip?

(A) 55   (B) $53\frac{1}{3}$ (C) $56\frac{2}{3}$ (D) 53   (E) $54\frac{1}{2}$

86 AVERAGES

8. Mr. Maron employs three secretaries at a salary of $140 per week and five salespeople at a salary of $300 per week. What is the average weekly salary paid to an employee?

(A) $55   (B) $190   (C) $240   (D) $200   (E) $185

9. Which of the following statements are always true?

    I—The average of any three consecutive even integers is the middle integer.
    II—The average of any three consecutive odd integers is the middle integer.
    III—The average of any three consecutive multiples of 5 is the middle number.

(A) I only   (B) II only   (C) I and II only
(D) I and III only   (E) I, II, and III

10. Mark has an average of 88 on his first four math tests. What grade must he earn on his fifth test in order to raise his average to 90?

(A) 92   (B) 94   (C) 96   (D) 98   (E) 100

1. SIMPLE AVERAGE

Most students are familiar with the method for finding an average and use this procedure frequently during the school year. To find the average of n numbers, find the sum of all the numbers and divide this sum by n.

    Example: Find the average of 12, 17, and 61.

    Solution:
$$\begin{array}{r} 12 \\ 17 \\ \underline{61} \\ 3\overline{)90} \\ 30 \end{array}$$

When the numbers to be averaged form an evenly spaced series, the average is simply the middle number. If we are finding the average of an even number of terms, there will be no middle number. In this case, the average is halfway between the two middle numbers.

    Example: Find the average of the first 40 positive even integers.

    Solution: Since these 40 addends are evenly spaced, the average will be half way between the 20th and 21st even integers. The 20th even integer is 40 (use your fingers to count if needed) and the 21st is 42, so the average of the first 40 positive even integers which range from 2 to 80 is 41.

The above concept must be clearly understood, as it would use up much too much time to add the 40 numbers and divide by 40. Using the method described, it is no harder to find the average of 100 evenly spaced terms than it is of 40 terms.

In finding averages, be sure the numbers being added are all of the same form or in terms of the same units. To average fractions and decimals, they must all be written as fractions or all as decimals.

Example: Find the average of $87\frac{1}{2}\%$, $\frac{1}{4}$, and .6

Solution: Rewrite each number as a decimal before adding.

$$\begin{array}{r} .875 \\ .25 \\ \underline{.6} \\ 3\overline{)1.725} \\ .575 \end{array}$$

Practice 1

Answers on page 92

Work out each problem in the space provided. Circle the letter before your answer.

1. Find the average of $\sqrt{.49}$, $\frac{3}{4}$, and 80%.
 (A) .72   (B) .75   (C) .78   (D) .075   (E) .073

2. Find the average of the first 5 positive integers that end in 3.
 (A) 3   (B) 13   (C) 18   (D) 23   (E) 28

3. The five men on a basketball team weigh 160, 185, 210, 200, and 195 pounds. Find the average weight of these players.
 (A) 190   (B) 192   (C) 195   (D) 198   (E) 180

4. Find the average of a, 2a, 3a, 4a, and 5a.
 (A) $3a^5$ (B) $3a$ (C) $2.8a$ (D) $2.8a^5$ (E) 3

5. Find the average of $\frac{1}{2}$, $\frac{1}{3}$, and $\frac{1}{4}$.
 (A) $\frac{1}{9}$ (B) $\frac{13}{36}$ (C) $\frac{1}{27}$ (D) $\frac{13}{12}$ (E) $\frac{1}{3}$

2. TO FIND A MISSING NUMBER WHEN AN AVERAGE IS GIVEN

In solving this type of problem, it is easiest to use an algebraic equation which applies the definition of average. That is,

$$\text{average} = \frac{\text{sum of terms}}{\text{number of terms}}$$

Example: The average of four numbers is 26. If three of the numbers are 50, 12, and 28, find the fourth number.

Solution: $\dfrac{50 + 12 + 28 + x}{4} = 26$

$50 + 12 + 28 + x = 104$
$90 + x = 104$
$x = 14$

An alternative method of solution is to realize that the number of units below 26 must balance the number of units above 26. 50 is 24 units *above* 26. 12 is 14 units *below* 26. 28 is 2 units *above* 26. Therefore, we presently have 26 units (24 + 2) *above* 26 and only 14 units *below* 26. Therefore the missing number must be 12 units *below* 26, making it 14. When the numbers are easy to work with, this method is usually the fastest. Just watch your arithmetic.

Practice 2

Answers on page 93

Work out each problem in the space provided. Circle the letter before your answer.

1. Dick's average for his freshman year was 88, his sophomore year was 94 and his junior year was 91. What average must he have in his senior year to leave high school with an average of 92?

(A) 92   (B) 93   (C) 94   (D) 95   (E) 96

2. The average of X, Y, and another number is M. Find the missing number.

(A) 3M − X + Y   (B) 3M − X − Y   (C) $\dfrac{M + X + Y}{3}$

(D) M − X − Y   (E) M − X + Y

3. The average of two numbers is 2x. If one of the numbers is x + 3, find the other number.

(A) x − 3   (B) 2x − 3   (C) 3x − 3   (D) −3   (E) 3x + 3

4. On consecutive days, the high temperature in Great Neck was 86°, 82°, 90°, 92°, 80°, and 81°. What was the high temperature on the seventh day, if the average high for the week was 84°?

(A) 79°   (B) 85°   (C) 81°   (D) 77°   (E) 76°

5. If the average of five consecutive integers is 17, find the largest of these integers.

(A) 17   (B) 18   (C) 19   (D) 20   (E) 21

3. WEIGHTED AVERAGE

When some numbers among terms to be averaged occur more than once, they must be given the appropriate weight. For example, if a student received four grades of 80 and one of 90, his average would not be the average of 80 and 90, but rather the average of 80, 80, 80, 80, and 90.

> Example: Mr. Martin drove for 6 hours at an average rate of 50 miles per hour and for 2 hours at an average rate of 60 miles per hour. Find his average rate for the entire trip.
>
> Solution: $\dfrac{6(50) + 2(60)}{8} = \dfrac{300 + 120}{8} = \dfrac{420}{8} = 52\tfrac{1}{2}$

Since he drove many more hours at 50 miles per hour than at 60 miles per hour, his average rate should be closer to 50 than to 60, which it is. In general, average rate can always be found by dividing the total distance covered by the time spent traveling.

Practice 3

Answers on page 93

Work out each problem in the space provided. Circle the letter before your answer.

1. In a certain gym class, 6 girls weigh 120 pounds each, 8 girls weigh 125 pounds each, and 10 girls weigh 116 pounds each. What is the average weight of these girls?

(A) 120   (B) 118   (C) 121   (D) 122   (E) 119

2. In driving from San Francisco to Los Angeles, Arthur drove for three hours at 60 miles per hour and for 4 hours at 55 miles per hour. What was his average rate, in miles per hour, for the entire trip?

(A) 57.5   (B) 56.9   (C) 57.1   (D) 58.2   (E) 57.8

3. In the Linwood School, five teachers earn $15,000 per year, three teachers earn $17,000 per year and one teacher earns $18,000 per year. Find the average yearly salary of these teachers.

(A) $16,667   (B) $16,000   (C) $17,000   (D) $16,448   (E) $16,025

4. During the first four weeks of summer vacation, Danny worked at a camp earning $50 per week. During the remaining six weeks of vacation, he worked as a stock boy earning $100 per week. What was his average weekly wage for the summer?

(A) $80   (B) $75   (C) $87.50   (D) $83.33   (E) $82

5. If M students each received a grade of P on a physics test and N students each received a grade of Q, what was the average grade for this group of students?

(A) $\dfrac{P+Q}{M+N}$ (B) $\dfrac{PQ}{M+N}$ (C) $\dfrac{MP+NQ}{M+N}$

(D) $\dfrac{MP+NQ}{P+Q}$ (E) $\dfrac{M+N}{P+Q}$

Retest

Answers on page 93

Work out each problem in the space provided. Circle the letter before your answer.

1. Find the average of the first 14 positive odd integers.

(A) 7.5 (B) 13 (C) 14 (D) 15 (E) 14.5

2. What is the average of $2x - 3$, $x + 1$, and $3x + 8$?

(A) $6x + 6$ (B) $2x - 2$ (C) $2x + 4$ (D) $2x + 2$ (E) $2x - 4$

3. Find the average of $\frac{1}{5}$, 25% and .09

(A) $\frac{2}{3}$ (B) .18 (C) .32 (D) 20% (E) $\frac{1}{4}$

4. Andy received test grades of 75, 82, and 70 on three French tests. What grade must he earn on the fourth test to have an average of 80 on these four tests?

(A) 90 (B) 93 (C) 94 (D) 89 (E) 96

5. The average of 2P, 3Q, and another number is S. Represent the third number in terms of P, Q, and S.

(A) $S - 2P - 3Q$ (B) $S - 2P + 3Q$ (C) $3S - 2P + 3Q$
(D) $3S - 2P - 3Q$ (E) $S + 2P - 3Q$

6. The students of South High spent a day on the street collecting money to help cure birth defects. In counting up the collections, they found that 10 cans contained $5.00 each, 14 cans contained $6.50 each, and 6 cans contained $7.80 each. Find the average amount contained in each of these cans.

(A) $6.14 (B) $7.20 (C) $6.26 (D) $6.43 (E) $5.82

7. The heights of the five starters on the Princeton basketball team are 6'6", 6'7", 6'11", 6'9", and 7'. Find the average height of these men.

(A) 6'8$\frac{1}{5}$" (B) 6'9" (C) 6'9$\frac{3}{5}$" (D) 6'9$\frac{1}{5}$" (E) 6'9$\frac{1}{2}$"

8. Which of the following statements is always true?

   I—The average of the first twenty integers is 10.5
   II—The average of the first ten positive integers is 5.
   III—The average of the first 4 positive integers which end in 2 is 17.

(A) I only (B) II only (C) III only (D) I and III only
(E) I, II, and III

9. Karen drove 40 miles into the country at 40 miles per hour and returned home by bus at 20 miles per hour. What was her average rate in miles per hour for the round trip?

(A) 30 (B) $25\frac{1}{2}$ (C) $26\frac{2}{3}$ (D) 20 (E) $27\frac{1}{3}$

10. Mindy's average monthly salary for the first four months she worked was $300. What must be her average monthly salary for each of the next 8 months, so that her average monthly salary for the year is $350?

(A) $400 (B) $380 (C) $390 (D) $375 (E) $370

SOLUTIONS TO PRACTICE EXERCISES

Diagnostic Test

1. (C) The integers are 2, 4, 6, 8, 10, 12, 14, 16, 18, 20. Since these are evenly spaced, the average is the average of the two middle numbers, 10 and 12, or 11.

2. (B) These numbers are evenly spaced, so the average is the middle number x.

3. (D) $\sqrt{.09} = .3$
   $\frac{1}{2} = .5$
   $.4 = .4$
   $3\overline{)1.2}$
   $.4$

4. (A) 93 is 1 above 92; 88 is 4 below 92. So far, she has 1 point above 92 and 4 points below 92. Therefore, she needs another 3 points above 92, making a required grade of 95.

5. (E) $\frac{W + x}{2} = A$

   $W + x = 2A$

   $x = 2A - W$

6. (C) 4 lb. 10 oz.
        6 lb. 13 oz.
       +3 lb. 6 oz.
       13 lb. 29 oz.

   $\frac{13 \text{ lb. } 29 \text{ oz.}}{3} = \frac{12 \text{ lb. } 45 \text{ oz.}}{3} = 4 \text{ lb. } 15 \text{ oz.}$

7. (B) 4(50) = 200
       2(60) = 120
       $6\overline{)320}$
       $53\frac{1}{3}$

8. (C) 3(140) = 420
       5(300) = 1500
       $8\overline{)1920}$
       240

9. (E) The average of any three numbers which are evenly spaced is the middle number.

10. (D) Since 88 is 2 below 90, Mark is 8 points below 90 after the first four tests. Thus, he needs a 98 to make the required average of 90.

Practice 1

1. (B) $\sqrt{.49} = .7$
   $\frac{3}{4} = .75$
   $80\% = .80$
   $3\overline{)2.25}$
   $.75$

2. (D) The integers are 3, 13, 23, 33, 43. Since these are evenly spaced, the average is the middle integer, 23.

3. (A) $160 + 185 + 210 + 200 + 195 = 950$

   $\frac{950}{5} = 190$

4. (B) These numbers are evenly spaced, so the average is the middle number, 3a.

5. (B) $\frac{1}{2} + \frac{1}{3} + \frac{1}{4} = \frac{6}{12} + \frac{4}{12} + \frac{3}{12} = \frac{13}{12}$

   To divide this sum by 3, multiply by $\frac{1}{3}$.
   $\frac{13}{12} \cdot \frac{1}{3} = \frac{13}{36}$

AVERAGES

Practice 2

1. (D) 88 is 4 below 92; 94 is 2 above 92; 91 is 1 below 92. So far, he has 5 points below 92 and only 2 above. Therefore, he needs another 3 points above 92, making the required grade 95.

2. (B) $\dfrac{X + Y + x}{3} = M$

    $X + Y + x = 3M$

    $x = 3M - X - Y$

3. (C) $\dfrac{(x + 3) + n}{2} = 2x$

    $x + 3 + n = 4x$

    $n = 3x - 3$

4. (D) 86° is 2 above the average of 84; 82° is 2 below; 90° is 6 above; 92° is 8 above; 80° is 4 below; 81° is 3 below. So far, there are 16° above and 9° below. Therefore, the missing term is 7° below the average, or 77°.

5. (C) 17 must be the middle integer, since the five integers are consecutive and the average is, therefore, the middle number. The numbers are 15, 16, 17, 18, and 19.

Practice 3

1. (A) $6(120) = 720$
    $8(125) = 1000$
    $10(116) = 1160$
    $24 \overline{)2880}$
    120

2. (C) $3(60) = 180$
    $4(55) = 220$
    $7 \overline{)400}$
    $57\tfrac{1}{7}$ which is 57.1 to the nearest tenth.

3. (B) $5(15,000) = 75,000$
    $3(17,000) = 51,000$
    $1(18,000) = 18,000$
    $9 \overline{)144,000}$
    $16,000$

4. (A) $4(50) = 200$
    $6(100) = 600$
    $10 \overline{)800}$
    80

5. (C) $M(P) = MP$
    $N(Q) = NQ$
    $\overline{MP + NQ}$

    Divide by the number of students, $M + N$.

Retest

1. (C) The integers are 1, 3, 5, 7, 9, 11, 13, 15, 17, 19, 21, 23, 25, 27. Since these are evenly spaced, the average is the average of the two middle numbers 13 and 15, or 14.

2. (D) $2x - 3$
    $x + 1$
    $\underline{3x + 8}$
    $6x + 6$

    $\dfrac{6x + 6}{3} = 2x + 2$

3. (B) $\frac{1}{5} = .20$
         $25\% = .25$
         $.09 = .09$
         $3\overline{).54}$
         $.18$

4. (B) 75 is 5 below 80; 82 is 2 above 80; 70 is 10 below 80. So far, he is 15 points below and 2 points above 80. Therefore, he needs another 13 points above 80, or 93.

5. (D) $\frac{2P + 3Q + x}{3} = S$

    $2P + 3Q + x = 3S$

    $x = 3S - 2P - 3Q$

6. (C) $10(\$5.00) = \$50$
        $14(\$6.50) = \$91$
        $6(\$7.80) = \underline{\$46.80}$
        $30\overline{)\$187.80}$
        $\$6.26$

7. (B) $6'6'' + 6'7'' + 6'11'' + 6'9'' + 7'$
        $= 31'33'' = 33'9''$

    $\frac{33'9''}{5} = 6'9''$

8. (C) I. The average of the first twenty *positive* integers is 10.5.
    II. The average of the first ten positive integers is 5.5.
    III. The first four positive integers which end in 2 are 2, 12, 22, and 32. Their average is 17.

9. (C) Karen drove for 1 hour into the country and returned home by bus in 2 hours. Since the total distance traveled was 80 miles, her average rate for the round trip was $\frac{80}{3}$ or $26\frac{2}{3}$ miles per hour.

10. (D) Since $300 is $50 below $350, Mindy's salary for the first four months is $200 below $350. Therefore, her salary for each of the next 8 months must be $\frac{\$200}{8}$ or $25 above the average of $350, thus making the required salary $375.

Concepts of Algebra—Signed Numbers and Equations

DIAGNOSTIC TEST

Answers on page 106

Work out each problem in the space provided. Circle the letter before your answer.

1. When +4 is added to −6, the sum is

   (A) −10 (B) +10 (C) −24 (D) −2 (E) +2

2. The product of $(-3)(+4)(-\frac{1}{2})(-\frac{1}{3})$ is

   (A) −1 (B) −2 (C) +2 (D) −6 (E) +6

3. When the product of (-12) and $(+\frac{1}{4})$ is divided by the product of (-18) and $(-\frac{1}{3})$, the quotient is

   (A) +2 (B) −2 (C) $+\frac{1}{2}$ (D) $-\frac{1}{2}$ (E) $-\frac{2}{3}$

4. Solve for x: $ax + b = cx + d$

   (A) $\dfrac{d-b}{ac}$ (B) $\dfrac{d-b}{a+c}$ (C) $\dfrac{d-b}{a-c}$ (D) $\dfrac{b-d}{ac}$ (E) $\dfrac{b-d}{a-c}$

5. Solve for y: $7x - 2y = 2$
   $3x + 4y = 30$

   (A) 2 (B) 6 (C) 1 (D) 11 (E) −4

6. Solve for x: $x + y = a$
   $x - y = b$

   (A) $a + b$ (B) $a - b$ (C) $\frac{1}{2}(a+b)$ (D) $\frac{1}{2}ab$ (E) $\frac{1}{2}(a-b)$

7. Solve for x: $4x^2 - 2x = 0$

   (A) $\frac{1}{2}$ only (B) 0 only (C) $-\frac{1}{2}$ only (D) $\frac{1}{2}$ or 0 (E) $-\frac{1}{2}$ or 0

96 CONCEPTS OF ALGEBRA—SIGNED NUMBERS AND EQUATIONS

8. Solve for x: $x^2 - 4x - 21 = 0$

(A) 7 or 3   (B) -7 or -3   (C) -7 or 3   (D) 7 or -3
(E) none of these

9. Solve for x: $\sqrt{x+1} - 3 = -7$

(A) 15   (B) 47   (C) 51   (D) 39
(E) no solution

10. Solve for x: $\sqrt{x^2 + 7} - 1 = x$

(A) 9   (B) 3   (C) -3   (D) 2
(E) no solution

1. SIGNED NUMBERS

The rules for operations with signed numbers are basic to successful work in algebra. Be sure you know, and can apply, the following rules.

Addition: To add numbers with the same sign, add the magnitudes of the numbers and keep the same sign. To add numbers with different signs, subtract the magnitudes of the numbers and use the sign of the number with the greater magnitude.

Example: Add the following:

```
  +4        -4        -4        +4
  +7        -7        +7        -7
  ---       ---       ---       ---
 +11       -11        +3        -3
```

Subtraction: Change the sign of the number to be subtracted and proceed with the rules for addition. Remember that subtracting is really adding the additive inverse.

Example: Subtract the following:

```
  +4        -4        -4        +4
  +7        -7        +7        -7
  ---       ---       ---       ---
  -3        +3       -11       +11
```

Multiplication: If there are an odd number of negative factors, the product is negative. An even number of negative signs gives a positive product.

Example: Find the following products:

$(+4)(+7) = +28$ $(-4)(-7) = +28$

$(+4)(-7) = -28$ $(-4)(+7) = -28$

Division: If the signs are the same, the quotient is positive. If the signs are different, the quotient is negative.

CONCEPTS OF ALGEBRA—SIGNED NUMBERS AND EQUATIONS

Example: Divide the following:

$$\frac{+28}{+4} = +7 \qquad \frac{-28}{-4} = +7 \qquad \frac{-28}{+4} = -7 \qquad \frac{+28}{-4} = -7$$

Practice 1

Answers on page 106

Work out each problem in the space provided. Circle the letter before your answer.

1. At 8 A.M. the temperature was $-4°$. If the temperature rose 7 degrees during the next hour, what was the thermometer reading at 9 A.M.?

(A) $+11°$ (B) $-11°$ (C) $+7°$ (D) $+3°$ (E) $-3°$

2. In Asia, the highest point is Mount Everest, with an altitude of 29,002 feet, while the lowest point is the Dead Sea, 1286 feet below sea level. What is the difference in their elevations?

(A) 27,716 feet   (B) 30,288 feet   (C) 28,284 feet
(D) 30,198 feet   (E) 27,284 feet

3. Find the product of $(-6)(-4)(-4)$ and (-2).

(A) -16 (B) $+16$ (C) -192 (D) $+192$ (E) -98

4. The temperatures reported at hour intervals on a winter evening were $+4°, 0°, -1°, -5°,$ and $-8°$. Find the average temperature for these hours.

(A) $-10°$ (B) $-2°$ (C) $+2°$ (D) $-2\frac{1}{2}°$ (E) $-3°$

5. Evaluate the expression $5a - 4x - 3y$ if $a = -2$, $x = -10$ and $y = 5$.

(A) $+15$ (B) $+25$ (C) -65 (D) -35 (E) $+35$

2. SOLUTION OF LINEAR EQUATIONS

Equations are the basic tools of algebra. The techniques of solving an equation are not difficult. Whether an equation involves numbers, or only letters, the basic steps are the same.

1. If there are fractions or decimals, remove them by multiplication.
2. Remove any parentheses by using the distributive law.
3. Collect all terms containing the unknown for which you are solving on the same side of the equal sign. Remember that whenever a term crosses the equal sign from one side of the

98 CONCEPTS OF ALGEBRA—SIGNED NUMBERS AND EQUATIONS

equation to the other, it must pay a toll. That is, it must change its sign.
4. Determine the coefficient of the unknown by combining similar terms or factoring when terms cannot be combined.
5. Divide both sides of the equation by the coefficient.

Example: Solve for x: $5x - 3 = 3x + 5$

Solution: $2x = 8$
$x = 4$

Example: Solve for x: $\frac{2}{3}x - 10 = \frac{1}{4}x + 15$

Solution: Multiply by 12. $8x - 120 = 3x + 180$
$5x = 300$
$x = 60$

Example: Solve for x: $.3x + .15 = 1.65$

Solution: Multiply by 100. $30x + 15 = 165$
$30x = 150$
$x = 5$

Example: Solve for x: $ax - r = bx - s$

Solution: $ax - bx = r - s$
$x(a - b) = r - s$
$x = \dfrac{r - s}{a - b}$

Example: Solve for x: $6x - 2 = 8(x - 2)$

Solution: $6x - 2 = 8x - 16$
$14 = 2x$
$x = 7$

Practice 2

Answers on page 107

Work out each problem in the space provided. Circle the letter before your answer.

1. Solve for x: $3x - 2 = 3 + 2x$

    (A) 1   (B) 5   (C) -1   (D) 6   (E) -5

2. Solve for a: $8 - 4(a - 1) = 2 + 3(4 - a)$

    (A) $-\frac{5}{3}$ (B) $-\frac{7}{3}$ (C) 1   (D) -2   (E) 2

3. Solve for x: $\frac{1}{8}y + 6 = \frac{1}{4}y$

    (A) 48   (B) 14   (C) 6   (D) 1   (E) 2

4. Solve for x: .02(x − 2) = 1
   (A) 2.5 (B) 52 (C) 1.5 (D) 51 (E) 6

5. Solve for x: 4(x − r) = 2x + 10r
   (A) 7r (B) 3r (C) r (D) 5.5r (E) $2\frac{1}{3}r$

3. SIMULTANEOUS EQUATIONS IN TWO UNKNOWNS

In solving equations with two unknowns, it is necessary to work with two equations simultaneously. The object is to eliminate one of the unknowns, resulting in an equation with one unknown, which can be solved by the methods of the previous section. This can be done by multiplying one or both equations by suitable constants in order to make the coefficients of one of the unknowns the same. Remember that multiplying *all* terms in an equation by the same constant does not change its value. The unknown can then be removed by adding or subtracting the two equations. When working with simultaneous equations, always be sure to have the terms containing the unknowns on one side of the equation and the remaining terms on the other side.

Example: Solve for x: 7x + 5y = 15
                     5x − 9y = 17

Solution: Since we wish to solve for x, we would like to eliminate the y terms. This can be done by multiplying the top equation by 9 and the bottom equation by 5. In doing this, both y coefficients will have the same magnitude.

Multiplying the first by 9, we have

$$63x + 45y = 135$$

Multiplying the second by 5, we have

$$25x − 45y = 85$$

Since the y terms now have opposite signs, we can eliminate y by adding the two equations. If they had the same signs, we would eliminate by subtracting the two equations.

Adding, we have

$$\begin{array}{r} 63x + 45y = 135 \\ 25x - 45y = 85 \\ \hline 88x = 220 \\ x = 2\frac{1}{2} \end{array}$$

Since we were only asked to solve for x, we stop here. If we were asked to solve for both x and y, we would now substitute $2\frac{1}{2}$ for x in either equation and solve the resulting equation for y.

$$7(2.5) + 5y = 15$$
$$17.5 + 5y = 15$$
$$5y = -2.5$$
$$y = -.5 \text{ or } -\tfrac{1}{2}$$

Example: Solve for x: $ax + by = r$
$cx - dy = s$

Solution: Multiply the first equation by d and the second by b, to eliminate the y terms by addition.

$$adx + bdy = dr$$
$$\underline{bcx - bdy = bs}$$
$$adx + bcx = dr + bs$$

Factor out x to determine the coefficient of x.

$$x(ad + bc) = dr + bs$$
$$x = \frac{dr + bs}{ad + bc}$$

Practice 3

Answers on page 107

Work out each problem in the space provided. Circle the letter before your answer.

1. Solve for x: $x - 3y = 3$
$2x + 9y = 11$

(A) 2 (B) 3 (C) 4 (D) 5 (E) 6

2. Solve for x: $.6x + .2y = 2.2$
$.5x - .2y = 1.1$

(A) 1 (B) 3 (C) 30 (D) 10 (E) 11

3. Solve for y: $2x + 3y = 12b$
$3x - y = 7b$

(A) $7\frac{1}{7}b$ (B) $2b$ (C) $3b$ (D) $1\frac{2}{7}$ (E) $-b$

4. If $2x = 3y$ and $5x + y = 34$, find y.

(A) 4 (B) 5 (C) 6 (D) 6.5 (E) 10

5. If x + y = -1 and x - y = 3, find y.

(A) 1   (B) -2   (C) -1   (D) 2   (E) 0

4. QUADRATIC EQUATIONS

In solving quadratic equations, there will always be two roots, even though these roots may be equal. A complete quadratic equation is of the form $ax^2 + bx + c = 0$, where a, b, and c are integers. At the level of this examination, $ax^2 + bx + c$ can always be factored. If b and/or c is equal to 0, we have an incomplete quadratic equation, which can still be solved by factoring and will still have two roots.

Example: $x^2 + 5x = 0$

Solution: Factor out a common factor of x.

$x(x + 5) = 0$

If the product of two factors is 0, either factor may be set equal to 0, giving $x = 0$ or $x + 5 = 0$. From these two linear equations, we find the two roots of the given quadratic equation to be $x = 0$ and $x = -5$.

Example: $6x^2 - 8x = 0$

Solution: Factor out a common factor of 2x.

$2x(3x - 4) = 0$

Set each factor equal to 0 and solve the resulting linear equations for x.

$2x = 0$ $3x - 4 = 0$
$x = 0$ $3x = 4$
            $x = \frac{4}{3}$

The roots of the given quadratic are 0 and $\frac{4}{3}$.

Example: $x^2 - 9 = 0$

Solution: $x^2 = 9$
$x = \pm 3$

Remember there must be two roots. This equation could also have been solved by factoring $x^2 - 9$ into $(x + 3)(x - 3)$ and setting each factor equal to 0. Remember that the difference of two perfect squares can always be factored, with one factor being the sum of the two square roots and the second being the difference of the two square roots.

Example: $x^2 - 8 = 0$

Solution: Since 8 is not a perfect square, this cannot be solved by factoring.

$$x^2 = 8$$
$$x = \pm\sqrt{8}$$

Simplifying the radical, we have $\sqrt{4}\;\sqrt{2}$, or $x = \pm 2\sqrt{2}$

Example: $16x^2 - 25 = 0$

Solution: Factoring, we have

$$(4x - 5)(4x + 5) = 0$$

Setting each factor equal to 0, we have

$$x = \pm \tfrac{5}{4}$$

If we had solved without factoring, we would have found $16x^2 = 25$

$$x^2 = \tfrac{25}{16}$$
$$x = \pm \tfrac{5}{4}$$

Example: $x^2 + 6x + 8 = 0$

Solution: $(x + 2)(x + 4) = 0$

If the last term of the trinomial is positive, both binomial factors must have the same sign, since the last two terms multiply to a positive product. If the middle term is also positive, both factors must be positive, since they also add to a positive sum. Setting each factor equal to 0, we have

$$x = -4 \quad \text{or} \quad x = -2$$

Example: $x^2 - 2x - 15 = 0$

Solution: We are now looking for two numbers which multiply to -15, therefore they must have opposite signs. To give -2 as a middle coefficient, the numbers must be -5 and $+3$.

$$(x - 5)(x + 3) = 0$$

This equation gives the roots 5 and -3.

Practice 4

Answers on page 107

Work out each problem in the space provided. Circle the letter before your answer.

1. Solve for x: $x^2 - 8x - 20 = 0$

(A) 5 and -4 (B) 10 and -2 (C) -5 and 4
(D) -10 and -2 (E) -10 and 2

2. Solve for x: $25x^2 - 4 = 0$

(A) $\frac{4}{25}$ and $-\frac{4}{25}$ (B) $\frac{2}{5}$ and $-\frac{2}{5}$ (C) $\frac{2}{5}$ only
(D) $-\frac{2}{5}$ only (E) none of these

3. Solve for x: $6x^2 - 42x = 0$

(A) 7 only (B) -7 only (C) 0 only (D) 7 and 0 (E) -7 and 0

4. Solve for x: $x^2 - 19x + 48 = 0$

(A) 8 and 6 (B) 24 and 2 (C) -16 and -3
(D) 12 and 4 (E) none of these

5. Solve for x: $3x^2 = 81$

(A) $9\sqrt{3}$ (B) $\pm 9\sqrt{3}$ (C) $3\sqrt{3}$ (D) $\pm 3\sqrt{3}$ (E) ± 9

5. EQUATIONS CONTAINING RADICALS

In solving equations containing radicals, it is important to get the radical alone on one side of the equation. Then square both sides to eliminate the radical sign. Solve the resulting equation. Remember that all solutions to radical equations must be checked, as squaring both sides may sometimes result in extraneous roots. In squaring each side of an equation, do not make the mistake of simply squaring each term. The entire side of the equation must be multiplied by itself.

Example: $\sqrt{x - 3} = 4$

Solution: $x - 3 = 16$
$x = 19$

Checking, we have $\sqrt{16} = 4$, which is true.

Example: $\sqrt{x - 3} = -4$

Solution: $x - 3 = 16$
$x = 19$

Checking, we have $\sqrt{16} = -4$, which is not true, since the radical sign means the principal, or positive, square root only. $\sqrt{16}$ is 4 not -4 and, therefore, this equation has no solution.

Example: $\sqrt{x^2 - 7} + 1 = x$

Solution: First get the radical alone on one side, then square.

$$\sqrt{x^2 - 7} = x - 1$$
$$x^2 - 7 = x^2 - 2x + 1$$
$$-7 = -2x + 1$$
$$2x = 8$$
$$x = 4$$

Checking, we have

$$\sqrt{9} + 1 = 4$$
$$3 + 1 = 4,$$

which is true.

Practice 5

Answers on page 108

Work out each problem in the space provided. Circle the letter before your answer.

1. Solve for y: $\sqrt{2y} + 11 = 15$

   (A) 4   (B) 2   (C) 8   (D) 1   (E) no solution

2. Solve for x: $4\sqrt{2x - 1} = 12$

   (A) 18.5   (B) 4   (C) 10   (D) 5   (E) no solution

3. Solve for x: $\sqrt{x^2 - 35} = 5 - x$

   (A) 6   (B) -6   (C) 3   (D) -3   (E) no solution

4. Solve for y: $26 = 3\sqrt{2y} + 8$

   (A) 6   (B) 18   (C) 3   (D) -6   (E) no solution

5. Solve for x: $\sqrt{\dfrac{2x}{5}} = 4$

   (A) 10   (B) 20   (C) 30   (D) 40   (E) no solution

Retest

Answers on page 108

Work out each problem in the space provided. Circle the letter before your answer.

1. When -5 is subtracted from the sum of -3 and +7, the result is

   (A) +15   (B) -1   (C) -9   (D) +9   (E) +1

2. The product of $(-\frac{1}{2})(-4)(+12)(-\frac{1}{6})$ is

(A) 2   (B) -2   (C) 4   (D) -4   (E) -12

3. When the sum of -4 and -5 is divided by the product of 9 and $-\frac{1}{27}$, the result is

(A) -3   (B) +3   (C) -27   (D) +27   (E) $-\frac{1}{3}$

4. Solve for x: $7b + 5d = 5x - 3b$

(A) 2bd   (B) 2b + d   (C) 5b + d   (D) 3bd   (E) 2b

5. Solve for y: $2x + 3y = 7$
$3x - 2y = 4$

(A) 6   (B) $5\frac{4}{5}$ (C) 2   (D) 1   (E) $5\frac{1}{3}$

6. Solve for x: $3x + 2y = 5a + b$
$4x - 3y = a + 7b$

(A) a + b   (B) a - b   (C) 2a + b   (D) 17a + 17b
(E) 4a - 6b

7. Solve for x: $8x^2 + 7x = 6x + 4x^2$

(A) $-\frac{1}{4}$ (B) 0 and $\frac{1}{4}$ (C) 0   (D) 0 and $-\frac{1}{4}$
(E) none of these

8. Solve for x: $x^2 + 9x - 36 = 0$

(A) -12 and +3   (B) +12 and -3
(C) -12 and -3   (D) 12 and 3
(E) none of these

9. Solve for x: $\sqrt{x^2 + 3} = x + 1$

(A) ±1   (B) 1   (C) -1   (D) 2   (E) no solution

10. Solve for x: $2\sqrt{x} = -10$

(A) 25   (B) -25   (C) 5   (D) -5   (E) no solution

SOLUTIONS TO PRACTICE EXERCISES

Diagnostic Test

1. (D) $(+4) + (-6) = -2$

2. (B) An odd number of negative signs gives a negative product.
$$(-\overset{1}{\cancel{3}})(+\overset{2}{\cancel{4}})(-\tfrac{1}{\cancel{2}})(-\tfrac{1}{\cancel{3}}) = -2$$

3. (D) The product of (-12) and $(+\tfrac{1}{4})$ is -3. The product of (-18) and $(-\tfrac{1}{3})$ is 6.
$$\frac{-3}{6} = -\frac{1}{2}$$

4. (C) $ax + b = cx + d$
$ax - cx = d - b$
$(a - c)x = d - b$
$$x = \frac{d - b}{a - c}$$

5. (B) Multiply the first equation by 3, the second by 7, and subtract.
$$\begin{array}{r} 21x - 6y = 6 \\ 21x + 28y = 210 \\ \hline -34y = -204 \\ y = 6 \end{array}$$

6. (C) Add the two equations.
$$\begin{array}{r} x + y = a \\ x - y = b \\ \hline 2x = a + b \end{array}$$
$x = \tfrac{1}{2}(a + b)$

7. (D) $2x(2x - 1) = 0$
$2x = 0 \quad 2x - 1 = 0$
$x = 0 \text{ or } \tfrac{1}{2}$

8. (D) $(x - 7)(x + 3) = 0$
$x - 7 = 0 \quad x + 3 = 0$
$x = 7 \text{ or } -3$

9. (E) $\sqrt{x + 1} - 3 = -7$
$\sqrt{x + 1} = -4$
$x + 1 = 16$
$x = 15$
Checking, $\sqrt{16} - 3 = -7$, which is not true.

10. (B) $\sqrt{x^2 + 7} - 1 = x$
$\sqrt{x^2 + 7} = x + 1$
$x^2 + 7 = x^2 + 2x + 1$
$7 = 2x + 1$
$6 = 2x$
$x = 3$
Checking, $\sqrt{16} - 1 = 3$, which is true.

Practice 1

1. (D) $(-4) + (+7) = +3$

2. (B) $(29{,}002) - (-1286) = 30{,}288$

3. (D) An even number of negative signs gives a positive product.
$6 \times 4 \times 4 \times 2 = 192$

4. (B) $\dfrac{(+4) + 0 + (-1) + (-5) + (-8)}{5}$
$= \dfrac{-10}{5} = -2°$

5. (A) $5(-2) - 4(-10) - 3(5)$
$= -10 + 40 - 15 = +15$

Practice 2

1. (B) $3x - 2 = 3 + 2x$
   $x = 5$

2. (D) $8 - 4a + 4 = 2 + 12 - 3a$
   $12 - 4a = 14 - 3a$
   $-2 = a$

3. (A) Multiply by 8 to clear fractions.
   $y + 48 = 2y$
   $48 = y$

4. (B) Multiply by 100 to clear decimals.
   $2(x - 2) = 100$
   $2x - 4 = 100$
   $2x = 104$
   $x = 52$

5. (A) $4x - 4r = 2x + 10r$
   $2x = 14r$
   $x = 7r$

Practice 3

1. (C) Multiply first equation by 3, then add.
   $3x - 9y = 9$
   $2x + 9y = 11$
   $\overline{5x = 20}$
   $x = 4$

2. (B) Multiply each equation by 10, then add.
   $6x + 2y = 22$
   $5x - 2y = 11$
   $\overline{11x = 33}$
   $x = 3$

3. (B) Multiply first equation by 3, second by 2, then subtract.
   $6x + 9y = 36b$
   $6x - 2y = 14b$
   $\overline{ 11y = 22b}$
   $y = 2b$

4. (A) $2x - 3y = 0$
   $5x + y = 34$

   Multiply first equation by 5, second by 2 and subtract.
   $10x - 15y = 0$
   $10x + 2y = 68$
   $\overline{ -17y = -68}$
   $y = 4$

5. (B) Subtract equations.
   $x + y = -1$
   $x - y = 3$
   $\overline{ 2y = -4}$
   $y = -2$

Practice 4

1. (B) $(x - 10)(x + 2) = 0$
   $x - 10 = 0 \qquad x + 2 = 0$
   $x = 10 \quad \text{or} \quad -2$

2. (B) $(5x - 2)(5x + 2) = 0$
   $5x - 2 = 0 \qquad 5x + 2 = 0$
   $x = \tfrac{2}{5} \quad \text{or} \quad -\tfrac{2}{5}$

3. (D) $6x(x - 7) = 0$
   $6x = 0 \qquad x - 7 = 0$
   $x = 0 \quad \text{or} \quad 7$

4. (E) $(x - 16)(x - 3) = 0$
   $x - 16 = 0 \qquad x - 3 = 0$
   $x = 16 \quad \text{or} \quad 3$

5. (D) $x^2 = 27$
   $x = \pm\sqrt{27}$
   But $\sqrt{27} = \sqrt{9}\sqrt{3} = 3\sqrt{3}$
   Therefore $x = \pm 3\sqrt{3}$

Practice 5

1. (C) $\sqrt{2y} = 4$
   $2y = 16$
   $y = 8$
   Checking, $\sqrt{16} = 4$, which is true.

2. (D) $4\sqrt{2x - 1} = 12$
   $\sqrt{2x - 1} = 3$
   $2x - 1 = 9$
   $2x = 10$
   $x = 5$
   Checking, $4\sqrt{9} = 12$, which is true.

3. (E) $x^2 - 35 = 25 - 10x + x^2$
   $-35 = 25 - 10x$
   $10x = 60$
   $x = 6$
   Checking, $\sqrt{1} = 5 - 6$, which is not true.

4. (B) $18 = 3\sqrt{2y}$
   $6 = \sqrt{2y}$
   $36 = 2y$
   $y = 18$
   Checking, $26 = 3\sqrt{36} + 8$
   $26 = 3(6) + 8$, which is true.

5. (D) $\dfrac{2x}{5} = 16$
   $2x = 80$
   $x = 40$
   Checking, $\sqrt{\dfrac{80}{5}} = \sqrt{16} = 4$, which is true.

Retest

1. (D) $(-3) + (+7) - (-5) = +9$

2. (D) An odd number of negative signs gives a negative product.
   $(-\tfrac{1}{2})(-\tfrac{2}{4})(+1\tfrac{2}{2})(-\tfrac{1}{8}) = -4$

3. (D) The sum of (-4) and (-5) is -9. The product of 9 and $-\tfrac{1}{27}$ is $-\tfrac{1}{3}$.
   $\dfrac{-9}{-\tfrac{1}{3}} = +27$

4. (B) $7b + 5d = 5x - 3b$
   $10b + 5d = 5x$
   $x = 2b + d$

5. (D) Multiply first equation by 3, second by 2, then subtract.
   $6x + 9y = 21$
   $6x - 4y = 8$
   $\overline{13y = 13}$
   $y = 1$

6. (A) Multiply first equation by 3, second by 2, then add.
   $9x + 6y = 15a + 3b$
   $8x - 6y = 2a + 14b$
   $\overline{17x = 17a + 17b}$
   $x = a + b$

7. (D) $4x^2 + x = 0$
   $x(4x + 1) = 0$
   $x = 0$ $\quad 4x + 1 = 0$
   $x = 0$ or $-\tfrac{1}{4}$

8. (A) $(x + 12)(x - 3) = 0$
   $x + 12 = 0 \quad x - 3 = 0$
   $x = -12$ or $+3$

9. (B) $\sqrt{x^2 + 3} = x + 1$
   $x^2 + 3 = x^2 + 2x + 1$
   $3 = 2x + 1$
   $2 = 2x$
   $x = 1$
   Checking, $\sqrt{4} = 1 + 1$, which is true.

10. (E) $2\sqrt{x} = -10$
$\sqrt{x} = -5$
$x = 25$

Checking, $2\sqrt{25} = -10$, which is not true.

Literal Expressions

DIAGNOSTIC TEST

Answers on page 115

Work out each problem in the space provided. Circle the letter before your answer.

1. If one book costs c dollars, what is the cost, in dollars, of m books?

   (A) $m + c$ (B) $\dfrac{m}{c}$ (C) $\dfrac{c}{m}$ (D) mc (E) $\dfrac{mc}{100}$

2. Represent the cost, in dollars, of k pounds of apples at c cents per pound.

   (A) kc (B) $100kc$ (C) $\dfrac{kc}{100}$ (D) $100k + c$
   (E) $\dfrac{k}{100} + c$

3. If p pencils cost c cents, what is the cost of one pencil?

   (A) $\dfrac{c}{p}$ (B) $\dfrac{p}{c}$ (C) pc (D) $p - c$ (E) $p + c$

4. Express the number of miles covered by a train in one hour if it covers r miles in h hours.

   (A) rh (B) $\dfrac{h}{r}$ (C) $\dfrac{r}{h}$ (D) $r + h$ (E) $r - h$

5. Express the number of minutes in h hours and m minutes.

   (A) mh (B) $\dfrac{h}{60} + m$ (C) $60(h + m)$ (D) $\dfrac{h + m}{60}$
   (E) $60h + m$

6. Express the number of seats in the school auditorium if there are r rows with s seats each and s rows with r seats each.

   (A) $2rs$ (B) $2r + 2s$ (C) $rs + 2$ (D) $2r + s$ (E) $r + 2s$

LITERAL EXPRESSIONS 111

7. How many dimes are there in n nickels and q quarters?

(A) 10nq (B) $\frac{n+q}{10}$ (C) $\frac{1}{2}$n + $\frac{5}{2}$q (D) 10n + 10q

(E) 2n + $\frac{q}{10}$

8. Roger rents a car at a cost of D dollars per day plus c cents per mile. How many dollars must he pay if he uses the car for 5 days and drives 1000 miles?

(A) 5D + 1000c (B) 5D + $\frac{c}{1000}$ (C) 5D + 100c

(D) 5D + 10c (E) 5D + c

9. The cost of a long-distance telephone call is c cents for the first three minutes and m cents for each additional minute. Represent the price of a call lasting d minutes, if d is more than 3.

(A) c + md (B) c + md - 3m (C) c + md + 3m
(D) c + 3md (E) cmd

10. The sales tax in Morgan County is m%. Represent the total cost of an article priced at $D.

(A) D + mD (B) D + 100mD (C) D + $\frac{mD}{100}$

(D) D + $\frac{m}{100}$ (E) D + 100m

Many students who have no trouble computing with numbers panic at the sight of letters. If you understand the concepts of a problem in which numbers are given, you need simply to apply the same concepts to letters. The computational processes are exactly the same. Just figure out what you would do if you had numbers and do exactly the same thing with the given letters.

> Example: Express the number of inches in y yards, f feet and i inches.
>
> Solution: We must change everything to inches and add. Since a yard contains 36 inches, y yards will contain 36y inches. Since a foot contains 12 inches, f feet will contain 12f inches. The total number of inches is 36y + 12f + i.
>
> Example: Find the number of cents in 2x - 1 dimes.
>
> Solution: To change dimes to cents we must multiply by 10. Think that 7 dimes would be 7 times 10 or 70 cents.

LITERAL EXPRESSIONS

Therefore the number of cents in 2x − 1 dimes is 10(2x − 1) or 20x − 10.

Example: Find the total cost of sending a telegram of w words if the charge is c cents for the first 15 words and d cents for each additional word, if w is greater than 15.

Solution: To the basic charge of c cents, we must add d for each word over 15. Therefore, we add d for (w − 15) words. The total charge is c + d(w − 15) or c + dw − 15d.

Example: Kevin bought d dozen apples at c cents per apple and had 20 cents left. Represent the number of cents he had before this purchase.

Solution: In d dozen, there are 12d apples. 12d apples at c cents each, cost 12dc cents. Adding this to the 20 cents he has left, we find he started with 12dc + 20 cents.

Practice 1   Answers on page 115

Work out each problem in the space provided. Circle the letter before your answer.

1. Express the number of days in w weeks and w days.

(A) $7w^2$ (B) 8w   (C) 7w   (D) 7 + 2w   (E) w^2

2. The charge on the Newport Ferry is D dollars for the car and driver and m cents for each additional passenger. Find the charge, in dollars, for a car containing four people.

(A) D + .03m   (B) D + 3m   (C) D + 4m
(D) D + 300m   (E) D + 400m

3. If g gallons of gasoline cost m dollars, express the cost of r gallons.

(A) $\frac{mr}{g}$ (B) $\frac{rg}{m}$ (C) rmg   (D) $\frac{mg}{r}$ (E) $\frac{m}{rg}$

4. How many quarters are equivalent to n nickels and d dimes?

(A) 5n + 10d   (B) 25n + 50d   (C) $\frac{n+d}{25}$

(D) 25n + 25d   (E) $\frac{n+2d}{5}$

5. A salesman earns a basic salary of $100 per week plus a 5% commission on all sales over $500. Find his total earnings in a week in which he sells r dollars worth of merchandise, with r being greater than 500.

(A) $125 + .05r$ (B) $75 + .05r$ (C) $125r$
(D) $100 + .05r$ (E) $100 - .05r$

Retest

Answers on page 116

Work out each problem in the space provided. Circle the letter before your answer.

1. If a school consists of b boys, g girls, and t teachers, represent the number of students in each class if each class contains the same number of students.

(A) $\dfrac{b+g}{t}$ (B) $t(b+g)$ (C) $\dfrac{b}{t} + g$ (D) $bt + g$ (E) $\dfrac{bg}{t}$

2. Represent the total cost, in cents, of b books at D dollars each and r books at c cents each.

(A) $\dfrac{bD}{100} + rc$ (B) $\dfrac{bD + rc}{100}$

(C) $100bD + rc$ (D) $bD + 100rc$

(E) $bD + \dfrac{rc}{100}$

3. Represent the number of feet in y yards, f feet, and i inches.

(A) $\dfrac{y}{3} + f + 12i$ (B) $\dfrac{y}{3} + f + \dfrac{i}{12}$

(C) $3y + f + i$ (D) $3y + f + \dfrac{i}{12}$

(E) $3y + f + 12i$

4. In a group of m men, b men earn D dollars per week and the rest earn half that amount each. Represent the total number of dollars paid to these men in a week.

(A) $bD + b - m$ (B) $\tfrac{1}{2}D(b + m)$
(C) $\tfrac{3}{2}bD + mD$ (D) $\tfrac{3}{2}D(b + m)$
(E) $bD + \tfrac{1}{2}mD$

114   LITERAL EXPRESSIONS

5. Ken bought d dozen roses for r dollars. Represent the cost of one rose.

(A) $\dfrac{r}{d}$ (B)   (B) $\dfrac{d}{r}$ (C) $\dfrac{12d}{r}$ (D) $\dfrac{12r}{d}$ (E) $\dfrac{r}{12d}$

6. The cost of mailing a package is c cents for the first b ounces and d cents for each additional ounce. Find the cost, in cents, for mailing a package weighing f ounces, if f is more than b.

(A) (c + d) (f - b)   (B) c + d (f - b)   (C) c + bd
(D) c + (d - b)   (E) b + (f - b)

7. Josh's allowance is m cents per week. Represent the number of dollars he gets in a year.

(A) $\dfrac{3m}{25}$ (B) 5200m   (C) 1200m   (D) $\dfrac{13m}{25}$ (E) $\dfrac{25m}{13}$

8. If it takes T tablespoons of coffee to make c cups, how many tablespoons of coffee are needed to make d cups?

(A) $\dfrac{Tc}{d}$ (B) $\dfrac{T}{dc}$ (C) $\dfrac{Td}{c}$ (D) $\dfrac{d}{Tc}$ (E) $\dfrac{cd}{T}$

9. The charge for renting a rowboat on Loon Lake is D dollars per hour plus c cents for each minute into the next hour. How many dollars will Mr. Wilson pay if he used a boat from 3:40 P.M. to 6:20 P.M.?

(A) D + 40c   (B) 2D + 40c   (C) 2D + 4c
(D) 2D + .4c   (E) D + 4.c

10. The cost for developing and printing a roll of film is c cents for processing the roll and d cents for each print. How much will it cost, in cents, to develop and print a roll of film with 20 exposures?

(A) 20c + d   (B) 20(c + d)   (C) c + 20d
(D) $c + \dfrac{d}{20}$ (E) $\dfrac{c + d}{20}$

LITERAL EXPRESSIONS   115

SOLUTIONS TO PRACTICE EXERCISES

Diagnostic Test

1. (D) This can be solved by a proportion, comparing books to dollars.

$$\frac{1}{c} = \frac{m}{x}$$

$$x = mc$$

2. (C) The cost in cents of k pounds at c cents per pound is kc. To convert this to dollars, we divide by 100.

3. (A) This can be solved by a proportion, comparing pencils to cents.

$$\frac{p}{c} = \frac{1}{x}$$

$$x = \frac{c}{p}$$

4. (C) This can be solved by a proportion, comparing miles to hours.

$$\frac{r}{h} = \frac{x}{1}$$

$$\frac{r}{h} = x$$

5. (E) There are 60 minutes in an hour. In h hours there are 60h minutes. With m additional minutes, the total is 60h + m.

6. (A) r rows with s seats each have a total of rs seats. s rows with r seats each have a total of sr seats. Therefore, the school auditorium has a total of rs + sr or 2rs seats.

7. (C) In n nickels, there are 5n cents. In q quarters, there are 25q cents. Altogether we have 5n + 25q cents. To see how many dimes this is, divide by 10.

$$\frac{5n + 25q}{10} = \frac{n + 5q}{2} = \frac{1}{2}n + \frac{5}{2}q$$

8. (D) The daily charge for 5 days at D dollars per day is 5D dollars. The charge, in cents, for 1000 miles at c cents per mile is 1000c cents. To change this to dollars, we divide by 100 and get 10c dollars. Therefore, the total cost in dollars is 5D + 10c.

9. (B) The cost for the first 3 minutes is c cents. The number of additional minutes is (d - 3) and the cost at m cents for each additional minute is thus m(d - 3) or md - 3m. Therefore, the total cost is c + md - 3m.

10. (C) The sales tax is $\frac{m}{100} \cdot D$ or $\frac{mD}{100}$. Therefore, the total cost is $D + \frac{mD}{100}$.

Practice 1

1. (B) There are 7 days in a week. w weeks contain 7w days. With w additional days, the total number of days is 8w.

2. (A) The charge is D dollars for car and driver. The three additional persons pay m cents each, for a total of 3m cents. To change this to dollars, divide by 100, for a total of $\frac{3m}{100}$ dollars. This can be written in decimal form as .03m. The total charge in dollars is then D + .03m.

3. (A) This can be solved by a proportion, comparing gallons to dollars.

$$\frac{g}{m} = \frac{r}{x}$$

$$gx = mr$$

$$x = \frac{mr}{g}$$

4. (E) In n nickels, there are 5n cents. In d dimes, there are 10d cents. Altogether, we have 5n + 10d cents. To see how many quarters this gives, divide by 25.

$$\frac{5n + 10d}{25} = \frac{n + 2d}{5},$$

since a fraction can be reduced when *every* term is divided by the same factor, in this case 5.

5. (B) Commission is paid on (r − 500) dollars. His commission is .05(r − 500) or .05r − 25. When this is added to his basic salary of 100, we have 100 + .05r − 25, or 75 + .05r.

Retest

1. (A) The total number of boys and girls is b + g. Since there are t teachers, and thus t classes, the number of students in each class is $\frac{b + g}{t}$.

2. (C) The cost, in dollars, of b books at D dollars each is bD dollars. To change this to cents, we multiply by 100 and get 100bD cents. The cost of r books at c cents each is rc cents. Therefore, the total cost, in cents, is 100bD + rc.

3. (D) In y yards there are 3y feet. In i inches there are $\frac{i}{12}$ feet. Therefore, the total number of feet is $3y + f + \frac{i}{12}$.

4. (B) The money earned by b men at D dollars per week is bD dollars. The number of men remaining is (m − b) and since they earn $\frac{1}{2}$D dollars per week, the money they earn is $\frac{1}{2}$D(m − b) = $\frac{1}{2}$mD − $\frac{1}{2}$bD. Therefore, the total amount earned is bD + $\frac{1}{2}$mD − $\frac{1}{2}$bD = $\frac{1}{2}$bD + $\frac{1}{2}$mD = $\frac{1}{2}$D(b + m).

5. (E) This can be solved by a proportion, comparing roses to dollars. Since d dozen roses equals 12d roses,

$$\frac{12d}{r} = \frac{1}{x}$$

$$12d \cdot x = r$$

$$x = \frac{r}{12d}$$

6. (B) The cost for the first b ounces is c cents. The number of additional ounces is (f − b) and the cost at d cents for each additional ounce is (f − b)d. Therefore, the total cost is c + d(f − b).

7. (D) Since there are 52 weeks in a year, his allowance in cents is 52m. To change to dollars, we divide by 100 and get $\frac{52m}{100}$ or $\frac{13m}{25}$.

8. **(C)** This can be solved by a proportion comparing tablespoons to cups.

$$\frac{T}{c} = \frac{x}{d}$$

$$cx = Td$$

$$x = \frac{Td}{c}$$

9. **(D)** The amount of time from 3:40 P.M. to 6:20 P.M. is 2 hrs. 40 min. Therefore, the charge at D dollars per hour and c cents per minute into the next hour is 2D dollars + 40c cents or 2D + .4c dollars.

10. **(C)** The cost for processing the roll is c cents. The cost for printing 20 exposures at d cents per print is 20d cents. Therefore, the total cost is c + 20d.

Roots and Radicals

DIAGNOSTIC TEST

Answers on page 125

Work out each problem in the space provided. Circle the letter before your answer.

1. The sum of $\sqrt{75}$ and $\sqrt{12}$ is

   (A) $\sqrt{87}$ (B) $7\sqrt{3}$ (C) $3\sqrt{5} + 3\sqrt{2}$ (D) $29\sqrt{3}$
   (E) $3\sqrt{3}$

2. The difference between $\sqrt{125}$ and $\sqrt{45}$

   (A) $4\sqrt{5}$ (B) $2\sqrt{5}$ (C) 2 (D) $5\sqrt{2}$ (E) 10

3. The product of $\sqrt{9x}$ and $\sqrt{4x}$ is

   (A) $6\sqrt{x}$ (B) $36\sqrt{x}$ (C) $36x$ (D) $6x$ (E) $6x^2$

4. If $\dfrac{2}{x} = \sqrt{.16}$, then x equals

   (A) 50 (B) 5 (C) .5 (D) .05 (E) .005

5. The square root of 17,956 is exactly

   (A) 132 (B) 133 (C) 134 (D) 135 (E) 137

6. The square root of 139.24 is exactly

   (A) 1.18 (B) 11.8 (C) 118 (D) .118 (E) 1180

7. Find $\sqrt{\dfrac{x^2}{36} + \dfrac{x^2}{25}}$.

   (A) $\dfrac{11x}{30}$ (B) $\dfrac{9x}{30}$ (C) $\dfrac{x}{11}$ (D) $\dfrac{2x}{11}$ (E) $\dfrac{x\sqrt{61}}{30}$

8. $\sqrt{x^2 + y^2}$ is equal to

   (A) $x + y$ (B) $x - y$ (C) $(x + y)(x - y)$
   (D) $\sqrt{x^2} + \sqrt{y^2}$ (E) none of these

118

9. Divide $8\sqrt{12}$ by $2\sqrt{3}$.
   (A) 16   (B) 9   (C) 8   (D) 12   (E) 96

10. $(\sqrt{2})^5$ is equal to
    (A) 2   (B) $2\sqrt{2}$ (C) 4   (D) $4\sqrt{2}$ (E) 8

1. ADDITION AND SUBTRACTION OF RADICALS

The conditions under which radicals can be added or subtracted are much the same as the conditions for letters in an algebraic expression. The radicals act as a label, or unit, and must therefore be exactly the same. In adding or subtracting, we add or subtract the coefficients, or rational parts and carry the radical along as a label, which does not change.

Example: $\sqrt{2} + \sqrt{3}$ cannot be added

$\sqrt{2} + \sqrt[3]{2}$ cannot be added

$4\sqrt{2} + 5\sqrt{2} = 9\sqrt{2}$

Often, when radicals to be added or subtracted are not the same, simplification of one or more radicals will make them the same. To simplify a radical, we remove any perfect square factors from underneath the radical sign.

Example: $\sqrt{12} = \sqrt{4}\sqrt{3} = 2\sqrt{3}$

$\sqrt{27} = \sqrt{9}\sqrt{3} = 3\sqrt{3}$

If we wish to add $\sqrt{12} + \sqrt{27}$, we must first simplify each one. Adding the simplified radicals gives a sum of $5\sqrt{3}$.

Example: $\sqrt{125} + \sqrt{20} - \sqrt{500}$

Solution: $\sqrt{25}\sqrt{5} + \sqrt{4}\sqrt{5} - \sqrt{100}\sqrt{5}$

$5\sqrt{5} + 2\sqrt{5} - 10\sqrt{5}$

$-3\sqrt{5}$

Practice 1

Answers on page 125

Work out each problem in the space provided. Circle the letter before your answer.

1. Combine $4\sqrt{27} - 2\sqrt{48} + \sqrt{147}$
   (A) $27\sqrt{3}$ (B) $-3\sqrt{3}$ (C) $9\sqrt{3}$ (D) $10\sqrt{3}$ (E) $11\sqrt{3}$

ROOTS AND RADICALS

2. Combine $\sqrt{80} + \sqrt{45} - \sqrt{20}$

(A) $9\sqrt{5}$ (B) $5\sqrt{5}$ (C) $-\sqrt{5}$ (D) $3\sqrt{5}$ (E) $-2\sqrt{5}$

3. Combine $6\sqrt{5} + 3\sqrt{2} - 4\sqrt{5} + \sqrt{2}$

(A) 8   (B) $2\sqrt{5} + 3\sqrt{2}$ (C) $2\sqrt{5} + 4\sqrt{2}$
(D) $5\sqrt{7}$ (E) 5

4. Combine $\frac{1}{2}\sqrt{180} + \frac{1}{3}\sqrt{45} - \frac{2}{5}\sqrt{20}$

(A) $3\sqrt{10} + \sqrt{15} + 2\sqrt{2}$ (B) $\frac{16}{5}\sqrt{5}$ (C) $\sqrt{97}$
(D) $\frac{24}{5}\sqrt{5}$ (E) none of these

5. Combine $5\sqrt{mn} - 3\sqrt{mn} - 2\sqrt{mn}$

(A) 0   (B) 1   (C) $\sqrt{mn}$ (D) mn   (E) $-\sqrt{mn}$

2. MULTIPLICATION AND DIVISION OF RADICALS

In multiplication and division, we again treat the radicals as we would treat letters in an algebraic expression. They are factors and must be treated as such.

Example: $\sqrt{2} \cdot \sqrt{3} = \sqrt{6}$

Example: $4\sqrt{2} \cdot 5\sqrt{3} = 20 \cdot \sqrt{6}$

Example: $(3\sqrt{2})^2 = 3\sqrt{2} \cdot 3\sqrt{2} = 9 \cdot 2 = 18$

Example: $\frac{\sqrt{8}}{\sqrt{2}} = \sqrt{4} = 2$

Example: $\frac{10\sqrt{20}}{2\sqrt{4}} = 5\sqrt{5}$

Example: $\sqrt{2}(\sqrt{8} + \sqrt{18}) = \sqrt{16} + \sqrt{36} = 4 + 6 = 10$

Practice 2

Answers on page 126

Work out each problem in the space provided. Circle the letter before your answer.

1. Multiply and simplify: $2\sqrt{18} \cdot 6\sqrt{2}$

(A) 72   (B) 48   (C) $12\sqrt{6}$ (D) $8\sqrt{6}$ (E) 36

2. Find $(3\sqrt{3})^3$.

(A) $27\sqrt{3}$ (B) $81\sqrt{3}$ (C) 81   (D) $9\sqrt{3}$ (E) 243

ROOTS AND RADICALS 121

3. Multiply and simplify: $\frac{1}{2}\sqrt{2}(\sqrt{6} + \frac{1}{2}\sqrt{2})$
   (A) $\sqrt{3} + \frac{1}{2}$ (B) $\frac{1}{2}\sqrt{3}$ (C) $\sqrt{6} + 1$ (D) $\sqrt{6} + \frac{1}{2}$ (E) $\sqrt{6} + 2$

4. Divide and simplify: $\dfrac{\sqrt{32b^3}}{\sqrt{8b}}$
   (A) $2\sqrt{b}$ (B) $\sqrt{2b}$ (C) $2b$ (D) $\sqrt{2b^2}$ (E) $b\sqrt{2b}$

5. Divide and simplify: $\dfrac{15\sqrt{96}}{5\sqrt{2}}$
   (A) $7\sqrt{3}$ (B) $7\sqrt{12}$ (C) $11\sqrt{3}$ (D) $12\sqrt{3}$ (E) $40\sqrt{3}$

3. SIMPLIFYING RADICALS CONTAINING A SUM OR DIFFERENCE

In simplifying radicals which contain several terms under the radical sign, we must combine terms before taking the square root.

Example: $\sqrt{16 + 9} = \sqrt{25} = 5$

It is not true that $\sqrt{16 + 9} = \sqrt{16} + \sqrt{9}$ which would be 4 + 3, or 7.

Example: $\sqrt{\dfrac{x^2}{16} - \dfrac{x^2}{25}} = \sqrt{\dfrac{25x^2 - 16x^2}{400}} = \sqrt{\dfrac{9x^2}{400}} = \dfrac{3x}{20}$

Practice 3

Answers on page 126

Work out each problem in the space provided. Circle the letter before your answer.

1. Simplify $\sqrt{\dfrac{x^2}{9} + \dfrac{x^2}{16}}$
   (A) $\dfrac{25x^2}{144}$ (B) $\dfrac{5x}{12}$ (C) $\dfrac{5x^2}{12}$ (D) $\dfrac{x}{7}$ (E) $\dfrac{7x}{12}$

2. Simplify $\sqrt{36y^2 + 64x^2}$
   (A) $6y + 8x$ (B) $10xy$ (C) $6y^2 + 8x^2$ (D) $10x^2y^2$
   (E) cannot be done

3. Simplify $\sqrt{\dfrac{x^2}{64} - \dfrac{x^2}{100}}$
   (A) $\dfrac{x}{40}$ (B) $-\dfrac{x}{2}$ (C) $\dfrac{x}{2}$ (D) $\dfrac{3x}{40}$ (E) $\dfrac{3x}{80}$

122 ROOTS AND RADICALS

4. Simplify $\sqrt{\dfrac{y^2}{2} - \dfrac{y^2}{18}}$

(A) $\dfrac{2y}{3}$ (B) $\dfrac{y\sqrt{5}}{3}$ (C) $\dfrac{10y}{3}$ (D) $\dfrac{y\sqrt{3}}{6}$ (E) cannot be done

5. $\sqrt{a^2 + b^2}$ is equal to

(A) $a + b$ (B) $a - b$ (C) $\sqrt{a^2} + \sqrt{b^2}$
(D) $(a + b)(a - b)$ (E) none of these

4. FINDING THE SQUARE ROOT OF A NUMBER

In finding the square root of a number, the first step is to pair off the digits in the square root sign in each direction from the decimal point. If there is an odd number of digits *before* the decimal point, insert a zero at the *beginning* of the number in order to pair digits. If there is an odd number of digits *after* the decimal point, add a zero at the *end*. It should be clearly understood that these zeros are place holders only and in no way change the value of the number. Every *pair* of numbers in the radical sign gives one digit of the square root.

    Example: Find the number of digits in the square root of 328,329.

    Solution: Pair the numbers beginning at the decimal point.

$$\sqrt{\overline{32}\,\overline{83}\,\overline{29}.}$$

    Each pair will give one digit in the square root. Therefore the square root of 328,329 has three digits.

If we were asked to find the square root of 328,329, we would look among the multiple-choice answers for a three-digit number. If there were more than one, we would have to use additional criteria for selection. Since our number ends in 9, its square root must end in a digit which, when multiplied by itself, ends in 9. Going through the digits from 0 to 9, this could be 3 ($3 \cdot 3 = 9$) or 7 ($7 \cdot 7 = 49$). Only one of these would appear among the choices, as this examination will not call for extensive computation, but rather for sound mathematical reasoning.

    Example: The square root of 4624 is exactly

        (A) 64   (B) 65   (C) 66   (D) 67   (E) 68

    Solution: Since all choices contain two digits, we must reason using the last digit. It must be a number which, when multiplied by itself, will end in 4. Among the choices, the only possibility is 68 as 64^2 will end in 6, 65^2 will end in 5, 66^2 in 6, and 67^2 in 9.

Practice 4

Answers on page 126

Work out each problem in the space provided. Circle the letter before your answer.

1. The square root of 17,689 is exactly

    (A) 131   (B) 132   (C) 133   (D) 134   (E) 136

2. The number of digits in the square root of 64,048,009 is

    (A) 4   (B) 5   (C) 6   (D) 7   (E) 8

3. The square root of 222.01 is exactly

    (A) 14.3   (B) 14.4   (C) 14.6   (D) 14.8   (E) 14.9

4. The square root of 25.6036 is exactly

    (A) 5.6   (B) 5.06   (C) 5.006   (D) 5.0006   (E) 5.00006

5. Which of the following square roots can be found exactly?

    (A) $\sqrt{.4}$ (B) $\sqrt{.9}$ (C) $\sqrt{.09}$ (D) $\sqrt{.02}$ (E) $\sqrt{.025}$

Retest

Answers on page 127

Work out each problem in the space provided. Circle the letter before your answer.

1. The sum of $2\sqrt{8}$, $4\sqrt{50}$, and $3\sqrt{18}$ is

    (A) $33\sqrt{6}$ (B) $9\sqrt{76}$ (C) $33\sqrt{2}$ (D) $135\sqrt{6}$ (E) $135\sqrt{2}$

2. The difference between $\frac{1}{2}\sqrt{180}$ and $\frac{2}{5}\sqrt{20}$ is

    (A) $\frac{1}{10}\sqrt{160}$ (B) $16\frac{2}{5}\sqrt{5}$ (C) $16\frac{2}{5}$
    (D) $\frac{11}{5}\sqrt{5}$ (E) $\frac{2}{5}\sqrt{5}$

3. The product of $a\sqrt{2x}$ and $x\sqrt{6x}$ is

    (A) $2ax^2\sqrt{3}$ (B) $12ax^3$ (C) $(2ax)^2\sqrt{3}$
    (D) $12ax^2$ (E) $12ax$

4. Divide $42\sqrt{40r^3t^6}$ by $3\sqrt{5rt^2}$

    (A) $56rt^2\sqrt{2}$ (B) $28rt\sqrt{2rt}$ (C) $28rt^2\sqrt{2}$
    (D) $28rt\sqrt{2t}$ (E) $56rt\sqrt{2t}$

124 ROOTS AND RADICALS

5. Solve for x: $\dfrac{3}{x} = \sqrt{.09}$

(A) 10   (B) 1   (C) .1   (D) .01   (E) 1.1

6. Find $\sqrt{\dfrac{a^2}{b^2} + \dfrac{a^2}{b^2}}$

(A) $\dfrac{a^2}{b^2}$ (B) $\dfrac{a}{b}$ (C) $\dfrac{2a}{b}$ (D) $\dfrac{a\sqrt{2}}{b}$ (E) $\dfrac{a\sqrt{2}}{b^2}$

7. The square root of 213.16 is exactly

(A) 14.2   (B) 14.3   (C) 14.8   (D) 14.9   (E) 14.6

8. The number of digits in the square root of 14,161 is

(A) 5   (B) 4   (C) 3   (D) 2   (E) 6

9. $(2\sqrt{3})^5$ is equal to

(A) $32\sqrt{3}$ (B) $288\sqrt{3}$ (C) $10\sqrt{3}$ (D) $90\sqrt{3}$ (E) $16\sqrt{3}$

10. Find $\sqrt{\dfrac{25m^4}{36c^{64}d^{16}}}$

(A) $\dfrac{5m^2}{6c^8 d^4}$ (B) $\dfrac{5m^2}{6c^{32} d^4}$ (C) $\dfrac{5m^2}{6c^{32} d^8}$ (D) $\dfrac{5m^2}{6c^8 d^8}$ (E) $\dfrac{5m}{6c^{16} d^4}$

SOLUTIONS TO PRACTICE EXERCISES

Diagnostic Test

1. (B) $\sqrt{75} = \sqrt{25}\sqrt{3} = 5\sqrt{3}$
$\sqrt{12} = \sqrt{4}\sqrt{3} = 2\sqrt{3}$
$5\sqrt{3} + 2\sqrt{3} = 7\sqrt{3}$

2. (B) $\sqrt{125} = \sqrt{25}\sqrt{5} = 5\sqrt{5}$
$\sqrt{45} = \sqrt{9}\sqrt{5} = 3\sqrt{5}$
$5\sqrt{5} - 3\sqrt{5} = 2\sqrt{5}$

3. (D) $\sqrt{9x} \cdot \sqrt{4x} = \sqrt{36x^2} = 6x$

4. (B) $\sqrt{.16} = .4$
$\frac{2}{x} = .4$ Multiply by x.
$2 = .4x$
$x = 5$

5. (C) Since the last digit is 6, the square root must end in 4 or 6.

6. (B) Since the number has two digits to the right of the decimal point, its square root will have one digit to the right of the decimal point.

7. (E) $\sqrt{\frac{25x^2 + 36x^2}{900}} = \sqrt{\frac{61x^2}{900}} = \frac{x\sqrt{61}}{30}$

8. (E) It is not possible to find the square root of separate terms.

9. (C) $\frac{8\sqrt{12}}{2\sqrt{3}} = 4\sqrt{4} = 4 \cdot 2 = 8$

10. (D) $(\sqrt{2})(\sqrt{2}) = 2$. Therefore, $(\sqrt{2}) \cdot (\sqrt{2}) \cdot (\sqrt{2}) \cdot (\sqrt{2}) \cdot (\sqrt{2}) = 4\sqrt{2}$

Practice 1

1. (E) $4\sqrt{27} = 4\sqrt{9}\sqrt{3} = 12\sqrt{3}$
$2\sqrt{48} = 2\sqrt{16}\sqrt{3} = 8\sqrt{3}$
$\sqrt{147} = \sqrt{49}\sqrt{3} = 7\sqrt{3}$
$12\sqrt{3} - 8\sqrt{3} + 7\sqrt{3} = 11\sqrt{3}$

2. (B) $\sqrt{80} = \sqrt{16}\sqrt{5} = 4\sqrt{5}$
$\sqrt{45} = \sqrt{9}\sqrt{5} = 3\sqrt{5}$
$\sqrt{20} = \sqrt{4}\sqrt{5} = 2\sqrt{5}$
$4\sqrt{5} + 3\sqrt{5} - 2\sqrt{5} = 5\sqrt{5}$

3. (C) Only terms with the same radical may be combined.
$6\sqrt{5} - 4\sqrt{5} = 2\sqrt{5}$
$3\sqrt{2} + \sqrt{2} = 4\sqrt{2}$
Therefore we have $2\sqrt{5} + 4\sqrt{2}$

4. (B) $\frac{1}{2}\sqrt{180} = \frac{1}{2}\sqrt{36}\sqrt{5} = 3\sqrt{5}$
$\frac{1}{3}\sqrt{45} = \frac{1}{3}\sqrt{9}\sqrt{5} = \sqrt{5}$
$\frac{2}{5}\sqrt{20} = \frac{2}{5}\sqrt{4}\sqrt{5} = \frac{4}{5}\sqrt{5}$
$3\sqrt{5} + \sqrt{5} - \frac{4}{5}\sqrt{5} = 4\sqrt{5} - \frac{4}{5}\sqrt{5}$
$= 3\frac{1}{5}\sqrt{5} = \frac{16}{5}\sqrt{5}$

5. (A) $5\sqrt{mn} - 5\sqrt{mn} = 0$

Practice 2

1. (A) $2\sqrt{18} \cdot 6\sqrt{2} = 12\sqrt{36} = 12 \cdot 6 = 72$

2. (B) $3\sqrt{3} \cdot 3\sqrt{3} \cdot 3\sqrt{3}$
   $= 27(3\sqrt{3}) = 81\sqrt{3}$

3. (A) Using the distributive law, we have
   $\frac{1}{2}\sqrt{12} + \frac{1}{4} \cdot 2 = \frac{1}{2}\sqrt{4}\sqrt{3} + \frac{1}{2} = \sqrt{3} + \frac{1}{2}$

4. (C) Dividing the numbers in the radical sign, we have $\sqrt{4b^2} = 2b$

5. (D) $3\sqrt{48} = 3\sqrt{16}\sqrt{3} = 12\sqrt{3}$

Practice 3

1. (B) $\sqrt{\dfrac{16x^2 + 9x^2}{144}} = \sqrt{\dfrac{25x^2}{144}} = \dfrac{5x}{12}$

2. (E) The terms cannot be combined and it is not possible to take the square root of separated terms.

3. (D) $\sqrt{\dfrac{100x^2 - 64x^2}{6400}} = \sqrt{\dfrac{36x^2}{6400}} = \dfrac{6x}{80}$
   $= \dfrac{3x}{40}$

4. (A) $\sqrt{\dfrac{18y^2 - 2y^2}{36}} = \sqrt{\dfrac{16y^2}{36}} = \dfrac{4y}{6} = \dfrac{2y}{3}$

5. (E) It is not possible to find the square root of separate terms.

Practice 4

1. (C) Since the last digit is 9, the square root must end in 3 or 7.

2. (A) Every pair of digits in the given number gives one digit of the square root.

3. (E) Since the number ends in 1, its square root must end in 1 or 9.

4. (B) Since the number has four digits to the right of the decimal point, its square root will have two digits to the right of the decimal point.

5. (C) In order to take the square root of a decimal, it must have an even number of decimal places so that its square root will have exactly half as many. In addition to this, the digits must form a perfect square ($\sqrt{.09} = .3$).

Retest

1. (C) $2\sqrt{8} = 2\sqrt{4}\sqrt{2} = 4\sqrt{2}$
   $4\sqrt{50} = 4\sqrt{25}\sqrt{2} = 20\sqrt{2}$
   $3\sqrt{18} = 3\sqrt{9}\sqrt{2} = 9\sqrt{2}$
   $4\sqrt{2} + 20\sqrt{2} + 9\sqrt{2} = 33\sqrt{2}$

2. (D) $\frac{1}{2}\sqrt{180} = \frac{1}{2}\sqrt{36}\sqrt{5} = 3\sqrt{5}$
   $\frac{2}{5}\sqrt{20} = \frac{2}{5}\sqrt{4}\sqrt{5} = \frac{4}{5}\sqrt{5}$
   $3\sqrt{5} - \frac{4}{5}\sqrt{5} = \frac{11}{5}\sqrt{5}$

3. (A) $a\sqrt{2x} \cdot x\sqrt{6x} = ax\sqrt{12x^2}$
   $= 2ax^2\sqrt{3}$

4. (C) $\frac{42\sqrt{40r^3t^6}}{3\sqrt{5rt^2}} = 14\sqrt{8r^2t^4}$
   $14\sqrt{8r^2t^4} = 28rt^2\sqrt{2}$

5. (A) $\sqrt{.09} = .3$
   $\frac{3}{x} = .3$ Multiply by x.
   $3 = .3x$
   $x = 10$

6. (D) $\sqrt{\frac{2a^2}{b^2}} = \frac{a\sqrt{2}}{b}$

7. (E) Since the last digit is 6, the square root must end in 4 or 6.

8. (C) A five-digit number has a three-digit square root.

9. (B) $2\sqrt{3} \cdot 2\sqrt{3} \cdot 2\sqrt{3} \cdot 2\sqrt{3} \cdot 2\sqrt{3}$
   $= 32(9\sqrt{3}) = 288\sqrt{3}$

10. (C) $\sqrt{\frac{25m^4}{36c^{64}d^{16}}} = \frac{5m^2}{6c^{32}d^8}$

Factoring and Algebraic Fractions

DIAGNOSTIC TEST

Answers on page 139

Work out each problem in the space provided. Circle the letter before your answer.

1. Find the sum of $\dfrac{n}{4}$ and $\dfrac{2n}{3}$.

   (A) $\dfrac{2n^2}{7}$ (B) $\dfrac{3n}{7}$ (C) $\dfrac{11n}{12}$ (D) $\dfrac{2n^2}{12}$ (E) $\dfrac{9n}{12}$

2. Combine into a single fraction: $2 - \dfrac{a}{b}$

   (A) $\dfrac{2-a}{b}$ (B) $\dfrac{2-a}{2-b}$ (C) $\dfrac{a-2b}{b}$ (D) $\dfrac{2b-a}{b}$ (E) $\dfrac{2a-b}{b}$

3. Divide $\dfrac{x-5}{x+5}$ by $\dfrac{5-x}{5+x}$.

   (A) 1 (B) -1 (C) $\dfrac{(x-5)^2}{(x+5)^2}$ (D) $-\dfrac{(x-5)^2}{(x+5)^2}$

   (E) 0

4. Find an expression equivalent to $\left(\dfrac{3x^2}{y}\right)^3$.

   (A) $\dfrac{27x^5}{3y}$ (B) $\dfrac{9x^6}{y^3}$ (C) $\dfrac{9x^5}{y^3}$ (D) $\dfrac{27x^5}{y^3}$ (E) $\dfrac{27x^6}{y^3}$

5. Simplify $\dfrac{2 + \dfrac{1}{a}}{\dfrac{b}{a}}$

   (A) $\dfrac{2a+1}{b}$ (B) $\dfrac{2a+1}{a}$ (C) $\dfrac{2a+1}{ab}$ (D) $\dfrac{4a^2+1}{xy}$ (E) $\dfrac{2b+1}{b}$

128

FACTORING AND ALGEBRAIC FRACTIONS

6. Simplify $\dfrac{\frac{1}{a} - \frac{1}{b}}{2}$

(A) $\dfrac{b-a}{2}$ (B) $\dfrac{a-b}{2}$ (C) $\dfrac{b-a}{2ab}$ (D) $\dfrac{ba}{2}$ (E) $\dfrac{2ab}{b+a}$

7. If $x + y = 16$ and $x^2 - y^2 = 48$, then $x - y$ equals

(A) 3 (B) 32 (C) 4 (D) 36 (E) 6

8. If $(x + y)^2 = 100$ and $xy = 20$, find $x^2 + y^2$.

(A) 100 (B) 20 (C) 40 (D) 60 (E) 80

9. If $\dfrac{1}{x} + \dfrac{1}{y} = \dfrac{1}{2}$ and $\dfrac{1}{x} - \dfrac{1}{y} = \dfrac{1}{4}$, find $\dfrac{1}{x^2} - \dfrac{1}{y^2}$

(A) $\frac{3}{4}$ (B) $\frac{1}{4}$ (C) $\frac{3}{16}$ (D) $\frac{1}{8}$ (E) $\frac{7}{8}$

10. The trinomial $x^2 - x - 20$ is exactly divisible by

(A) $x - 4$ (B) $x - 10$ (C) $x + 4$ (D) $x - 2$ (E) $x + 5$

1. REDUCING FRACTIONS

In reducing fractions, we must divide the numerator and denominator by the same factor. We can multiply or divide both the numerator and denominator of a fraction by the same number without changing the value of the fraction. However, if we were to add or subtract the same number in the numerator and denominator, the value of the fraction would not remain the same. When we reduce $\dfrac{9}{12}$ to $\dfrac{3}{4}$, we are really saying that $\dfrac{9}{12} = \dfrac{3 \cdot 3}{3 \cdot 4}$ and then dividing the numerator and denominator by 3. We may not say that $\dfrac{9}{12} = \dfrac{5+4}{5+7}$ and then say that $\dfrac{9}{12} = \dfrac{4}{7}$. This is a serious error in algebra as well. $\dfrac{9t}{12t} = \dfrac{3}{4}$, because we divide numerator and denominator by 3t. However, $\dfrac{9+t}{12+t}$ cannot be reduced, as there is no factor which divides into the *entire* numerator as well as the *entire* denominator. *Never cancel terms!!!* That is, never cancel parts of numerators or denominators containing + or − signs, unless they are enclosed in parentheses as parts of factors. This is one of the most frequent student errors. Be very careful to avoid it.

FACTORING AND ALGEBRAIC FRACTIONS

Example: Reduce $\dfrac{4b^2 + 8b}{3b^3 + 6b^2}$

Solution: Factoring the numerator and denominator by removing the largest common factor in both cases, we have $\dfrac{4b(b + 2)}{3b^2(b + 2)}$.

The factors common to both numerator and denominator are b and (b + 2). Dividing these out, we have $\dfrac{4}{3b}$.

Example: Reduce $\dfrac{x^2 + 6x + 8}{x^2 + x - 12}$ to lowest terms.

Solution: There are no common factors here, but both numerator and denominator may be factored as trinomials. $\dfrac{(x + 4)(x + 2)}{(x + 4)(x - 3)}$ gives $\dfrac{x + 2}{x - 3}$ as a final answer. Remember not to cancel the x's as they are *terms* and not *factors*.

Example: Reduce $\dfrac{10 - 2x}{x^2 - 4x - 5}$ to lowest terms.

Solution: The numerator contains a common factor, while the denominator must be factored as a trinomial.

$$\dfrac{2(5 - x)}{(x - 5)(x + 1)}$$

When numbers are reversed around a minus sign, they may be turned around by factoring out a (-1). 5 - x = (-1)(x - 5). Doing this will enable us to reduce the fraction to $\dfrac{-2}{x + 1}$. Remember that if the terms had been reversed around a plus sign, the factors could have been canceled without factoring further, as a + b = b + a, by the commutative law of addition. Subtraction, however, is not commutative, necessitating the factoring of -1.

Practice 1

Answers on page 139

Work out each problem in the space provided. Circle the letter before your answer.

1. Reduce to lowest terms: $\dfrac{3x^3 - 3x^2y}{9x^2 - 9xy}$

(A) $\dfrac{x}{6}$ (B) $\dfrac{x}{3}$ (C) $\dfrac{2x}{3}$ (D) 1 (E) $\dfrac{x - y}{3}$

FACTORING AND ALGEBRAIC FRACTIONS 131

2. Reduce to lowest terms: $\dfrac{2x - 8}{12 - 3x}$

(A) $-\dfrac{2}{3}$ (B) $\dfrac{2}{3}$ (C) $-\dfrac{4}{3}$ (D) $\dfrac{4}{3}$ (E) $-\dfrac{3}{2}$

3. Find the value of $\dfrac{3x - y}{y - 3x}$ when $x = \dfrac{2}{7}$ and $y = \dfrac{3}{10}$, $y \neq 3x$.

(A) $\dfrac{24}{70}$ (B) $\dfrac{11}{70}$ (C) 0 (D) 1 (E) -1

4. Reduce to lowest terms: $\dfrac{b^2 + b - 12}{b^2 + 2b - 15}$

(A) $\dfrac{4}{5}$ (B) $-\dfrac{4}{3}$ (C) $\dfrac{b+4}{b+5}$ (D) $\dfrac{b-4}{b-5}$ (E) $-\dfrac{b+4}{b+5}$

5. Reduce to lowest terms: $\dfrac{2x + 4y}{6x + 12y}$

(A) $\dfrac{2}{3}$ (B) $-\dfrac{2}{3}$ (C) $-\dfrac{1}{3}$ (D) $\dfrac{1}{3}$ (E) 3

2. ADDITION OR SUBTRACTION OF FRACTIONS

In adding or subtracting fractions, it is necessary to have the fractions expressed in terms of the same common denominator. When adding or subtracting two fractions, use the same shortcuts used in arithmetic. Remember that $\dfrac{a}{b} + \dfrac{c}{d} = \dfrac{ad + bc}{bd}$, and that $\dfrac{a}{b} - \dfrac{c}{d} = \dfrac{ad - bc}{bd}$. All sums or differences should be reduced to lowest terms.

Example: Add $\dfrac{3}{a} + \dfrac{2}{b}$

Solution: Add the two cross products and put the sum over the denominator product: $\dfrac{3b + 2a}{ab}$.

Example: Add $\dfrac{2a}{3} + \dfrac{4a}{5}$

Solution: $\dfrac{10a + 12a}{15} = \dfrac{22a}{15}$

Example: Add $\dfrac{5a}{a + b} + \dfrac{5b}{a + b}$

Solution: Since both fractions have the same denominator, we must simply add the numerators and put the sum over the same denominator.

$$\dfrac{5a + 5b}{a + b} = \dfrac{5(a + b)}{a + b} = 5$$

132 FACTORING AND ALGEBRAIC FRACTIONS

Example: Subtract $\dfrac{4r-s}{6} - \dfrac{2r-7s}{6}$

Solution: Since both fractions have the same denominator, we subtract the numerators and place the difference over the same denominator. Be very careful of the minus sign between the fractions, as it will change the sign of each term in the second numerator.

$$\frac{4r-s-(2r-7s)}{6} = \frac{4r-s-2r+7s}{6} = \frac{2r+6s}{6} =$$

$$\frac{2(r+3s)}{6} = \frac{r+3s}{3}$$

Practice 2

Answers on page 140

Work out each problem in the space provided. Circle the letter before your answer.

1. Subtract $\dfrac{6x+5y}{2x} - \dfrac{4x+y}{2x}$

   (A) $1+4y$ (B) $4y$ (C) $1+2y$ (D) $\dfrac{x+2y}{x}$ (E) $\dfrac{x+3y}{x}$

2. Add $\dfrac{3c}{c+d} + \dfrac{3d}{c+d}$

   (A) $\dfrac{6cd}{c+d}$ (B) $\dfrac{3cd}{c+d}$ (C) $\dfrac{3}{2}$ (D) 3 (E) $\dfrac{9cd}{c+d}$

3. Add $\dfrac{a}{5} + \dfrac{3a}{10}$

   (A) $\dfrac{4a}{15}$ (B) $\dfrac{a}{2}$ (C) $\dfrac{3a^2}{50}$ (D) $\dfrac{2a}{25}$ (E) $\dfrac{3a^2}{15}$

4. Add $\dfrac{x+4}{6} + \dfrac{1}{2}$

   (A) $\dfrac{x+7}{6}$ (B) $\dfrac{x+5}{8}$ (C) $\dfrac{x+4}{12}$ (D) $\dfrac{x+5}{12}$ (E) $\dfrac{x+5}{6}$

5. Subtract $\dfrac{3b}{4} - \dfrac{7b}{10}$

   (A) $-\dfrac{2b}{3}$ (B) $\dfrac{b}{5}$ (C) $\dfrac{b}{20}$ (D) b (E) $\dfrac{2b}{3}$

3. MULTIPLICATION AND DIVISION OF FRACTIONS

In multiplying or dividing fractions, we must first factor all numerators and denominators and may then cancel all factors common to any numerator and any denominator. Remember always to invert the fraction following the division sign. Where exponents are involved, they are added in multiplication and subtracted in division.

Example: Find the product of $\dfrac{x^3}{y^2}$ and $\dfrac{y^3}{x^2}$.

Solution: Factors common to both numerator and denominator are x^2 in the first numerator and second denominator and, also, y^2 in the first denominator and second numerator. Dividing by these common factors, we are left with $\dfrac{x}{1} \cdot \dfrac{y}{1}$. Finally, we multiply the resulting fractions, giving an answer of xy.

Example: Divide $\dfrac{15a^2 b}{2}$ by $5a^3$.

Solution: We invert the divisor and multiply.

$$\frac{15a^2 b}{2} \cdot \frac{1}{5a^3}$$

We can divide the first numerator and second denominator by $5a^2$, giving $\dfrac{3b}{2} \cdot \dfrac{1}{a}$ or $\dfrac{3b}{2a}$.

Practice 3

Answers on page 140

Work out each problem in the space provided. Circle the letter before your answer.

1. Find the product of $\dfrac{x^2}{y^3}$ and $\dfrac{y^4}{x^5}$

(A) $\dfrac{y^2}{x^3}$ (B) $\dfrac{y}{x^3}$ (C) $\dfrac{x^3}{y}$ (D) $\dfrac{x^8}{y^7}$ (E) $\dfrac{x}{y}$

2. Multiply c by $\dfrac{b}{c}$

(A) $\dfrac{b}{c^2}$ (B) $\dfrac{c^2}{b}$ (C) b (D) c (E) bc^2

3. Divide $\dfrac{ax}{by}$ by $\dfrac{x}{y}$

(A) $\dfrac{ax^2}{by^2}$ (B) $\dfrac{b}{a}$ (C) $\dfrac{a}{b}$ (D) $\dfrac{by^2}{ax^2}$ (E) $\dfrac{ay}{bx}$

4. Divide $4abc$ by $\dfrac{2a^2b}{3d^2}$

(A) $\dfrac{8a^3b^2c}{3d^2}$ (B) $\dfrac{a}{6cd^2}$ (C) $\dfrac{2ac}{bd^2}$ (D) $\dfrac{6cd^2}{a}$ (E) $\dfrac{5cd^2}{a}$

5. Divide $\dfrac{3a^2c^4}{4b^2}$ by $6ac^2$

(A) $\dfrac{ac^2}{8b^2}$ (B) $\dfrac{ac^2}{4b^2}$ (C) $\dfrac{4b^2}{ac^2}$ (D) $\dfrac{8b^2}{ac^2}$ (E) $\dfrac{ac^2}{6b^2}$

4. COMPLEX ALGEBRAIC FRACTIONS

Complex algebraic fractions are simplified by the same methods reviewed earlier for arithmetic fractions. To eliminate the fractions within the fraction, multiply *each term* of the entire complex fraction by the lowest quantity which will eliminate them all.

Example: Simplify $\dfrac{\dfrac{3}{x} + \dfrac{2}{y}}{6}$

Solution: We must multiply *each term* by xy, giving $\dfrac{3y + 2x}{6xy}$.

No reduction is possible beyond this. Remember *never* to cancel terms or parts of terms. We may only reduce by canceling factors.

Example: Simplify $\dfrac{1}{1 - \dfrac{b}{a}}$

Solution: Multiply every term by a, giving $\dfrac{a}{a - b}$. Remember that nothing can be canceled here.

Practice 4

Answers on page 140

Work out each problem in the space provided. Circle the letter before your answer.

1. Simplify $\dfrac{x}{x - \dfrac{x}{2}}$

   (A) 2 (B) 2x (C) 1 (D) $\dfrac{1}{x}$ (E) $-\dfrac{1}{x}$

2. Simplify $\dfrac{\dfrac{a}{x^2}}{\dfrac{a^2}{x}}$

   (A) $\dfrac{x}{a}$ (B) $\dfrac{1}{a^2 x}$ (C) $\dfrac{1}{ax}$ (D) ax (E) $\dfrac{a}{x}$

3. Simplify $\dfrac{\dfrac{1}{x} - \dfrac{1}{y}}{\dfrac{1}{x} + \dfrac{1}{y}}$

   (A) $\dfrac{x-y}{x+y}$ (B) $\dfrac{x+y}{x-y}$ (C) $\dfrac{y-x}{x+y}$ (D) -1 (E) $-xy$

4. Simplify $\dfrac{1 + \dfrac{1}{x}}{\dfrac{1}{y}}$

   (A) $\dfrac{xy+y}{x}$ (B) 2y (C) $x+1$ (D) $\dfrac{y+1}{x}$ (E) $\dfrac{xy+1}{y}$

5. Simplify $\dfrac{2 + \dfrac{1}{t}}{\dfrac{2}{t^2}}$

   (A) $t^2 + t$ (B) t^3 (C) $\dfrac{2t+1}{2}$ (D) $t+1$ (E) $\dfrac{2t^2+t}{2}$

5. USING FACTORING TO FIND MISSING VALUES

Certain types of problems may involve the ability to factor in order to evaluate a given expression. In particular, you should be able to factor the difference of two perfect squares. If an expression consists of two terms which are separated by a minus sign, the expression can always be factored into two binomials, with one containing the sum of the square roots and the other their difference. This can be stated by the identity $x^2 - y^2 = (x + y)(x - y)$.

Example: If $m^2 - n^2 = 48$ and $m + n = 12$, find $m - n$.

Solution: Since $m^2 - n^2$ is equal to $(m + n)(m - n)$, these two factors must multiply to 48. If one of them is 12, the other must be 4.

Example: If $(a + b)^2 = 48$ and $ab = 6$, find $a^2 + b^2$.

Solution: $(a + b)^2$ is equal to $a^2 + 2ab + b^2$. Substituting 6 for ab, we have $a^2 + 2(6) + b^2 = 48$ and $a^2 + b^2 = 36$.

Practice 5

Answers on page 141

Work out each problem in the space provided. Circle the letter before your answer.

1. If $a + b = \frac{1}{3}$ and $a - b = \frac{1}{4}$ find $a^2 - b^2$.

(A) $\frac{1}{12}$ (B) $\frac{1}{7}$ (C) $\frac{2}{7}$ (D) $\frac{1}{6}$
(E) none of these

2. If $(a - b)^2 = 40$ and $ab = 8$, find $a^2 + b^2$.

(A) 5 (B) 24 (C) 48 (D) 56 (E) 32

3. If $a + b = 8$ and $a^2 - b^2 = 24$, then $a - b =$

(A) 16 (B) 4 (C) 3 (D) 32 (E) 6

4. The trinomial $x^2 + 4x - 45$ is exactly divisible by

(A) $x + 9$ (B) $x - 9$ (C) $x + 5$ (D) $x + 15$ (E) $x - 3$

5. If $\dfrac{1}{c} - \dfrac{1}{d} = 5$ and $\dfrac{1}{c} + \dfrac{1}{d} = 3$, then $\dfrac{1}{c^2} - \dfrac{1}{d^2} =$

(A) 16 (B) 34 (C) 2 (D) 15
(E) cannot be determined

Retest

Answers on page 141

Work out each problem in the space provided. Circle the letter before your answer.

1. Find the sum of $\dfrac{2n}{5}$ and $\dfrac{n}{10}$.

   (A) $\dfrac{3n}{50}$ (B) $\tfrac{1}{2}n$ (C) $\dfrac{2n^2}{50}$ (D) $\dfrac{2n^2}{10}$ (E) $\dfrac{3n}{10}$

2. Combine into a single fraction: $\dfrac{x}{y} - 3$

   (A) $\dfrac{x-3y}{y}$ (B) $\dfrac{x-3}{y}$ (C) $\dfrac{x-9}{3y}$ (D) $\dfrac{x-3y}{3}$ (E) $\dfrac{x-3y}{3y}$

3. Divide $\dfrac{x^2+2x-8}{4+x}$ by $\dfrac{2-x}{3}$.

   (A) 3   (B) -3 (C) $3(x-2)$ (D) $\dfrac{3}{2-x}$

   (E) none of these

4. Find an expression equivalent to $\left(\dfrac{5a^3}{b}\right)^3$.

   (A) $\dfrac{15a^6}{b^3}$ (B) $\dfrac{15a^9}{b^3}$ (C) $\dfrac{125a^6}{b^3}$ (D) $\dfrac{125a^9}{b^3}$ (E) $\dfrac{25a^6}{b^3}$

5. Simplify $\dfrac{3-\dfrac{1}{x}}{\dfrac{y}{x}}$

   (A) $\dfrac{2}{y}$ (B) $\dfrac{2x}{y}$ (C) $\dfrac{3-x}{y}$ (D) $\dfrac{3x-1}{x}$ (E) $\dfrac{3x-1}{y}$

6. $\dfrac{3-\dfrac{1}{x}}{\dfrac{3}{x^2}}$ is equal to

   (A) $\dfrac{x^2-x}{3}$ (B) $\dfrac{3x^2-x}{3}$ (C) x^2-x (D) $\dfrac{3x-1}{3}$ (E) $\dfrac{3-x}{3}$

138   FACTORING AND ALGEBRAIC FRACTIONS

7. If $a^2 - b^2 = 100$ and $a + b = 25$, then $a - b =$
(A) 4   (B) 75   (C) −4   (D) −75   (E) 5

8. The trinomial $x^2 - 8x - 20$ is exactly divisible by
(A) $x - 5$ (B) $x - 4$ (C) $x - 2$ (D) $x - 10$ (E) $x - 1$

9. If $\dfrac{1}{a} - \dfrac{1}{b} = 6$ and $\dfrac{1}{a} + \dfrac{1}{b} = 5$, find $\dfrac{1}{a^2} - \dfrac{1}{b^2}$.
(A) 30   (B) −11   (C) 61   (D) 11   (E) 1

10. If $(x - y)^2 = 30$ and $xy = 17$, find $x^2 + y^2$.
(A) −4   (B) 4   (C) 13   (D) 47   (E) 64

SOLUTIONS TO PRACTICE EXERCISES

Diagnostic Test

1. (C) $\dfrac{3n + 8n}{12} = \dfrac{11n}{12}$

2. (D) $\dfrac{2}{1} - \dfrac{a}{b} = \dfrac{2b - a}{b}$

3. (B) $\dfrac{x - 5}{x + 5} \cdot \dfrac{5 + x}{5 - x}$ Cancel $x + 5$.

   $\dfrac{x - 5}{5 - x} = \dfrac{x - 5}{-1(x - 5)} = -1$

4. (E) $\dfrac{3x^2}{y} \cdot \dfrac{3x^2}{y} \cdot \dfrac{3x^2}{y} = \dfrac{27x^6}{y^3}$

5. (A) Multiply every term by a.

   $\dfrac{2a + 1}{b}$

6. (C) Multiply every term by ab.

   $\dfrac{b - a}{2ab}$

7. (A) $x^2 - y^2 = (x + y)(x - y) = 48$
   Substituting 16 for $x + y$, we have
   $$16(x - y) = 48$$
   $$x - y = 3$$

8. (D) $(x + y)^2 = x^2 + 2xy + y^2 = 100$
   Substituting 20 for xy, we have
   $$x^2 + 40 + y^2 = 100$$
   $$x^2 + y^2 = 60$$

9. (D) $\left(\dfrac{1}{x} + \dfrac{1}{y}\right)\left(\dfrac{1}{x} - \dfrac{1}{y}\right) = \dfrac{1}{x^2} - \dfrac{1}{y^2}$

   $\left(\dfrac{1}{2}\right)\left(\dfrac{1}{4}\right) = \dfrac{1}{x^2} - \dfrac{1}{y^2}$

   $\dfrac{1}{8} = \dfrac{1}{x^2} - \dfrac{1}{y^2}$

10. (C) $x^2 - x - 20 = (x - 5)(x + 4)$

Practice 1

1. (B) $\dfrac{3x^2(x - y)}{9x(x - y)} = \dfrac{x}{3}$

2. (A) $\dfrac{2(x - 4)}{3(4 - x)} = -\dfrac{2}{3}$

3. (E) $\dfrac{3x - y}{y - 3x} = -1$ regardless of the values of x and y, as long as the denominator is not 0.

4. (C) $\dfrac{(b + 4)(b - 3)}{(b + 5)(b - 3)} = \dfrac{b + 4}{b + 5}$

5. (D) $\dfrac{2(x + 2y)}{6(x + 2y)} = \dfrac{2}{6} = \dfrac{1}{3}$

Practice 2

1. (D) $\dfrac{6x + 5y - (4x + y)}{2x}$

    $= \dfrac{6x + 5y - 4x - y}{2x} = \dfrac{2x + 4y}{2x}$

    $= \dfrac{2(x + 2y)}{2x} = \dfrac{x + 2y}{x}$

2. (D) $\dfrac{3c + 3d}{c + d} = \dfrac{3(c + d)}{c + d} = 3$

3. (B) $\dfrac{2a + 3a}{10} = \dfrac{5a}{10} = \dfrac{a}{2}$

4. (A) $\dfrac{x + 4 + 3}{6} = \dfrac{x + 7}{6}$

5. (C) $\dfrac{3b(10) - 4(7b)}{4(10)} = \dfrac{30b - 28b}{40}$

    $= \dfrac{2b}{40} = \dfrac{b}{20}$

Practice 3

1. (B) Cancel x^2 and y^3.

    $\dfrac{1}{1} \cdot \dfrac{y}{x^3} = \dfrac{y}{x^3}$

2. (C) $c \cdot \dfrac{b}{c} = b$

3. (C) $\dfrac{ax}{by} \cdot \dfrac{y}{x}$ Cancel y and x. $\dfrac{a}{b}$

4. (D) $4abc \cdot \dfrac{3d^2}{2a^2b}$ Cancel 2, a, and ab.

    $2c \cdot \dfrac{3d^2}{a} = \dfrac{6cd^2}{a}$

5. (A) $\dfrac{3a^2c^4}{4b^2} \cdot \dfrac{1}{6ac^2}$ Cancel 3, a, and c^2.

    $\dfrac{ac^2}{4b^2} \cdot \dfrac{1}{2} = \dfrac{ac^2}{8b^2}$

Practice 4

1. (A) Multiply every term by 2.

    $\dfrac{2x}{2x - x} = \dfrac{2x}{x} = 2$

2. (C) Multiply every term by x^2.

    $\dfrac{a}{a^2x} = \dfrac{1}{ax}$

3. (C) Multiply every term by xy.

    $\dfrac{y - x}{y + x}$

4. (A) Multiply every term by xy.

    $\dfrac{xy + y}{x}$

5. (E) Multiply every term by t^2.

    $\dfrac{2t^2 + t}{2}$

Practice 5

1. (A) $(a+b)(a-b) = a^2 - b^2$
   $(\frac{1}{3})(\frac{1}{4}) = a^2 - b^2$
   $\frac{1}{12} = a^2 - b^2$

2. (D) $(a-b)^2 = a^2 - 2ab + b^2 = 40$
   Substituting 8 for ab, we have
   $a^2 - 16 + b^2 = 40$
   $a^2 + b^2 = 56$

3. (C) $(a+b)(a-b) = a^2 - b^2$
   $8(a-b) = 24$
   $(a-b) = 3$

4. (A) $x^2 + 4x - 45 = (x+9)(x-5)$

5. (D) $\left(\frac{1}{c} - \frac{1}{d}\right)\left(\frac{1}{c} + \frac{1}{d}\right) = \frac{1}{c^2} - \frac{1}{d^2}$
   $(5)(3) = \frac{1}{c^2} - \frac{1}{d^2}$
   $15 = \frac{1}{c^2} - \frac{1}{d^2}$

Retest

1. (B) $\frac{4n+n}{10} = \frac{5n}{10} = \frac{n}{2} = \frac{1}{2}n$

2. (A) $\frac{x}{y} - \frac{3}{1} = \frac{x-3y}{y}$

3. (B) $\frac{x^2 + 2x - 8}{4+x} \cdot \frac{3}{2-x}$
   $= \frac{(x+4)(x-2)}{4+x} \cdot \frac{3}{2-x}$
   Cancel $x+4$. $\frac{3(x-2)}{2-x} = \frac{3(x-2)}{-1(x-2)} = -3$

4. (D) $\frac{5a^3}{b} \cdot \frac{5a^3}{b} \cdot \frac{5a^3}{b} = \frac{125a^9}{b^3}$

5. (E) Multiply every term by x.
   $\frac{3x-1}{y}$

6. (B) Multiply every term by x^2.
   $\frac{3x^2 - x}{3}$

7. (A) $a^2 - b^2 = (a+b)(a-b) = 100$
   Substituting 25 for $a+b$, we have
   $25(a-b) = 100$
   $a-b = 4$

8. (D) $x^2 - 8x - 20 = (x-10)(x+2)$

9. (A) $\left(\frac{1}{a} - \frac{1}{b}\right)\left(\frac{1}{a} + \frac{1}{b}\right) = \frac{1}{a^2} - \frac{1}{b^2}$
   $(6)(5) = \frac{1}{a^2} - \frac{1}{b^2}$
   $30 = \frac{1}{a^2} - \frac{1}{b^2}$

10. (E) $(x-y)^2 = x^2 - 2xy + y^2 = 30$
    Substituting 17 for xy, we have
    $x^2 - 34 + y^2 = 30$
    $x^2 + y^2 = 64$

Problem Solving in Algebra

DIAGNOSTIC TEST

Answers on page 159

Work out each problem in the space provided. Circle the letter before your answer.

1. Find three consecutive odd integers such that the sum of the first two is four times the third.

(A) 3, 5, 7 (B) −3, −1, 1 (C) −11, −9, −7
(D) −7, −5, −3 (E) 9, 11, 13

2. Find the shortest side of a triangle whose perimeter is 64, if the ratio of two of its sides is 4:3 and the third side is 20 less than the sum of the other two.

(A) 6 (B) 18 (C) 20 (D) 22 (E) 24

3. A purse contains 16 coins in dimes and quarters. If the value of the coins is $2.50, how many dimes are there?

(A) 6 (B) 8 (C) 9 (D) 10 (E) 12

4. How many quarts of water must be added to 18 quarts of a 32% alcohol solution to dilute it to a solution which is only 12% alcohol?

(A) 10 (B) 14 (C) 20 (D) 30 (E) 34

5. Danny drove to Yosemite Park from his home at 60 miles per hour. On his trip home, his rate was 10 miles per hour less and the trip took one hour longer. How far is his home from the park?

(A) 65 mi. (B) 100 mi. (C) 200 mi. (D) 280 mi. (E) 300 mi.

6. Two cars leave a restaurant at the same time and travel along a straight highway in opposite directions. At the end of three hours they are 300 miles apart. Find the rate of the slower car, if one car travels at a rate 20 miles per hour faster than the other.

(A) 30 (B) 40 (C) 50 (D) 55 (E) 60

7. The numerator of a fraction is one half the denominator. If the numerator is increased by 2 and the denominator is decreased by 2, the value of the fraction is $\frac{2}{3}$. Find the numerator of the original fraction.

(A) 4   (B) 8   (C) 10   (D) 12   (E) 20

8. Darren can mow the lawn in 20 minutes, while Valerie needs 30 minutes to do the same job. How many minutes will it take them to mow the lawn if they work together?

(A) 10   (B) 8   (C) 16   (D) $6\frac{1}{2}$ (E) 12

9. Meredith is 3 times as old as Adam. Six years from now, she will be twice as old as Adam will be then. How old is Adam now?

(A) 6   (B) 12   (C) 18   (D) 20   (E) 24

10. Mr. Barry invested some money at 5% and an amount half as great at 4%. His total annual income from both investments was $210. Find the amount invested at 4%.

(A) $1000   (B) $1500   (C) $2000   (D) $2500   (E) $3000

In the following sections, we will review some of the major types of algebraic problems. Although not every problem you come across will fall into one of these categories, it will help you to be thoroughly familiar with these types of problems. By practicing with the problems which follow, you will learn to translate words into mathematical equations. You should then be able to handle other types of problems confidently.

In solving verbal problems, it is most important that you read carefully and know what it is that you are trying to find. Once this is done, represent your unknown algebraically. Write the equation which translates the words of the problem into the symbols of mathematics. Solve that equation by the techniques previously reviewed.

1. COIN PROBLEMS

In solving coin problems, it is best to change the value of all monies to cents before writing an equation. Thus, the number of nickels must be multiplied by 5 to give the value in cents, dimes by 10, quarters by 25, half dollars by 50, and dollars by 100.

Example: Sue has $1.35, consisting of nickels and dimes. If she has 9 more nickels than dimes, how many nickels does she have?

Solution: Let   x = the number of dimes
x + 9 = the number of nickels

$$10x = \text{the value of the dimes in cents}$$
$$5x + 45 = \text{the value of the nickels in cents}$$
$$135 = \text{the value of the money she has in cents}$$
$$10x + 5x + 45 = 135$$
$$15x = 90$$
$$x = 6$$

She has 6 dimes and 15 nickels.

In a problem such as this, you can be sure that 6 would be among the multiple choice answers given. You must be sure to read carefully what you are asked to find and then continue until you have found the quantity sought.

Practice 1

Answers on page 160

Work out each problem in the space provided. Circle the letter before your answer.

1. Marie has $2.20 in dimes and quarters. If the number of dimes is $\frac{1}{4}$ the number of quarters, how many dimes does she have?

(A) 2   (B) 4   (C) 6   (D) 8   (E) 10

2. Lisa has 45 coins which are worth a total of $3.50. If the coins are all nickels and dimes, how many more dimes than nickels does she have?

(A) 5   (B) 10   (C) 15   (D) 20   (E) 25

3. A postal clerk sold 40 stamps for $5.40. Some were 10-cent stamps and some were 15-cent stamps. How many 10-cent stamps were there?

(A) 10   (B) 12   (C) 20   (D) 24   (E) 28

4. Each of the 30 students in Homeroom 704 contributed either a nickel or a quarter to the Cancer Fund. If the total amount collected was $4.70, how many students contributed a nickel?

(A) 10   (B) 12   (C) 14   (D) 16   (E) 18

5. In a purse containing nickels and dimes, the ratio of nickels to dimes is 3:4. If there are 28 coins in all, what is the value of the dimes?

(A) 60¢   (B) $1.12   (C) $1.60   (D) 12¢   (E) $1.00

2. CONSECUTIVE INTEGER PROBLEMS

Consecutive integers are one apart and can be represented algebraically as x, x + 1, x + 2, and so on. Consecutive even and odd integers are both two apart and can be represented by x, x + 2, x + 4, and so on. *Never* try to represent consecutive odd integers by x, x + 1, x + 3, etc., for if x is odd, x + 1 would be even.

Example: Find three consecutive odd integers whose sum is 219.

Solution: Represent the integers as x, x + 2 and x + 4. Write an equation stating that their sum is 219.

$$3x + 6 = 219$$
$$3x = 213$$
$$x = 71, \text{ making the integers } 71, 73, \text{ and } 75.$$

Practice 2

Answers on page 160

Work out each problem in the space provided. Circle the letter before your answer.

1. If n + 1 is the largest of four consecutive integers, represent the sum of the four integers.

   (A) 4n + 10   (B) 4n − 2   (C) 4n − 4   (D) 4n − 5   (E) 4n − 8

2. If n is the first of two consecutive odd integers, which equation could be used to find these integers if the difference of their squares is 120?

   (A) $(n + 1)^2 - n^2 = 120$ (B) $n^2 - (n + 1)^2 = 120$
   (C) $n^2 - (n + 2)^2 = 120$ (D) $(n + 2)^2 - n^2 = 120$
   (E) $[(n + 2) - n]^2 = 120$

3. Find the average of four consecutive odd integers whose sum is 112.

   (A) 25   (B) 29   (C) 31   (D) 28   (E) 30

4. Find the second of three consecutive integers if the sum of the first and third is 26.

   (A) 11   (B) 12   (C) 13   (D) 14   (E) 15

5. If 2x − 3 is an odd integer, find the next even integer.

   (A) 2x − 5   (B) 2x − 4   (C) 2x − 2   (D) 2x − 1   (E) 2x + 1

3. AGE PROBLEMS

In solving age problems, you are usually called upon to represent a person's age at the present time, several years from now, or several years ago. A person's age x years from now is found by adding x to his present age. A person's age x years ago is found by subtracting x from his present age.

Example: Michelle was 15 years old y years ago. Represent her age x years from now.

Solution: Her present age is 15 + y. In x years, her age will be her present age plus x, or 15 + y + x.

Example: Jody is now 20 years old and her brother, Glenn, is 14. How many years ago was Jody three times as old as Glenn was then?

Solution: We are comparing their ages x years ago. At that time, Jody's age (20 - x) was three times Glenn's age (14 - x). This can be stated as the equation

20 - x = 3(14 - x)
20 - x = 42 - 3x
2x = 22
x = 11

To check, find their ages 11 years ago. Jody was 9 while Glenn was 3. Therefore, Jody was three times as old as Glenn was then.

Practice 3

Answers on page 161

Work out each problem in the space provided. Circle the letter before your answer.

1. Mark is now 4 times as old as his brother Stephen. In 1 year Mark will be 3 times as old as Stephen will be then. How old was Mark two years ago?

(A) 2   (B) 3   (C) 6   (D) 8   (E) 9

2. Mr. Burke is 24 years older than his son Jack. In 8 years, Mr. Burke will be twice as old as Jack will be then. How old is Mr. Burke now?

(A) 16   (B) 24   (C) 32   (D) 40   (E) 48

3. Lili is 23 years old and Melanie is 15 years old. How many years ago was Lili twice as old as Melanie?

(A) 7   (B) 16   (C) 9   (D) 5   (E) 8

4. Two years from now, Karen's age will be 2x + 1. Represent her age two years ago.

(A) 2x - 4   (B) 2x - 1   (C) 2x + 3   (D) 2x - 3   (E) 2x - 2

5. Alice is now 5 years younger than her brother Robert, whose age is 4x + 3. Represent her age 3 years from now.

(A) 4x - 5   (B) 4x - 2   (C) 4x   (D) 4x + 1   (E) 4x - 1

4. INVESTMENT PROBLEMS

The annual amount of interest paid on an investment is found by multiplying the amount invested, called the principal, by the percent of interest, called the rate.

$$\text{PRINCIPAL} \cdot \text{RATE} = \text{INTEREST INCOME}$$

Example: Mrs. Friedman invested some money in a bank paying 4% interest annually and a second amount, $500 less than the first, in a bank paying 6% interest. If her annual income from both investments was $50, how much money did she invest at 6%?

Solution: Represent the two investments algebraically.

x = amount invested at 4%
$x - 500$ = amount invested at 6%
$.04x$ = annual interest from 4% investment
$.06(x - 500)$ = annual interest from 6% investment
$.04x + .06(x - 500) = 50$

Multiply by 100 to remove decimals.

$$4x + 6(x - 500) = 5000$$
$$4x + 6x - 3000 = 5000$$
$$10x = 8000$$
$$x = 800$$
$$x - 500 = 300$$

She invested $300 at 6%.

Practice 4

Answers on page 161

Work out each problem in the space provided. Circle the letter before your answer.

1. Barbara invested x dollars at 3% and $400 more than this amount at 5%. Represent the annual income from the 5% investment.

(A) .05x   (B) .05(x + 400)   (C) .05x + 400
(D) 5x + 40000   (E) none of these

2. Mr. Blum invested $10,000, part at 6% and the rest at 5%. If x represents the amount invested at 6%, represent the annual income from the 5% investment.

(A) 5(x − 10,000)
(B) 5(10,000 − x)
(C) .05(x + 10,000)
(D) .05(x − 10,000)
(E) .05(10,000 − x)

3. Dr. Kramer invested $2000 in an account paying 6% interest annually. How many more dollars must she invest at 3% so that her total annual income is 4% of her entire investment?

(A) $120 (B) $1000 (C) $2000 (D) $4000 (E) $6000

4. Marion invested $7200, part at 4% and the rest at 5%. If the annual income from both investments was the same, find her total annual income from these investments.

(A) $160 (B) $320 (C) $4000 (D) $3200 (E) $1200

5. Mr. Maxwell inherited some money from his father. He invested $\frac{1}{2}$ of this amount at 5%, $\frac{1}{3}$ of this amount at 6% and the rest at 3%. If the total annual income from these investments was $300, what was the amount he inherited?

(A) $600 (B) $60 (C) $2000 (D) $3000 (E) $6000

5. FRACTION PROBLEMS

A fraction is a ratio between two numbers. If the value of a fraction is $\frac{3}{4}$, it does not mean that the numerator is 3 and the denominator 4. The numerator and denominator could be 9 and 12 respectively, or 1.5 and 2, or 45 and 60, or an infinite number of other combinations. All we know is that the ratio of numerator to denominator will be 3:4. Therefore, the numerator may be represented by 3x and the denominator by 4x. The fraction is then represented by $\frac{3x}{4x}$.

> Example: The value of a fraction is $\frac{2}{3}$. If one is subtracted from the numerator and added to the denominator, the value of the fraction is $\frac{1}{2}$. Find the original fraction.
>
> Solution: Represent the original fraction as $\frac{2x}{3x}$. If one is subtracted from the numerator and added to the denominator, the new fraction is $\frac{2x-1}{3x+1}$. The value of this new fraction is $\frac{1}{2}$.

$$\frac{2x-1}{3x+1} = \frac{1}{2}$$

Cross multiply to eliminate fractions.

$4x - 2 = 3x + 1$
$x = 3$

The original fraction is $\frac{2x}{3x}$, which is $\frac{6}{9}$.

Practice 5

Answers on page 162

Work out each problem in the space provided. Circle the letter before your answer.

1. A fraction is equivalent to $\frac{4}{5}$. If the numerator is increased by 4 and the denominator is increased by 10, the value of the resulting fraction is $\frac{2}{3}$. Find the numerator of the original fraction.

   (A) 4   (B) 5   (C) 12   (D) 16   (E) 20

2. What number must be added to both the numerator and denominator of the fraction $\frac{5}{21}$ to give a fraction equal to $\frac{3}{7}$?

   (A) 3   (B) 4   (C) 5   (D) 6   (E) 7

3. The value of a certain fraction is $\frac{3}{5}$. If both the numerator and denominator are increased by 5, the new fraction is equivalent to $\frac{7}{10}$. Find the original fraction.

   (A) $\frac{3}{5}$ (B) $\frac{6}{10}$ (C) $\frac{9}{15}$ (D) $\frac{12}{20}$ (E) $\frac{15}{25}$

4. The denominator of a certain fraction is 5 more than the numerator. If 3 is added to both numerator and denominator, the value of the new fraction is $\frac{2}{3}$. Find the original fraction.

   (A) $\frac{3}{8}$ (B) $\frac{4}{9}$ (C) $\frac{11}{16}$ (D) $\frac{12}{17}$ (E) $\frac{7}{12}$

5. The denominator of a fraction is twice as large as the numerator. If 4 is added to both the numerator and denominator, the value of the fraction is $\frac{5}{8}$. Find the denominator of the original fraction.

   (A) 6   (B) 10   (C) 12   (D) 14   (E) 16

6. MIXTURE PROBLEMS

There are two kinds of mixture problems with which you should be familiar. The first is sometimes referred to as dry mixture, in which we mix dry ingredients of different values, such as nuts or coffee. Also solved by the same method are problems dealing with tickets at different prices, and similar problems. In solving this type of problem it is best to organize the data in a chart with three rows and columns, labeled as illustrated in the following example.

Example: Mr. Sweet wishes to mix candy worth 36 cents a pound with candy worth 52 cents a pound to make 300 pounds of a mixture worth 40 cents a pound. How many pounds of the more expensive candy should he use?

Solution:

	No. of pounds	· Price per pound =	Total value
More expensive	x	52	52x
Less expensive	300 - x	36	36(300 - x)
Mixture	300	40	12000

The value of the more expensive candy plus the value of the less expensive candy must be equal to the value of the mixture. Almost all mixture problems derive their equation from adding the final column in the chart.

$52x + 36(300 - x) = 12000$

Notice that all values were computed in cents to avoid decimals.

$$52x + 10800 - 36x = 12000$$
$$16x = 1200$$
$$x = 75$$

He should use 75 pounds of the more expensive candy.

In solving the second type of mixture problem, we are dealing with percents instead of prices, and amounts of a certain ingredient instead of values. As we did with prices, we may omit the decimal point from the percents, as long as we do it in every line of the chart.

Example: How many quarts of pure alcohol must be added to 15 quarts of a solution which is 40% alcohol to strengthen it to a solution which is 50% alcohol?

PROBLEM SOLVING IN ALGEBRA   151

Solution:

	No. of quarts	· Percent alcohol	= Amount of alcohol
Original	15	40	600
Added	x	100	100x
New	15 + x	50	50(15 + x)

Notice that the percent of alcohol in pure alcohol is 100. If we had added pure water to weaken the solution, the percent of alcohol in pure water would have been 0. Again, the equation comes from adding the final column, since the amount of alcohol in the original solution plus the amount of alcohol added must equal the amount of alcohol in the new solution.

$$600 + 100x = 50(15 + x)$$
$$600 + 100x = 750 + 50x$$
$$50x = 150$$
$$x = 3$$

3 quarts of alcohol should be added.

Practice 6

Answers on page 163

Work out each problem in the space provided. Circle the letter before your answer.

1. Express, in terms of x, the value, in cents, of x pounds of 40-cent cookies and (30 − x) pounds of 50-cent cookies.

   (A) 150 + 10x
   (B) 150 − 50x
   (C) 1500 − 10x
   (D) 1500 − 50x
   (E) 1500 + 10x

2. How many pounds of nuts selling for 70 cents a pound must be mixed with 30 pounds of nuts selling at 90 cents a pound to make a mixture which will sell for 85 cents a pound?

   (A) 7.5   (B) 10   (C) 22.5   (D) 40   (E) 12

3. A container holds 10 pints of a solution which is 20% acid. If 3 quarts of pure acid are added to the container, what percent of the resulting mixture is acid?

   (A) 5   (B) 10   (C) 20   (D) 50   (E) $33\frac{1}{3}$

4. A solution of 60 quarts of sugar and water is 20% sugar. How much water must be added to make a solution which is 5% sugar?

(A) 180 qts.   (B) 120 qts.   (C) 100 qts.   (D) 80 qts.   (E) 20 qts.

5. How much water must be evaporated from 240 pounds of a solution which is 3% alcohol to strengthen it to a solution which is 5% alcohol?

(A) 120 lbs.   (B) 96 lbs.   (C) 100 lbs.   (D) 84 lbs.   (E) 140 lbs.

7. MOTION PROBLEMS

The fundamental relationship in all motion problems is that rate times time is equal to distance.

$$\text{RATE} \cdot \text{TIME} = \text{DISTANCE}$$

The problems at the level of this examination usually deal with a relationship between distances. Most motion problems fall into one of three categories.

A. Motion in opposite directions

This can occur when objects start at the same point and move apart, or when they start at a given distance apart and move toward each other. In either case, the distance covered by the first object plus the distance covered by the second is equal to the total distance covered. This can be shown in the following diagram.

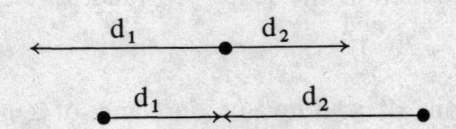

In either case, $d_1 + d_2$ = total distance covered.

B. Motion in the same direction

This type of problem is sometimes referred to as a "catch up" problem. Usually two objects leave the same place at different times and at different rates, but the one which leaves later "catches up" to the one which leaves earlier. In such cases the two distances must be equal. If one is still ahead of the other, then an equation must be written expressing this fact.

C. Round trip

In this type of problem, the rate going is different from the rate returning. The times are also different. But if we go somewhere and then return to the starting point, the distances must be equal.

PROBLEM SOLVING IN ALGEBRA 153

To solve any type of motion problem, it is helpful to organize the information in a chart with columns for rate, time, and distance. A separate line should be used for each moving object. Be very careful of units used. If the rate is given in *miles per hour*, the time must be in *hours* and the distance will be in *miles*.

Example: A passenger train and a freight train leave at 10:30 A.M. from stations which are 405 miles apart and travel toward each other. The rate of the passenger train is 45 miles per hour faster than that of the freight train. If they pass each other at 1:30 P.M., how fast was the passenger train traveling?

Solution: Notice that each train traveled exactly 3 hours.

	Rate ·	Time =	Distance
Passenger	x + 45	3	3x + 135
Freight	x	3	3x

$$3x + 135 + 3x = 405$$
$$6x = 270$$
$$x = 45$$

The rate of the passenger train was 90 m.p.h.

Example: Susie left her home at 11 A.M., traveling along Route 1 at 30 miles per hour. At 1 P.M., her brother Richard left home and started after her on the same road at 45 miles per hour. At what time did Richard catch up to Susie?

Solution:

	Rate ·	Time =	Distance
Susie	30	x	30x
Richard	45	x - 2	45x - 90

Since Richard left 2 hours later than Susie, he traveled for x - 2 hours, while Susie traveled for x hours. Notice that we do not fill in 11 and 1 in the time column, as these are times on the clock and not actual hours traveled. Since Richard caught up to Susie, the distances must be equal.

$$30x = 45x - 90$$
$$90 = 15x$$
$$x = 6$$

Susie traveled for 6 hours, which means it was 6 hours past 11 A.M., or 5 P.M. when Richard caught up to her.

Example: How far can Scott drive into the country if he drives out at 40 miles per hour and returns over the same road at 30 miles per hour and spends 8 hours away from home including a one-hour stop for lunch?

Solution: His actual driving time is 7 hours, which must be divided into two parts. If one part is x, the other is what is left, or 7 - x.

	Rate	Time	=	Distance
Going	40	x		40x
Return	30	7 - x		210 - 30x

The distances are equal.

40x = 210 - 30x
70x = 210
x = 3

If he traveled 40 miles per hour for 3 hours, he went 120 miles.

Practice 7

Answers on page 164

Work out each problem in the space provided. Circle the letter before your answer.

1. At 10 A.M. two cars started traveling toward each other from towns 287 miles apart. They passed each other at 1:30 P.M. If the rate of the faster car exceeded the rate of the slower car by 6 miles per hour, find the rate, in miles per hour, of the faster car.

(A) 38   (B) 40   (C) 44   (D) 48   (E) 50

2. A motorist covers 350 miles in 8 hours. Before noon he averages 50 miles per hour, but after noon he averages only 40 miles per hour. At what time did he leave?

(A) 7 A.M.   (B) 8 A.M.   (C) 9 A.M.   (D) 10 A.M.   (E) 11 A.M.

3. At 3 P.M. a plane left Kennedy Airport for Los Angeles traveling at 600 m.p.h. At 3:30 P.M. another plane left the same airport on the same route traveling at 650 m.p.h. At what time did the second plane overtake the first?

(A) 5:15 P.M. (B) 6:45 P.M. (C) 6:50 P.M. (D) 7:15 P.M. (E) 9:30 P.M.

4. Joe left home at 10 A.M. and walked out into the country at 4 miles per hour. He returned on the same road at 2 miles per hour. If he arrived home at 4 P.M., how many miles into the country did he walk?

(A) 6   (B) 8   (C) 10   (D) 11   (E) 12

5. Two cars leave a restaurant at the same time and proceed in the same direction along the same route. One car averages 36 miles per hour and the other 31 miles per hour. In how many hours will the faster car be 30 miles ahead of the slower car?

(A) 3   (B) $3\frac{1}{2}$ (C) 4   (D) 6   (E) $6\frac{1}{4}$

8. WORK PROBLEMS

In most work problems, a job is broken up into several parts, each representing a fractional portion of the entire job. For each part represented, the numerator should represent the time actually spent working, while the denominator should represent the total time needed to do the job alone. The sum of all the individual fractions must be 1, if the job is completed.

Example: John can complete a paper route in 20 minutes. Steve can complete the same route in 30 minutes. How long will it take them to complete the route if they work together?

Solution:

$$\frac{\text{Time actually spent}}{\text{Time needed to do entire job alone}} \quad \overset{\text{John}}{\frac{x}{20}} + \overset{\text{Steve}}{\frac{x}{30}} = 1$$

Multiply by 60 to clear fractions.

$3x + 2x = 60$
$5x = 60$
$x = 12$

Example: Mr. Powell can mow his lawn twice as fast as his son Dick. Together they do the job in 20 minutes. How many minutes would it take Mr. Powell to do the job alone?

Solution: If it takes Mr. Powell x hours to mow the lawn, Dick will take twice as long, or 2x hours, to mow the lawn.

Mr. Powell   Dick

$$\frac{20}{x} + \frac{20}{2x} = 1$$

Multiply by 2x to clear fractions.

$$40 + 20 = 2x$$
$$60 = 2x$$
$$x = 30 \text{ minutes}$$

Practice 8

Answers on page 165

Work out each problem in the space provided. Circle the letter before your answer.

1. Mr. White can paint his barn in 5 days. What part of the barn is still unpainted after he has worked for x days?

(A) $\frac{x}{5}$ (B) $\frac{5}{x}$ (C) $\frac{x-5}{x}$ (D) $\frac{5-x}{x}$ (E) $\frac{5-x}{5}$

2. Mary can clean the house in 6 hours. Her younger sister Ruth can do the same job in 9 hours. In how many hours can they do the job if they work together?

(A) $3\frac{1}{2}$ (B) $3\frac{3}{5}$ (C) 4   (D) $4\frac{1}{4}$ (E) $4\frac{1}{2}$

3. A swimming pool can be filled by an inlet pipe in 3 hours. It can be drained by a drainpipe in 6 hours. By mistake, both pipes are opened at the same time. If the pool is empty, in how many hours will it be filled?

(A) 4   (B) $4\frac{1}{2}$ (C) 5   (D) $5\frac{1}{2}$ (E) 6

4. Mr. Jones can plow his field with his tractor in 4 hours. If he uses his manual plow, it takes three times as long to plow the same field. After working with the tractor for two hours, he ran out of gas and had to finish with the manual plow. How long did it take to complete the job after the tractor ran out of gas?

(A) 4 hours   (B) 6 hours   (C) 7 hours   (D) 8 hours   (E) $8\frac{1}{2}$ hours

5. Michael and Barry can complete a job in 2 hours when working together. If Michael requires 6 hours to do the job alone, how many hours does Barry need to do the job alone?

(A) 2   (B) $2\frac{1}{2}$ (C) 3   (D) $3\frac{1}{2}$ (E) 4

Retest

Answers on page 165

Work out each problem in the space provided. Circle the letter before your answer.

1. Three times the first of three consecutive odd integers is 10 more than the third. Find the middle integer.

(A) 7   (B) 9   (C) 11   (D) 13   (E) 15

2. The denominator of a fraction is three times the numerator. If 8 is added to the numerator and 6 is subtracted from the denominator, the resulting fraction is equivalent to $\frac{8}{9}$. Find the original fraction.

(A) $\frac{16}{18}$ (B) $\frac{1}{3}$ (C) $\frac{8}{24}$ (D) $\frac{5}{3}$ (E) $\frac{8}{16}$

3. How many quarts of water must be added to 40 quarts of a 5% acid solution to dilute it to a 2% solution?

(A) 80   (B) 40   (C) 60   (D) 20   (E) 50

4. Miriam is 11 years older than Charles. In three years she will be twice as old as Charles will be then. How old was Miriam 2 years ago?

(A) 6   (B) 8   (C) 9   (D) 17   (E) 19

5. One printing press can print the school newspaper in 12 hours, while another press can print it in 18 hours. How long will the job take if both presses work simultaneously?

(A) 7 hrs. 12 min.   (B) 6 hrs. 36 min.
(C) 6 hrs. 50 min.   (D) 7 hrs. 20 min.
(E) 7 hrs. 15 min.

6. Janet has $2.05 in dimes and quarters. If she has four fewer dimes than quarters, how much money does she have in dimes?

(A) 30¢   (B) 80¢   (C) $1.20   (D) 70¢   (E) 90¢

7. Mr. Cooper invested a sum of money at 6%. He invested a second sum, $150 more than the first at 3%. If his total annual income was $54, how much did he invest at 3%?

(A) $700   (B) $650   (C) $500   (D) $550   (E) $600

8. Two busses are 515 miles apart. At 9:30 A.M. they start traveling toward each other at rates of 48 and 55 miles per hour. At what time will they pass each other?

(A) 1:30 P.M. (B) 2:30 P.M. (C) 2 P.M.   (D) 3 P.M.   (E) 3:30 P.M.

9. Carol started from home on a trip averaging 30 miles per hour. How fast must her mother drive to catch up to her in 3 hours if she leaves 30 minutes after Carol?

(A) 35 m.p.h. (B) 39 m.p.h. (C) 40 m.p.h.
(D) 55 m.p.h. (E) 60 m.p.h.

10. Dan has twice as many pennies as Frank. If Frank wins 12 pennies from Dan, both boys will have the same number of pennies. How many pennies did Dan have originally?

(A) 24 (B) 12 (C) 36 (D) 48 (E) 52

SOLUTIONS TO PRACTICE EXERCISES

Diagnostic Test

1. **(D)** Represent the integers as x, $x + 2$, and $x + 4$.

    $$x + x + 2 = 4(x + 4)$$
    $$2x + 2 = 4x + 16$$
    $$-14 = 2x$$
    $$x = -7, x + 2 = -5, x + 4 = -3$$

2. **(B)** Represent the first two sides as $4x$ and $3x$, then the third side is $7x - 20$.

    $$4x + 3x + (7x - 20) = 64$$
    $$14x - 20 = 64$$
    $$14x = 84$$
    $$x = 6$$

    The shortest side is $3(6) = 18$.

3. **(D)**
    Let x = the number of dimes
    $16 - x$ = the number of quarters
    $10x$ = value of dimes in cents
    $400 - 25x$ = value of quarters in cents

    $$10x + 400 - 25x = 250$$
    $$-15x = -150$$
    $$x = 10$$

4. **(D)**

	No. of Quarts ·	Percent Alcohol =	Amount of Alcohol
Original	18	32	576
Added	x	0	0
New	18 + x	12	216 + 12x

    $$576 = 216 + 12x$$
    $$360 = 12x$$
    $$x = 30$$

5. **(E)**

	R ·	T =	D
Going	60	x	60x
Return	50	x + 1	50x + 50

    $$60x = 50x + 50$$
    $$10x = 50$$
    $$x = 5$$

    If he drove for 5 hours at 60 miles per hour, he drove 300 miles.

6. **(B)**

	R ·	T =	D
Slow	x	3	3x
Fast	x + 20	3	3x + 60

    $$3x + 3x + 60 = 300$$
    $$6x = 240$$
    $$x = 40$$

7. **(C)** Represent the original fraction by $\frac{x}{2x}$.

    $$\frac{x + 2}{2x - 2} = \frac{2}{3}$$

    Cross multiply.

    $$3x + 6 = 4x - 4$$
    $$x = 10$$

8. **(E)** Darren   Valerie

    $$\frac{x}{20} + \frac{x}{30} = 1$$

    Multiply by 60.

    $$3x + 2x = 60$$
    $$5x = 60$$
    $$x = 12$$

9. (A) Let x = Adam's age now
 3x = Meredith's age now
 x + 6 = Adam's age in 6 years
 3x + 6 = Meredith's age in 6 years
 3x + 6 = 2(x + 6)
 3x + 6 = 2x + 12
 x = 6

10. (B) Let x = amount invested at 4%
 2x = amount invested at 5%

 .04x + .05(2x) = 210

 Multiply by 100 to eliminate decimals.

 4x + 5(2x) = 21,000
 14x = 21,000
 x = $1500

Practice 1

1. (A) Let x = number of dimes
 4x = number of quarters
 10x = value of dimes in cents
 100x = value of quarters in cents

 10x + 100x = 220
 110x = 220
 x = 2

2. (A) Let x = number of nickels
 45 − x = number of dimes
 5x = value of nickels in cents
 450 − 10x = value of dimes in cents

 5x + 450 − 10x = 350
 −5x = −100
 x = 20

 20 nickels and 25 dimes

3. (B) Let x = number of 10-cent stamps
 40 − x = number of 15-cent stamps
 10x = value of 10-cent stamps
 600 − 15x = value of 15-cent stamps

 10x + 600 − 15x = 540
 −5x = −60
 x = 12

4. (C) Let x = number of nickels
 30 − x = number of quarters
 5x = value of nickels in cents
 750 − 25x = value of quarters in cents

 5x + 750 − 25x = 470
 −20x = −280
 x = 14

5. (C) Let 3x = number of nickels
 4x = number of dimes

 3x + 4x = 28
 7x = 28
 x = 4

 There are 16 dimes, worth $1.60.

Practice 2

1. (B) Consecutive integers are 1 apart. If the fourth is n + 1, the third is n, the second is n − 1, and the first is n − 2. The sum of these is 4n − 2.

2. (D) The other integer is n + 2. If a difference is positive the larger quantity must come first.

3. **(D)** To find the average of any 4 numbers, divide their sum by 4.

4. **(C)** Represent the integers as x, x + 1, and x + 2.

$$x + x + 2 = 26$$
$$2x = 24$$
$$x = 12$$
$$x + 1 = 13$$

5. **(C)** An even integer follows an odd integer, so simply add 1.

Practice 3

1. **(C)** Let x = Stephen's age now
   4x = Mark's age now
   x + 1 = Stephen's age in 1 year
   4x + 1 = Mark's age in 1 year

   $$4x + 1 = 3(x + 1)$$
   $$4x + 1 = 3x + 3$$
   $$x = 2$$

   Mark is now 8, so 2 years ago he was 6.

2. **(D)** Let x = Jack's age now
   x + 24 = Mr. Burke's age now
   x + 8 = Jack's age in 8 years
   x + 32 = Mr. Burke's age in 8 years

   $$x + 32 = 2(x + 8)$$
   $$x + 32 = 2x + 16$$
   $$16 = x$$

   Jack is now 16, Mr. Burke is 40.

3. **(A)** The fastest reasoning here is from the answers. Subtract each number from both ages, to see which results in Lili being twice as old as Melanie. 7 years ago, Lili was 16 and Melanie was 8.

4. **(D)** Karen's age now can be found by subtracting 2 from her age 2 years from now. Her present age is 2x − 1. To find her age 2 years ago, subtract another 2.

5. **(D)** Alice's present age is 4x − 2. In 3 years her age will be 4x + 1.

Practice 4

1. **(B)** She invested x + 400 dollars at 5%. The income is .05(x + 400).

2. **(E)** He invested 10,000 − x dollars at 5%. The income is .05(10,000 − x).

3. **(D)** Let x = amount invested at 3%
   2000 + x = her total investment

   $$.06(2000) + .03x = .04(2000 + x)$$

   Multiply by 100 to eliminate decimals.

   $$6(2000) + 3x = 4(2000 + x)$$
   $$12,000 + 3x = 8000 + 4x$$
   $$4000 = x$$

4. **(B)** Let x = amount invested at 4%
   7200 − x = amount invested at 5%

   $$.04x = .05(7200 − x)$$

   Multiply by 100 to eliminate decimals.

   $$4x = 5(7200 − x)$$
   $$4x = 36,000 − 5x$$
   $$9x = 36,000$$
   $$x = 4000$$

   Her income is .04(4000) + .05(3200). This is $160 + $160, or $320.

5. **(E)** In order to avoid fractions, represent his inheritance as 6x. Then $\frac{1}{2}$ his inheritance is 3x and $\frac{1}{3}$ his inheritance is 2x.

Let 3x = amount invested at 5%
2x = amount invested at 6%
x = amount invested at 3%

$$.05(3x) + .06(2x) + .03(x) = 300$$

Multiply by 100 to eliminate decimals.

$$5(3x) + 6(2x) + 3(x) = 30,000$$
$$15x + 12x + 3x = 30,000$$
$$30x = 30,000$$
$$x = 1000$$

His inheritance was 6x, or $6000.

Practice 5

1. **(D)** Represent the original fraction as $\frac{4x}{5x}$.

$$\frac{4x + 4}{5x + 10} = \frac{2}{3}$$

Cross multiply.

$$12x + 12 = 10x + 20$$
$$2x = 8$$
$$x = 4$$

The original numerator was 4x, or 16.

2. **(E)** While this can be solved using the equation $\frac{5 + x}{21 + x} = \frac{3}{7}$, it is probably easier to work from the answers. Try adding each choice to the numerator and denominator of $\frac{5}{21}$ to see which gives a result equal to $\frac{3}{7}$.

$$\frac{5 + 7}{21 + 7} = \frac{12}{28} = \frac{3}{7}$$

3. **(C)** Here again, it is fastest to reason from the answers. Add 5 to each numerator and denominator to see which will result in a new fraction equal to $\frac{7}{10}$.

$$\frac{9 + 5}{15 + 5} = \frac{14}{20} = \frac{7}{10}$$

4. **(E)** Here again, add 3 to each numerator and denominator of the given choices to see which will result in a new fraction equal to $\frac{2}{3}$.

$$\frac{7 + 3}{12 + 3} = \frac{10}{15} = \frac{2}{3}$$

5. **(C)** Represent the original fraction by $\frac{x}{2x}$.

$$\frac{x + 4}{2x + 4} = \frac{5}{8}$$

Cross multiply.

$$8x + 32 = 10x + 20$$
$$12 = 2x$$
$$x = 6$$

The original denominator is 2x, or 12.

Practice 6

1. **(C)** Multiply the number of pounds by the price per pound to get the total value.

$$40(x) + 50(30 - x)$$
$$40x + 1500 - 50x$$
$$1500 - 10x$$

2. **(B)**

No. of Pounds	Price per Pound	Total Value
x	70	70x
30	90	2700
x + 30	85	85(x + 30)

$$70x + 2700 = 85(x + 30)$$
$$70x + 2700 = 85x + 2550$$
$$150 = 15x$$
$$x = 10$$

3. **(D)**

	No. of Pints	% of Acid	Amount of Acid
Original	10	.20	2
Added	6	1.00	6
New	16		8

Remember that 3 quarts of acid are 6 pints. There are now 8 pints of acid in 16 pints of solution. Therefore, the new solution is $\frac{1}{2}$ or 50% acid.

4. **(A)**

No. of Quarts	% of Sugar	Amount of Sugar
60	20	1200
x	0	0
60 + x	5	5(60 + x)

$$1200 = 5(60 + x)$$
$$1200 = 300 + 5x$$
$$900 = 5x$$
$$x = 180$$

5. **(B)**

No. of Pounds	% of Alcohol	Amount of Alcohol
240	3	720
x	0	0
240 - x	5	5(240 - x)

Notice that when x quarts were evaporated, x was *subtracted* from 240 to represent the number of pounds in the mixture.

$$720 = 5(240 - x)$$
$$720 = 1200 - 5x$$
$$5x = 480$$
$$x = 96$$

Practice 7

1. (C)

	R ·	T =	D
Slow	x	3.5	3.5x
Fast	x + 6	3.5	3.5(x + 6)

The cars each traveled from 10 A.M. to 1:30 P.M., which is $3\frac{1}{2}$ hours.

$$3.5x + 3.5(x + 6) = 287$$

Multiply by 10 to eliminate decimals.

$$35x + 35(x + 6) = 2870$$
$$35x + 35x + 210 = 2870$$
$$70x = 2660$$
$$x = 38$$

The rate of the faster car was x + 6 or 44 m.p.h.

2. (C)

	R ·	T =	D
Before noon	50	x	50x
After noon	40	8 - x	40(8 - x)

The 8 hours must be divided into 2 parts.

$$50x + 40(8 - x) = 350$$
$$50x + 320 - 40x = 350$$
$$10x = 30$$
$$x = 3$$

If he traveled 3 hours before noon, he left at 9 A.M.

3. (E)

	R ·	T =	D
	600	x	600x
	650	$x - \frac{1}{2}$	$650(x - \frac{1}{2})$

The later plane traveled $\frac{1}{2}$ hour less.

$$600x = 650(x - \tfrac{1}{2})$$
$$600x = 650x - 325$$
$$325 = 50x$$
$$6\tfrac{1}{2} = x$$

The plane which left at 3 P.M. traveled for $6\frac{1}{2}$ hours. The time is then 9:30 P.M.

4. (B)

	R ·	T =	D
Going	4	x	4x
Return	2	6 - x	2(6 - x)

He was gone for 6 hours.

$$4x = 2(6 - x)$$
$$4x = 12 - 2x$$
$$6x = 12$$
$$x = 2$$

If he walked for 2 hours at 4 miles per hour, he walked for 8 miles.

5. (D)

	R ·	T =	D
	36	x	36x
	31	x	31x

They travel the same number of hours.

$$36x - 31x = 30$$
$$5x = 30$$
$$x = 6$$

This problem may be reasoned without an equation. If the faster car gains 5 miles per hour on the slower car, it will gain 30 miles in 6 hours.

Practice 8

1. **(E)** In x days, he has painted $\frac{x}{5}$ of the barn. To find what part is still unpainted, subtract the part completed from 1. Think of 1 as $\frac{5}{5}$.

$$\frac{5}{5} - \frac{x}{5} = \frac{5-x}{5}$$

2. **(B)**   Mary   Ruth

$$\frac{x}{6} + \frac{x}{9} = 1$$

Multiply by 18.

$$3x + 2x = 18$$
$$5x = 18$$
$$x = 3\tfrac{3}{5}$$

3. **(E)**   Inlet   Drain

$$\frac{x}{3} - \frac{x}{6} = 1$$

Multiply by 6.

$$2x - x = 6$$
$$x = 6$$

Notice the two fractions are subtracted, as the drainpipe does not help the inlet pipe but works against it.

4. **(B)**   Tractor   Plow

$$\frac{2}{4} + \frac{x}{12} = 1$$

This can be done without algebra, as half the job was completed by the tractor; therefore, the second fraction must also be equal to $\frac{1}{2}$. x is therefore 6.

5. **(C)**   Michael   Barry

$$\frac{2}{6} + \frac{2}{x} = 1$$

Multiply by 6x.

$$2x + 12 = 6x$$
$$12 = 4x$$
$$x = 3$$

Retest

1. **(B)** Represent the integers as x, x + 2, and x + 4.

$$3x = (x + 4) + 10$$
$$2x = 14$$
$$x = 7$$
$$x + 2 = 9$$

2. **(C)** Represent the original fraction by $\frac{x}{3x}$.

$$\frac{x+8}{3x-6} = \frac{8}{9}$$

Cross multiply.

$$9x + 72 = 24x - 48$$
$$120 = 15x$$
$$x = 8$$
$$3x = 24$$

The original fraction is $\frac{8}{24}$

3. **(C)**

	No. of Quarts	· Percent Alcohol	= Amount of Alcohol
Original	40	5	200
Added	x	0	0
New	40 + x	2	80 + 2x

$$200 = 80 + 2x$$
$$120 = 2x$$
$$x = 60$$

4. (D) Let x = Charles' age now
x + 11 = Miriam's age now
x + 3 = Charles' age in 3 years
x + 14 = Miriam's age in 3 years

$$x + 14 = 2(x + 3)$$
$$x + 14 = 2x + 6$$
$$x = 8$$

Therefore Miriam is 19 now and 2 years ago was 17.

5. (A) Fast Press   Slow Press
$$\frac{x}{12} + \frac{x}{18} = 1$$

Multiply by 36.

$$3x + 2x = 36$$
$$5x = 36$$
$$x = 7\tfrac{1}{5} \text{ hours}$$
$$= 7 \text{ hours } 12 \text{ minutes}$$

6. (A) Let x = the number of dimes
x + 4 = the number of quarters
10x = the value of dimes in cents
25x + 100 = the value of quarters in cents

$$10x + 25x + 100 = 205$$
$$35x = 105$$
$$x = 3$$

She has 30¢ in dimes.

7. (A) Let x = amount invested at 6%
x + 150 = amount invested at 3%

$$.06x + .03(x + 150) = 54$$
Multiply by 100 to eliminate decimals
$$6x + 3(x + 150) = 5400$$
$$6x + 3x + 450 = 5400$$
$$9x = 4950$$
$$x = \$550$$
$$x + 150 = \$700$$

8. (B)

	R ·	T =	D
Slow	48	x	48x
Fast	55	x	55x

$$48x + 55x = 515$$
$$103x = 515$$
$$x = 5 \text{ hours}$$

Therefore, they will pass each other 5 hours after 9:30 A.M., 2:30 P.M.

9. (A)

	R ·	T =	D
Carol	30	3.5	105
Mother	x	3	3x

$$3x = 105$$
$$x = 35 \text{ m.p.h.}$$

10. (D) Let x = number of pennies Frank has
2x = number of pennies Dan has

$$x + 12 = 2x - 12$$
$$x = 24$$

Therefore, Dan originally had 48 pennies.

Geometry

DIAGNOSTIC TEST

Answers on page 190

Work out each problem in the space provided. Circle the letter before your answer.

1. If the angles of a triangle are in the ratio 5:6:7, the triangle is

   (A) acute (B) isosceles (C) obtuse
   (D) right (E) equilateral

2. If the area of a circle whose radius is x is 4, find the area of a circle whose radius is 3x.

   (A) 12 (B) 36 (C) $4\sqrt{3}$ (D) 48 (E) 144

3. A spotlight is 2 feet from one wall of a room and 3 feet from the wall at right angles to it. How many feet is it from the intersection of the two walls?

   (A) 4 (B) 5 (C) $3\sqrt{2}$ (D) $\sqrt{13}$ (E) $2\sqrt{3}$

4. In parallelogram ABCD, angle B is 5 times as large as angle C. What is the measure in degrees of angle B?

   (A) 30 (B) 60 (C) 100 (D) 120 (E) 150

5. A rectangular box with a square base contains 24 cubic feet. If the height of the box is 18 inches, how many feet are there in each side of the base?

   (A) 4 (B) 2 (C) $\frac{2\sqrt{3}}{3}$ (D) $\frac{\sqrt{3}}{2}$ (E) $\sqrt{3}$

6. In triangle ABC, AB = BC. If angle B contains x degrees, find the number of degrees in angle A.

   (A) x (B) 180 − x (C) $180 - \frac{x}{2}$ (D) $90 - \frac{x}{2}$ (E) 90 − x

167

168   GEOMETRY

7. In the diagram below, AB is perpendicular to BC. If XBY is a straight line and angle XBC contains 37°, find the number of degrees in angle ABY.

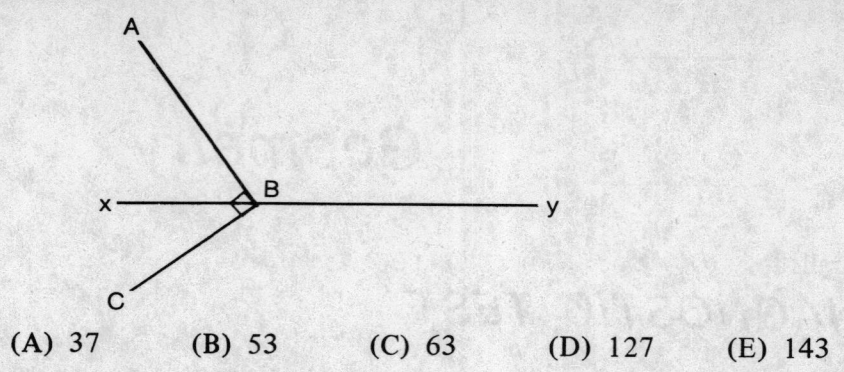

(A) 37   (B) 53   (C) 63   (D) 127   (E) 143

8. If AB is parallel to CD, angle 1 contains 40° and angle 2 contains 30°, find the number of degrees in angle FEG.

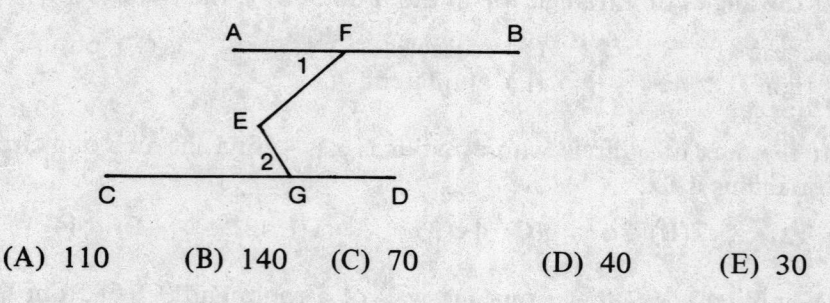

(A) 110   (B) 140   (C) 70   (D) 40   (E) 30

9. In a circle whose center is O, arc AB contains 100°. Find the number of degrees in angle ABO.

(A) 50   (B) 100   (C) 40   (D) 65   (E) 60

10. Find the length of the line segment joining the points whose coordinates are (-3, 1) and (5, -5).

(A) 10   (B) $2\sqrt{5}$ (C) $2\sqrt{10}$ (D) 100   (E) $\sqrt{10}$

The type of question which you should expect in this area will expect you to recall some of the numerical relationships learned in geometry. If you are thoroughly familiar with these relationships, you should not find these questions difficult. As mentioned earlier, be particularly careful with units. For example, you cannot multiply a dimension given in feet by another given in inches when you are finding area. Read each question very carefully for the units given. The following sections, which list all the needed formulas with illustrations of each and practice exercises for each section should be worked on very carefully.

GEOMETRY

1. AREAS

A. Rectangle = base · altitude = bh

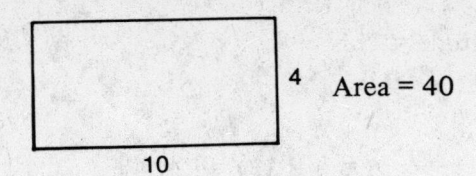

Area = 40

B. Parallelogram = base · altitude = bh

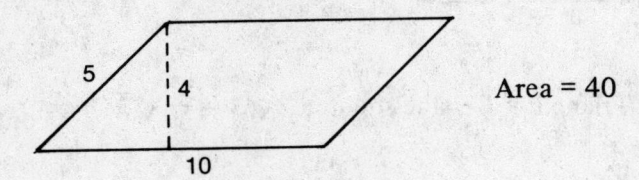

Area = 40

Notice that the altitude is different from the side. It is always shorter than the second side of the parallelogram, as a perpendicular is the shortest distance from a point to a line.

C. Rhombus = $\frac{1}{2}$ · product of the diagonals = $\frac{1}{2} d_1 d_2$

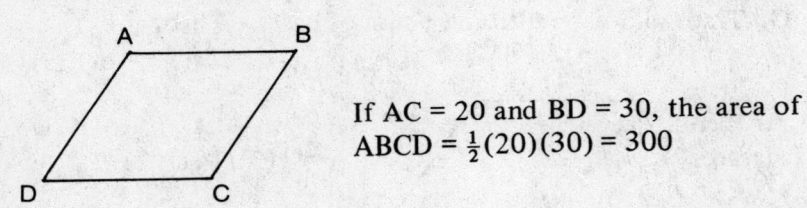

If AC = 20 and BD = 30, the area of ABCD = $\frac{1}{2}$(20)(30) = 300

D. Square = side · side = s^2

Area = 25

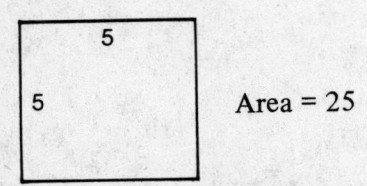

Remember that every square is a rhombus, so that the rhombus formula may be used for a square if the diagonal is given. The diagonals of a square are equal.

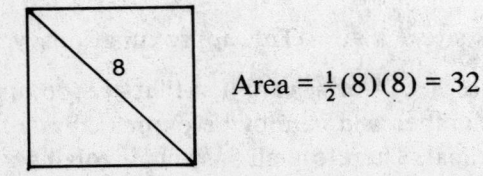

Area = $\frac{1}{2}$(8)(8) = 32

170   GEOMETRY

Remember also that a rhombus is *not* a square. Therefore do not use the s² formula for a rhombus. A rhombus, however, is a parallelogram, so you may use bh if you do not know the diagonals.

E. Triangle = $\frac{1}{2}$ · base · altitude = $\frac{1}{2}$bh

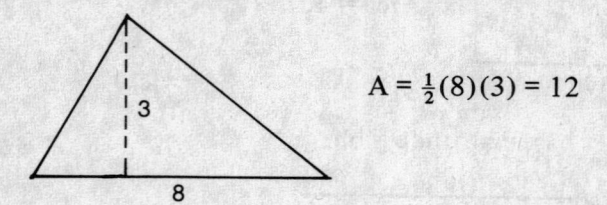

$A = \frac{1}{2}(8)(3) = 12$

F. Equilateral Triangle = $\frac{1}{4}$ · side squared · $\sqrt{3}$ = $\frac{s^2}{4}\sqrt{3}$

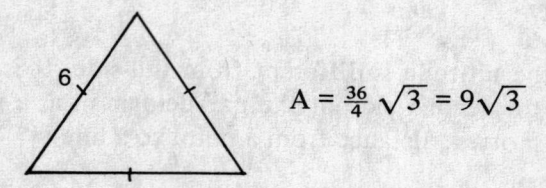

$A = \frac{36}{4}\sqrt{3} = 9\sqrt{3}$

G. Trapezoid = $\frac{1}{2}$ · altitude · sum of bases = $\frac{1}{2}h(b_1 + b_2)$

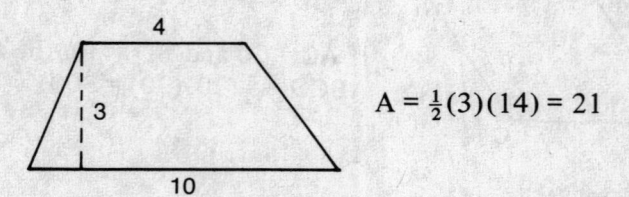

$A = \frac{1}{2}(3)(14) = 21$

H. Circle = π · radius squared = $\pi \cdot r^2$

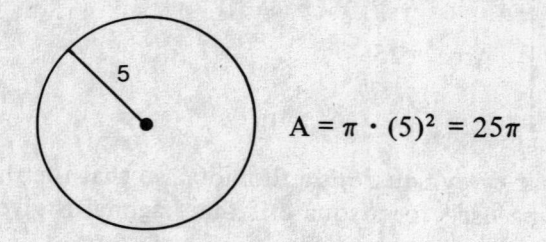

$A = \pi \cdot (5)^2 = 25\pi$

Remember that π is the ratio between the circumference of any circle and its diameter. $\pi = \frac{C}{d}$. The approximations you have used for π in the past (3.14 or $\frac{22}{7}$) are just that—approximations. π is an irrational number and cannot be expressed as a fraction or terminating decimal. Therefore all answers involving π should be left in terms of π unless you are given a specific value to substitute for π.

A word about units—Area is measured in square units. That is, we wish to compute how many squares one inch on each side (a square inch) or one foot on each side (a square foot), etc., can be used to cover a given surface. To change from square inches to square feet or square yards, remember that

$$144 \text{ square inches} = 1 \text{ square foot}$$
$$9 \text{ square feet} = 1 \text{ square yard}$$

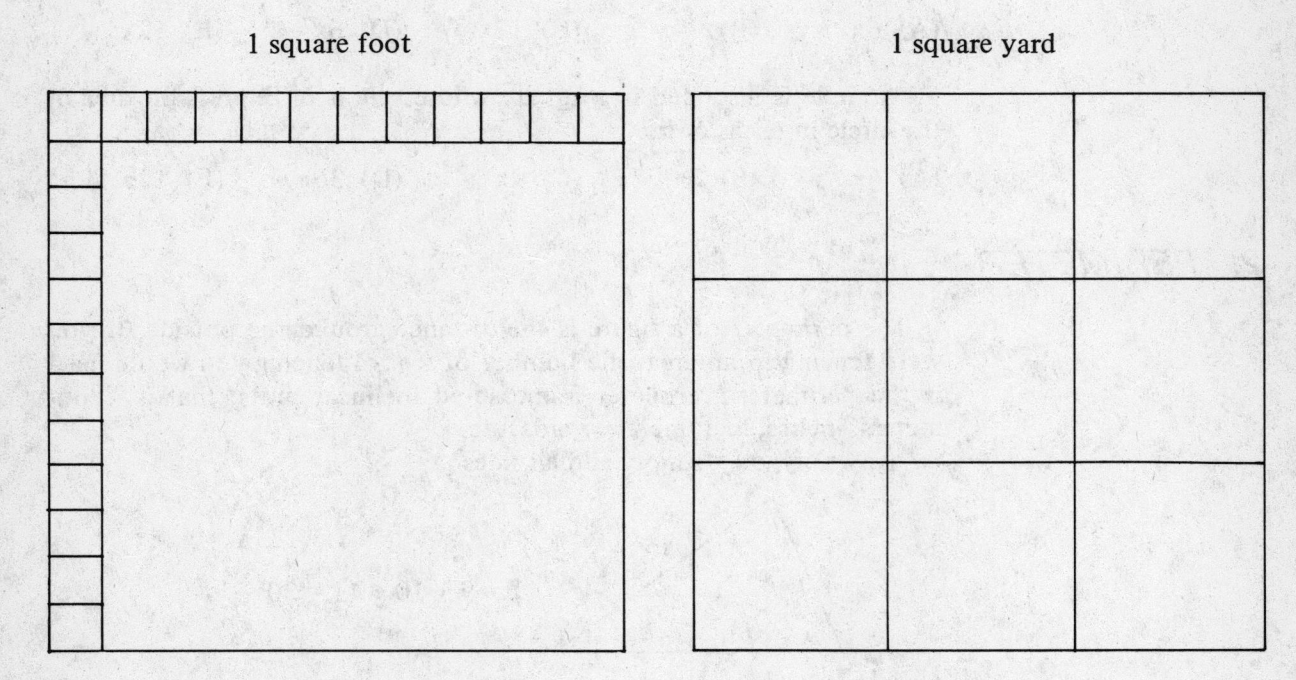

1 square foot

1 square yard

$12'' = 1'$
12 one inch squares in a row
12 rows
144 square inches in 1 sq. ft.

$3' = 1$ yd.
3 one foot squares in a row
3 rows
9 square feet in 1 sq. yd.

Practice 1

Answers on page 191

Work out each problem in the space provided. Circle the letter before your answer.

1. The dimensions of a rectangular living room are 18 feet by 20 feet. How many square yards of carpeting are needed to cover the floor?

(A) 360 (B) 42 (C) 40 (D) 240 (E) 90

2. In a parallelogram whose area is 15, the base is represented by x + 7 and the altitude is x − 7. Find the base of the parallelogram.

(A) 8   (B) 15   (C) 1   (D) 34   (E) 5

3. The sides of a right triangle are 6, 8, and 10. Find the altitude drawn to the hypotenuse.

(A) 2.4   (B) 4.8   (C) 3.4   (D) 3.5   (E) 4.2

4. If the diagonals of a rhombus are represented by 4x and 6x, the area may be represented by

(A) 6x   (B) 24x   (C) 12x   (D) $6x^2$ (E) $12x^2$

5. A circle is inscribed in a square whose side is 6. Express the area of the circle in terms of π.

(A) 6π (B) 3π (C) 9π (D) 36π (E) 12π

2. PERIMETER

The perimeter of a figure is the distance around the outside. If you were fencing in an area, the number of feet of fencing you would need is the perimeter. Perimeter is measured in linear units, that is, centimeters, inches, feet, meters, yards, etc.

A. Any polygon = simply add all sides

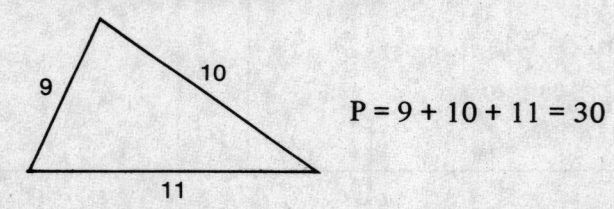

P = 9 + 10 + 11 = 30

B. Circle = π · diameter = πd

or

2 · π · radius = $2\pi r$

Since 2r = d, these formulas are the same. The perimeter of a circle is called its circumference.

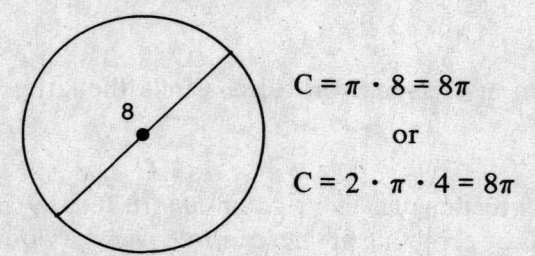

C = π · 8 = 8π

or

C = 2 · π · 4 = 8π

The distance covered by a wheel in one revolution is equal to the circumference of the wheel. In making one revolution, every point on the rim comes in contact with the ground. The distance covered is then the same as stretching the rim out into a straight line.

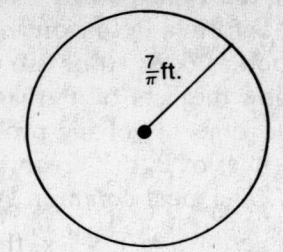

The distance covered by this wheel in one revolution is $2 \cdot \pi \cdot \dfrac{7}{\pi} = 14$ feet.

Practice 2

Answers on page 192

Work out each problem in the space provided. Circle the letter before your answer.

1. The area of an equilateral triangle is $16\sqrt{3}$. Find its perimeter.

   (A) 24   (B) 16   (C) 48   (D) $24\sqrt{3}$ (E) $48\sqrt{3}$

2. The hour hand of a clock is 3 feet long. How many feet does the tip of this hand move between 9:30 P.M. and 1:30 A.M. the following day?

   (A) π (B) 2π (C) 3π (D) 4π (E) 24π

3. If the radius of a circle is increased by 3, the circumference is increased by

   (A) 3   (B) 3π (C) 6   (D) 6π (E) 4.5

4. The radius of a wheel is 18 inches. Find the number of feet covered by this wheel in 20 revolutions.

   (A) 360π (B) 360   (C) 720π (D) 720   (E) 60π

5. A square is equal in area to a rectangle whose base is 9 and whose altitude is 4. Find the perimeter of the square.

   (A) 36   (B) 26   (C) 13
   (D) 24   (E) none of these

3. RIGHT TRIANGLES

A. Pythagorean theorem

$$(\text{leg})^2 + (\text{leg})^2 = (\text{hypotenuse})^2$$

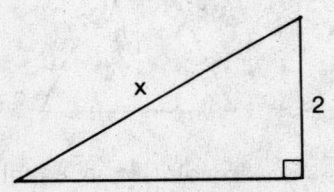

$(5)^2 + (2)^2 = x^2$
$25 + 4 = x^2$
$29 = x^2$
$x = \sqrt{29}$

B. Pythagorean triples

These are sets of numbers which satisfy the Pythagorean Theorem. When a given set of numbers such as 3, 4, 5 form a Pythagorean triple ($3^2 + 4^2 = 5^2$), any multiples of this set such as 6, 8, 10 or 30, 40, 50 also form a Pythagorean triple. Memorizing the sets of Pythagorean triples which follow will save you valuable time in solving problems, for, if you recognize given numbers as multiples of Pythagorean triples, you do not have to do any arithmetic at all. The most common Pythagorean triples which should be memorized are

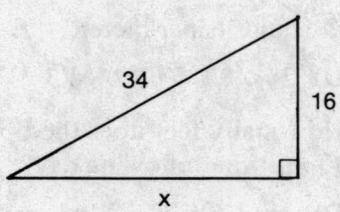

3, 4, 5
5, 12, 13
8, 15, 17
7, 24, 25

Squaring these numbers to apply the Pythagorean theorem would take too much time. Instead, recognize the hypotenuse as 2(17). Suspect an 8, 15, 17 triangle. Since the given leg is 2(8), the missing leg will be 2(15) or 30, without any computation at all.

C. 30°–60°–90° triangle

a) The leg opposite the 30° angle is one-half the hypotenuse.
b) The leg opposite the 60° angle is one-half the hypotenuse · $\sqrt{3}$.
c) An altitude in an equilateral triangle forms a 30°–60°–90° triangle and is therefore equal to one-half the side · $\sqrt{3}$.

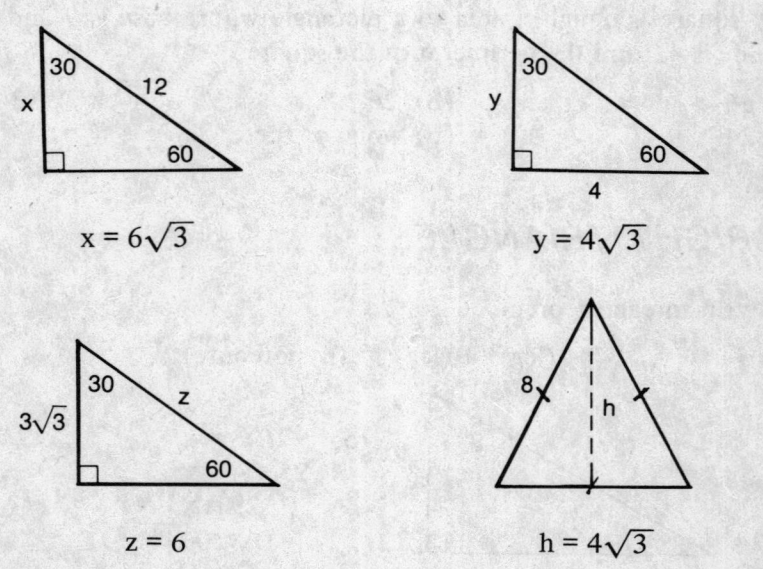

$x = 6\sqrt{3}$

$y = 4\sqrt{3}$

$z = 6$

$h = 4\sqrt{3}$

D. 45°-45°-90° triangle (isosceles right triangle)
   a) Each leg is one-half the hypotenuse times $\sqrt{2}$.
   b) Hypotenuse is leg times $\sqrt{2}$.
   c) The diagonal of a square forms a 45°-45°-90° triangle and is therefore equal to a side times $\sqrt{2}$.

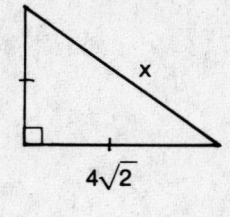

$x = 8$

$y = 3\sqrt{2}$

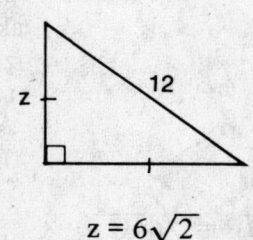

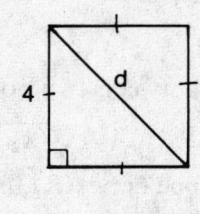

$z = 6\sqrt{2}$

$d = 4\sqrt{2}$

Practice 3

Answers on page 192

Work out each problem in the space provided. Circle the letter before your answer.

1. A farmer uses 140 feet of fencing to enclose a rectangular field. If the ratio of length to width is 3:4, find the diagonal, in feet, of the field.

(A) 50   (B) 100   (C) 20
(D) 10   (E) cannot be determined

2. Find the altitude of an equilateral triangle whose side is 20.

(A) 10   (B) $20\sqrt{3}$ (C) $10\sqrt{3}$ (D) $20\sqrt{2}$ (E) $10\sqrt{2}$

3. Two boats leave the same dock at the same time, one traveling due west at 8 miles per hour and the other due north at 15 miles per hour. How many miles apart are the boats after three hours?

(A) 17   (B) 69   (C) 75   (D) 51   (E) 39

4. Find the perimeter of a square whose diagonal is $6\sqrt{2}$.

(A) 24   (B) $12\sqrt{2}$ (C) 12   (D) 20   (E) $24\sqrt{2}$

5. Find the length of DB.

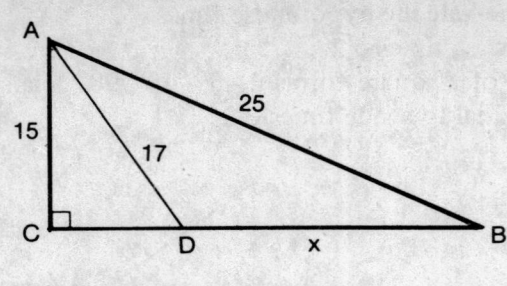

(A) 8 (B) 10 (C) 12
(D) 15 (E) 20

4. COORDINATE GEOMETRY

A. Distance between two points =
$$\sqrt{(x_2 - x_1)^2 + (y_2 - y_1)^2}$$

The distance between $(-3, 2)$ and $(5, -1)$ is
$$\sqrt{[-3 - 5]^2 + [2 - (-1)]^2} = \sqrt{(-8)^2 + (3)^2} = \sqrt{64 + 9} = \sqrt{73}$$

B. The midpoint of a line segment =
$$\left(\frac{x_1 + x_2}{2}, \frac{y_1 + y_2}{2}\right)$$

Since a midpoint is in the middle, its coordinates are found by averaging the x coordinates and averaging the y coordinates. Remember that to find the average of two numbers, you add them and divide by two. Be very careful of signs in adding signed numbers. Review the rules given earlier if necessary.

The midpoint of the segment joining $(-4, 1)$ to $(-2, -9)$ is
$$\left(\frac{-4 + (-2)}{2}, \frac{1 + (-9)}{2}\right) = \left(\frac{-6}{2}, \frac{-8}{2}\right) = (-3, -4).$$

Practice 4

Answers on page 193

Work out each problem in the space provided. Circle the letter before your answer.

1. AB is the diameter of a circle whose center is O. If the coordinates of A are (2, 6) and the coordinates of B are (6, 2), find the coordinates of O.

(A) (4, 4) (B) (4, -4) (C) (2, -2) (D) (0, 0) (E) (2, 2)

2. AB is the diameter of a circle whose center is O. If the coordinates of O are (2, 1) and the coordinates of B are (4, 6), find the coordinates of A.

(A) $(3, 3\frac{1}{2})$ (B) $(1, 2\frac{1}{2})$ (C) $(0, -4)$ (D) $(2\frac{1}{2}, 1)$ (E) $(-1, -2\frac{1}{2})$

3. Find the distance from the point whose coordinates are (4, 3) to the point whose coordinates are (8, 6).

(A) 5 (B) 25 (C) $\sqrt{7}$ (D) $\sqrt{67}$ (E) 15

4. The vertices of a triangle are (2, 1), (2, 5), and (5, 1). The area of the triangle is

(A) 12 (B) 10 (C) 8 (D) 6 (E) 5

5. The area of a circle whose center is at (0, 0) is 16π. The circle passes through each of the following points *except*

(A) (4, 4) (B) (0, 4) (C) (4, 0) (D) (-4, 0) (E) (0, -4)

5. PARALLEL LINES

A. If two lines are parallel and cut by a transversal, the alternate interior angles are congruent.

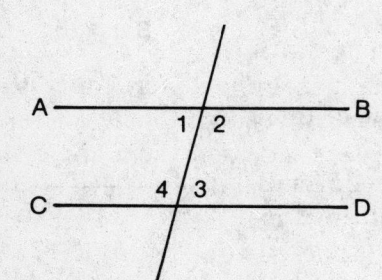

If AB is parallel to CD, then
angle 1 ≅ angle 3 and
angle 2 ≅ angle 4

B. If two parallel lines are cut by a transversal, the corresponding angles are congruent.

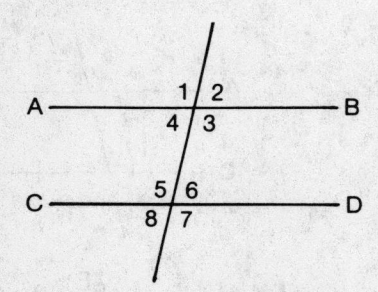

If AB is parallel to CD, then
angle 1 ≅ angle 5
angle 2 ≅ angle 6
angle 3 ≅ angle 7
angle 4 ≅ angle 8

C. If two parallel lines are cut by a transversal, interior angles on the same side of the transversal are supplementary.

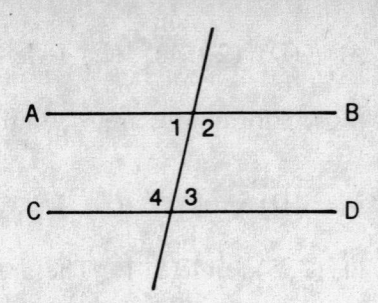

If AB is parallel to CD,
angle 1 + angle 4 = 180°
angle 2 + angle 3 = 180°

Practice 5

Answers on page 193

Work out each problem in the space provided. Circle the letter before your answer.

1. If AB is parallel to CD, BC is parallel to ED, and angle B = 30°, find the number of degrees in angle D.

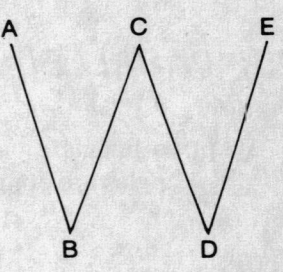

(A) 30   (B) 60   (C) 150
(D) 120   (E) none of these

2. If AB is parallel to CD, angle A = 35° and angle C = 45°, find the number of degrees in angle AEC.

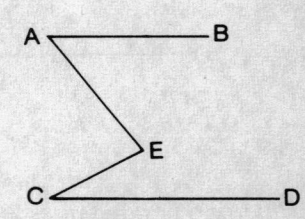

(A) 35   (B) 45   (C) 70   (D) 80   (E) 100

3. If AB is parallel to CD and angle 1 = 130°, find angle 2.

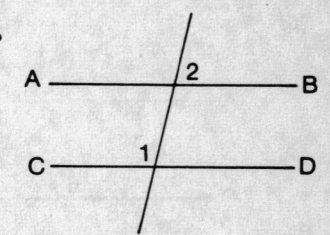

(A) 130°   (B) 100°   (C) 40°   (D) 60°   (E) 50°

4. If AB is parallel to CD, EF bisects angle BEG, GF bisects angle EGD, find the number of degrees in angle EFG.

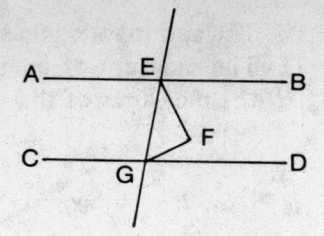

(A) 40 (B) 60 (C) 90
(D) 120 (E) cannot be determined

5. If AB is parallel to CD and angle 1 = x°, then the sum of angle 1 and angle 2 is

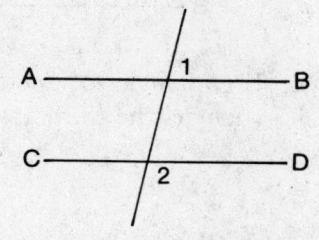

(A) $2x°$ (B) $(180 - x)°$ (C) $180°$
(D) $(180 + x)°$ (E) none of these

6. TRIANGLES

A. If two sides of a triangle are congruent, the angles opposite these sides are congruent.

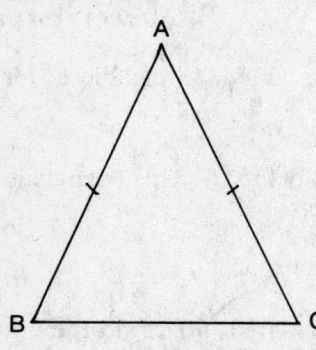

If AB ≅ AC, then angle B ≅ angle C.

B. If two angles of a triangle are congruent, the sides opposite these angles are congruent.

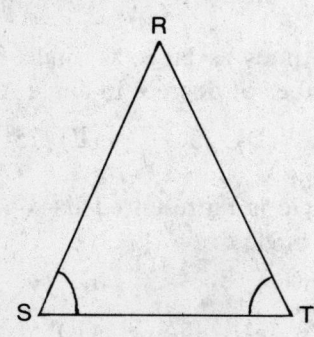

If angle S ≅ angle T, then RS ≅ RT.

C. The sum of the measures of the angles of a triangle is 180°.
D. The measure of an exterior angle of a triangle is equal to the sum of the measures of the two remote interior angles.

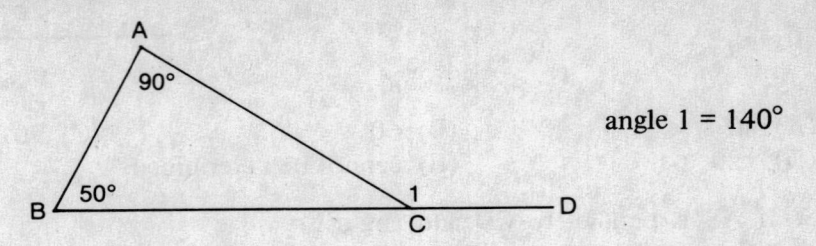

angle 1 = 140°

E. If two angles of one triangle are congruent to two angles of a second triangle, the third angles are congruent.

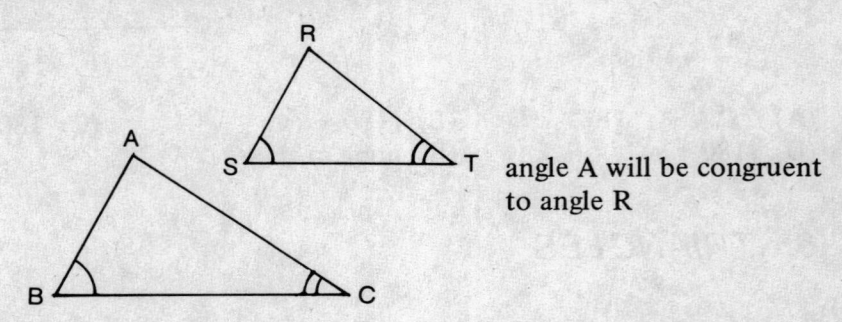

angle A will be congruent to angle R

Practice 6

Answers on page 194

Work out each problem in the space provided. Circle the letter before your answer.

1. The angles of a triangle are in the ratio 1:5:6. This triangle is

   (A) acute   (B) obtuse   (C) isosceles
   (D) right   (E) equilateral

2. If the vertex angle of an isosceles triangle is 50°, find the number of degrees in one of the base angles.

   (A) 50   (B) 130   (C) 60   (D) 65   (E) 55

3. In triangle ABC, angle A is three times as large as angle B. The exterior angle at C is 100°. Find the number of degrees in angle A.

   (A) 60   (B) 80   (C) 20   (D) 25   (E) 75

4. If a base angle of an isosceles triangle is represented by x°, represent the number of degrees in the vertex angle.

   (A) 180 - x   (B) x - 180   (C) 2x - 180
   (D) 180 - 2x   (E) 90 - 2x

5. In triangle ABC, AB = BC. If angle A = (4x - 30)° and angle C = (2x + 10)°, find the number of degrees in angle B.

(A) 20   (B) 40   (C) 50   (D) 100   (E) 80

7. POLYGONS

A. The sum of the measures of the angles of a polygon of n sides is (n - 2)180°.

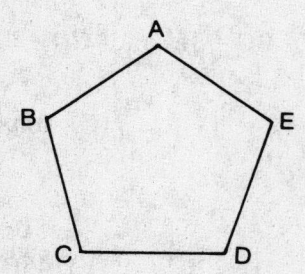

Since ABCDE has 5 sides, angle A + angle B + angle C + angle D + angle E = (5 - 2)180° = 3(180)° = 540°

B. Properties of a parallelogram

    a) Opposite sides are parallel
    b) Opposite sides are congruent
    c) Opposite angles are congruent
    d) Consecutive angles are supplementary
    e) Diagonals bisect each other

C. Properties of a rectangle

    a) All 5 properties of a parallelogram
    b) All angles are right angles
    c) Diagonals are congruent

D. Properties of a rhombus

    a) All 5 properties of a parallelogram
    b) All sides are congruent
    c) Diagonals are perpendicular to each other
    d) Diagonals bisect the angles

E. Properties of a square

    a) All 5 parallelogram properties
    b) Two additional rectangle properties
    c) Three additional rhombus properties

Practice 7

Answers on page 195

Work out each problem in the space provided. Circle the letter before your answer.

1. Find the number of degrees in the sum of the interior angles of a hexagon.

   (A) 360   (B) 540   (C) 720   (D) 900   (E) 1080

2. In parallelogram ABCD, AB = x + 4, BC = x - 6 and CD = 2x - 16. Find AD.

   (A) 20   (B) 24   (C) 28   (D) 14   (E) 10

3. In parallelogram ABCD, AB = x + 8, BC = 3x and CD = 4x - 4. ABCD must be a

   (A) rectangle   (B) rhombus   (C) trapezoid
   (D) square   (E) pentagon

4. The sum of the angles in a rhombus is

   (A) 180°   (B) 360°   (C) 540°   (D) 720°   (E) 450°

5. Which of the following statements is *false?*

   (A) A square is a rhombus.   (B) A rhombus is a parallelogram.
   (C) A rectangle is a rhombus.   (D) A rectangle is a parallelogram.
   (E) A square is a rectangle.

8. CIRCLES

A. A central angle is equal in degrees to its intercepted arc.

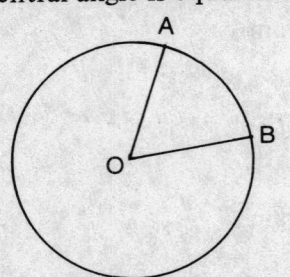

If arc AB = 50°, then angle AOB = 50°.

B. An inscribed angle is equal in degrees to one-half its intercepted arc.

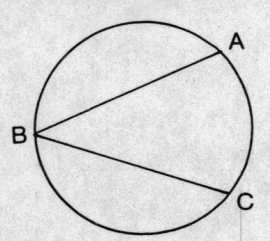

If arc AC = 100°, then angle ABC = 50°.

C. An angle formed by two chords intersecting in a circle is equal in degrees to one-half the sum of its intercepted arcs.

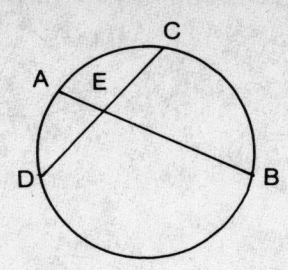

If arc AD = 30° and arc CB = 120°, then angle AED = 75°.

D. An angle outside the circle formed by two secants, a secant and a tangent, or two tangents is equal in degrees to one-half the difference of its intercepted arcs.

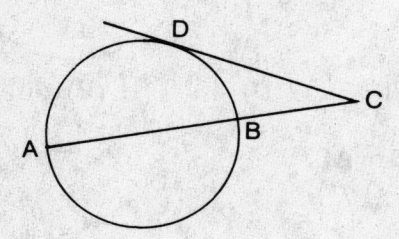

If arc AD = 120° and arc BD = 30°, then angle C = 45°.

E. Two tangent segments drawn to a circle from the same external point are congruent.

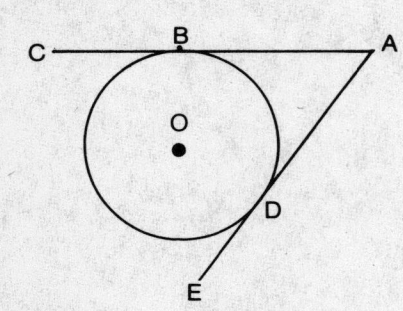

If AC and AE are tangent to circle O at B and D, then AB ≅ AD.

Practice 8

Answers on page 195

Work out each problem in the space provided. Circle the letter before your answer.

1. If circle O is inscribed in triangle ABC, find the length of side AB.

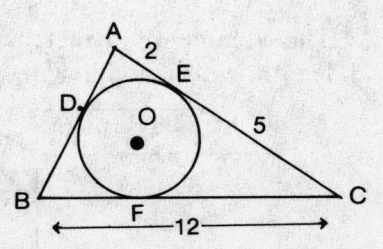

(A) 12 (B) 14 (C) 9
(D) 10 (E) 7

184   GEOMETRY

2. Find angle x.

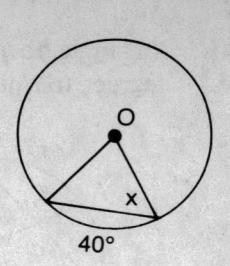

(A) 40°   (B) 20°   (C) 50°
(D) 70°   (E) 80°

3. Find angle x.

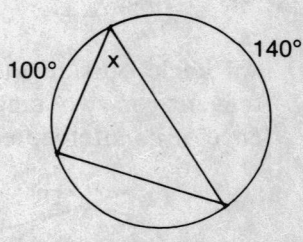

(A) 120°   (B) 50°   (C) 70°   (D) 40°   (E) 60°

4. Find the number of degrees in arc AC.

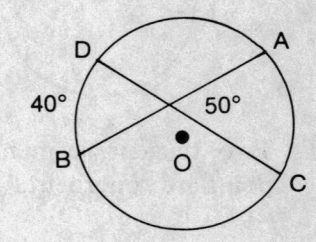

(A) 60   (B) 50   (C) 25
(D) 100   (E) 20

5. The number of degrees in angle ABC is

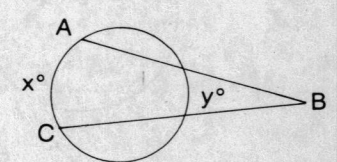

(A) $\frac{1}{2}y$ (B) y
(C) $\frac{1}{2}x$ (D) $\frac{1}{2}(x - y)$
(E) $\frac{1}{2}(x + y)$

9. VOLUMES

A. The volume of a rectangular solid is equal to the product of its length, width, and height.

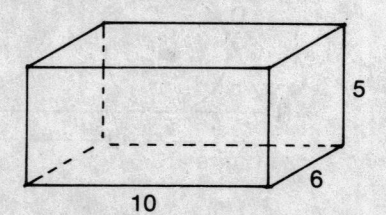

$V = (10)(6)(5) = 300$

B. The volume of a cube is equal to the cube of an edge, since the length, width, and height are all equal.

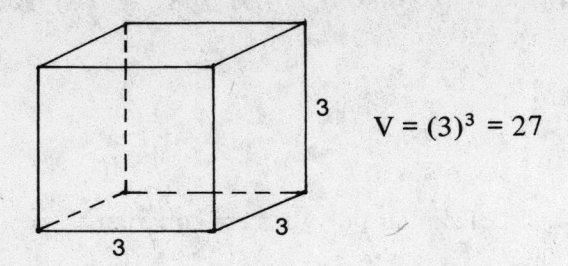

$V = (3)^3 = 27$

C. The volume of a cylinder is equal to π times the square of the radius of the base times the height.

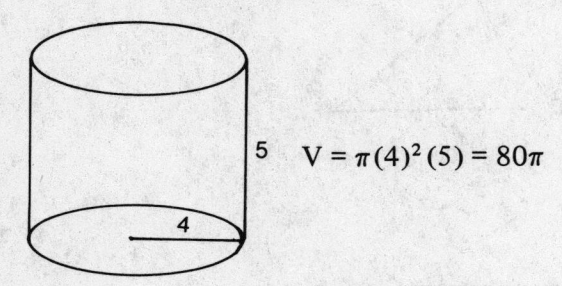

$V = \pi(4)^2(5) = 80\pi$

Practice 9

Answers on page 195

Work out each problem in the space provided. Circle the letter before your answer.

1. The surface of a cube is 96 square feet. How many cubic feet are there in the volume of the cube?

(A) 16   (B) 4   (C) 12   (D) 64   (E) 32

2. A cylindrical pail has a radius of 7 inches and a height of 10 inches. Approximately how many gallons will the pail hold, if there are 231 cubic inches to a gallon? (Use $\pi = \frac{22}{7}$.)

(A) .9   (B) 4.2   (C) 6.7   (D) 5.1   (E) 4.8

3. Water is poured into a cylindrical tank at the rate of 9 cubic inches a minute. How many minutes will it take to fill the tank if its radius is 3 inches and its height is 14 inches? (Use $\pi = \frac{22}{7}$.)

(A) $14\frac{2}{3}$ (B) 44   (C) 30   (D) $27\frac{2}{9}$ (E) 35

4. A rectangular tank 10 inches by 8 inches by 4 inches is filled with water. If the water is to be transferred to smaller tanks in the form of cubes 4 inches on a side, how many of these tanks are needed?

(A) 4   (B) 5   (C) 6   (D) 7   (E) 8

5. The base of a tank is 6 feet by 5 feet and its height is 16 inches. Find the number of cubic feet of water in the tank when it is $\frac{5}{8}$ full.

(A) 25   (B) 40   (C) 480   (D) 768   (E) 300

10. SIMILAR POLYGONS

A. Corresponding angles of similar polygons are congruent.

B. Corresponding sides of similar polygons are in proportion.

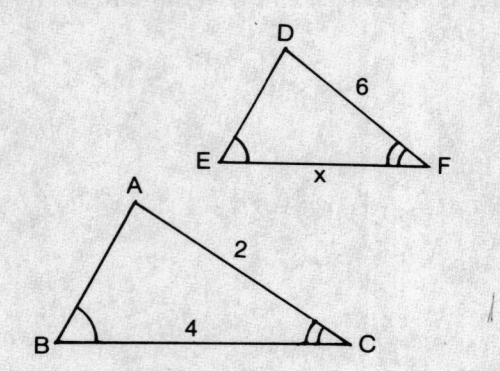

If triangle ABC is similar to triangle DEF and the sides and angles are given as marked, then EF must be equal to 12 as the ratio of corresponding sides is 2:6 or 1:3.

C. When figures are similar, all ratios between corresponding lines are equal. This includes the ratios of corresponding sides, medians, altitudes, angle bisectors, radii, diameters, perimeters, and circumferences. The ratio is referred to as the linear ratio or ratio of similitude.

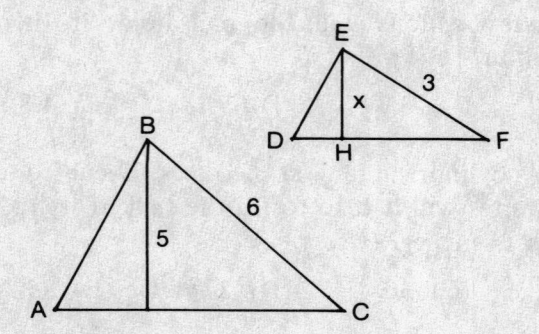

If triangle ABC is similar to triangle DEF and the segments are given as marked, then EH is equal to 2.5 because the linear ratio is 6:3 or 2:1.

D. When figures are similar, the ratio of their areas is equal to the square of the linear ratio.

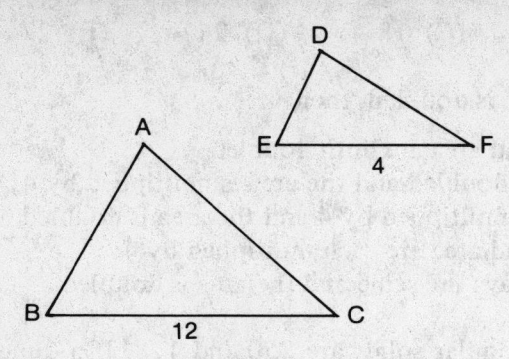

If triangle ABC is similar to triangle DEF, the area of triangle ABC will be 9 times as great as the area of triangle DEF. The linear ratio is 12:4 or 3:1. The area ratio will be the square of this or 9:1. If the area of triangle ABC had been given as 27, the area of triangle DEF would be 3.

E. When figures are similar, the ratio of their volumes is equal to the cube of their linear ratio.

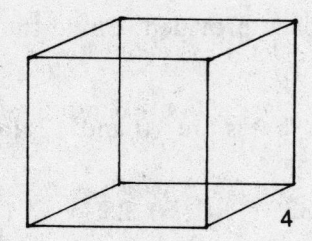

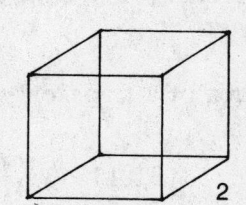

The volume of the larger cube is 8 times the volume of the smaller cube. The ratio of sides is 4:2 or 2:1. The ratio of areas would be 4:1. The ratio of volumes would be 8:1.

Practice 10

Answers on page 196

Work out each problem in the space provided. Circle the letter before your answer.

1. If the area of a circle of radius x is 5π, find the area of a circle of radius $3x$.

(A) 10π (B) 15π (C) 20π (D) 30π (E) 45π

2. If the length and width of a rectangle are each doubled, the area is increased by

(A) 50%   (B) 100%   (C) 200%   (D) 300%   (E) 400%

188   GEOMETRY

3. The area of one circle is 9 times as great as the area of another. If the radius of the smaller circle is 3, find the radius of the larger circle.

(A) 9 (B) 12 (C) 18 (D) 24 (E) 27

4. If the radius of a circle is doubled, then

(A) the circumference and area are both doubled
(B) the circumference is doubled and the area is multiplied by 4
(C) the circumference is multiplied by 4 and the area is doubled
(D) the circumference and area are each multiplied by 4
(E) the circumference stays the same and the area is doubled

5. The volumes of two similar solids are 250 and 128. If a dimension of the larger solid is 25, find the corresponding side of the smaller solid.

(A) 12.8   (B) 15   (C) 20
(D) 40   (E) cannot be determined

Retest

Answers on page 196

Work out each problem in the space provided. Circle the letter before your answer.

1. The area of a trapezoid whose bases are 10 and 12 and whose altitude is 3 is

(A) 66 (B) 11 (C) 33 (D) 25 (E) $16\frac{1}{2}$

2. The circumference of a circle whose area is 16π is

(A) 8π (B) 4π (C) 16π (D) 8 (E) 16

3. Find the perimeter of a square whose diagonal is 8.

(A) 32 (B) 16 (C) $32\sqrt{2}$ (D) $16\sqrt{2}$ (E) $32\sqrt{3}$

4. The length of the line segment joining the point A(4, -3) to B(7, -7) is

(A) $\sqrt{221}$ (B) $\sqrt{185}$ (C) 7 (D) $6\frac{1}{2}$ (E) 5

5. Find angle x if AB is parallel to CD.

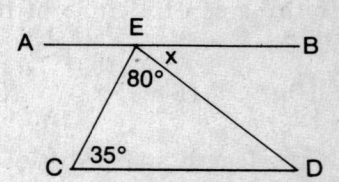

(A) 35°   (B) 80°   (C) 245°
(D) 65°   (E) 55°

GEOMETRY   189

6. In triangle ABC, the angles are in a ratio of 1:1:2. The largest angle of the triangle is

(A) 45°   (B) 60°   (C) 90°   (D) 120°   (E) 100°

7. Find the number of degrees in each angle of a regular pentagon.

(A) 72   (B) 108   (C) 60   (D) 180   (E) 120

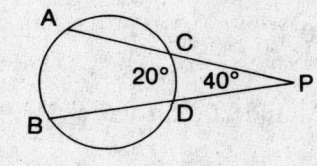

8. Find the number of degrees in arc AB.

(A) 80   (B) 20   (C) 60   (D) 100   (E) 90

9. Find the edge, in inches, of a cube whose volume is equal to the volume of a rectangular solid 2 in. by 6 in. by 18 in.

(A) 4   (B) 8   (C) 5   (D) 6   (E) 7

10. If the volume of one cube is 8 times as great as another, then the ratio of the area of a face of the larger cube to the area of a face of the smaller cube is

(A) 2:1   (B) 4:1   (C) $\sqrt{2}:1$ (D) 8:1   (E) $2\sqrt{2}:1$

SOLUTIONS TO PRACTICE EXERCISES

Diagnostic Test

1. **(A)** Represent the angles as 5x, 6x, and 7x. They must add up to 180°.

    $$18x = 180$$
    $$x = 10$$

    The angles are 50°, 60°, and 70°, an acute triangle.

2. **(B)** The area of a circle is πr^2. The area of a circle with radius x is πx^2, which equals 4. The area of a circle with radius 3x is $\pi(3x)^2 = 9\pi x^2 = 9 \cdot 4 = 36$.

3. **(D)**

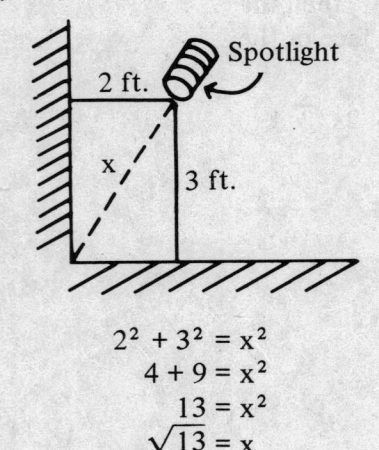

    $$2^2 + 3^2 = x^2$$
    $$4 + 9 = x^2$$
    $$13 = x^2$$
    $$\sqrt{13} = x$$

4. **(E)**

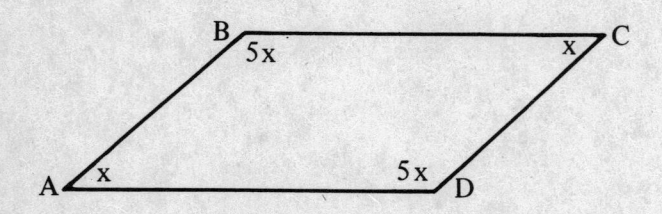

    The sum of the angles in a parallelogram is 360°.

    $$12x = 360°$$
    $$x = 30°$$

    Angle B = 5x = 5 · 30° = 150°

5. **(A)** The volume of a rectangular box is the product of its length, width, and height. Since the height is 18 inches, or $1\frac{1}{2}$ feet, and the length and width of the square base are the same, we have

    $$x \cdot x \cdot 1\tfrac{1}{2} = 24$$
    $$x^2 = 16$$
    $$x = 4$$

6. **(D)** The remaining degrees of the triangle are 180 - x. Since the triangle is isosceles, the remaining angles are equal, each $\frac{180 - x}{2} = 90 - \frac{x}{2}$.

7. **(D)**

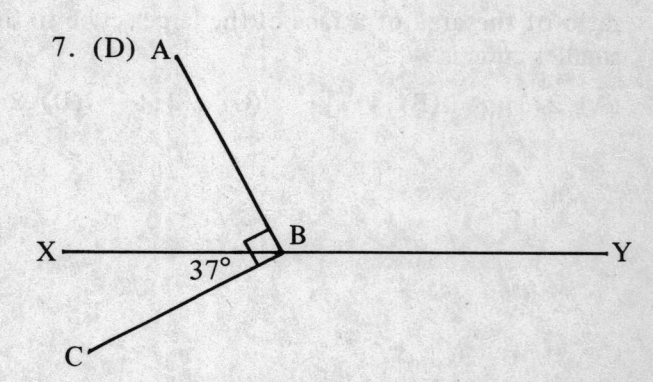

    Angle ABX = 90° - 37° = 53°
    Angle ABY = 180° - 53° = 127°

8. **(C)**

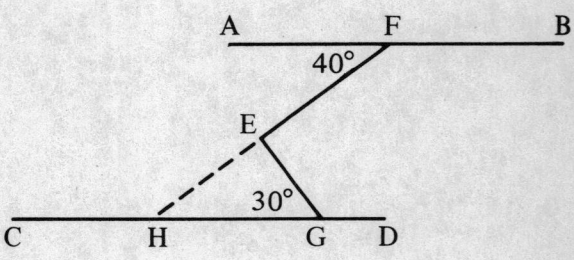

    Extend FE to H. ∡EHG = ∡AFE = 40°. ∡HEG must equal 110° because there are 180° in a triangle. Since ∡FEG is the supplement of ∡HEG, ∡FEG = 70°.

9. (C)

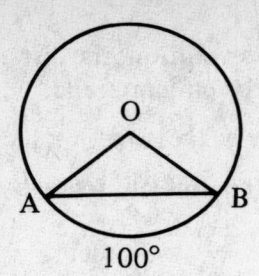

Angle O is a central angle equal to its arc, 100°. This leaves 80° for the other two angles. Since the triangle is isosceles (because the legs are both radii and therefore equal) angle ABO is 40°.

10. (A) $d = \sqrt{(5-(-3))^2 + (-5-1)^2}$
$= \sqrt{(8)^2 + (-6)^2} = \sqrt{64+36}$
$= \sqrt{100} = 10$

Practice 1

1. (C) Find the area in square feet and then convert to square yards by dividing by 9. Remember there are 9 square feet in one square yard.

    $(18 \cdot 20) \div 9 = 360 \div 9 = 40$ square yards

2. (B) Area of parallelogram = $b \cdot h$

    $(x+7)(x-7) = 15$
    $x^2 - 49 = 15$
    $x^2 = 64$
    $x = 8$
    Base = $x + 7 = 15$

3. (B) Area of triangle = $\frac{1}{2} \cdot b \cdot h$

    Using one leg as base and the other as altitude, the area is $\frac{1}{2} \cdot 6 \cdot 8 = 24$. Using the hypotenuse as base and the altitude to the hypotenuse must give the same area.

    $\frac{1}{2} \cdot 10 \cdot h = 24$
    $5h = 24$
    $h = 4.8 \therefore \frac{1}{2} \cdot 10 \cdot 4.8 = 24$

4. (E) Area of rhombus = $\frac{1}{2} \cdot$ product of diagonals

    Area = $\frac{1}{2}(4x)(6x) = \frac{1}{2}(24x^2) = 12x^2$

5. (C) radius of circle = 3
    Area = $\pi r^2 = 9\pi$

Practice 2

1. (A) Area of equilateral triangle $= \dfrac{s^2}{4}\sqrt{3}$

   Therefore $\dfrac{s^2}{4}$ must equal 16.

   $$s^2 = 64$$
   $$s = 8$$

   Perimeter is $8 + 8 + 8 = 24$

2. (B) In 4 hours the hour hand moves through one-third of the circumference of the clock.

   $$C = 2\pi r = 2\pi(3) = 6\pi$$
   $$\tfrac{1}{3} \cdot 6\pi = 2\pi$$

3. (D) Compare $2\pi r$ with $2\pi(r + 3)$.

   $$2\pi(r + 3) = 2\pi r + 6\pi$$

   Circumference was increased by 6π. Trying this with a numerical value for r will give the same result.

4. (E) In one revolution, the distance covered is equal to the circumference.

   $$C = 2\pi r = 2\pi(18) = 36\pi \text{ inches}$$

   To change this to feet, divide by 12.

   $$\dfrac{36\pi}{12} = 3\pi \text{ feet}$$

   In 20 revolutions, the wheel will cover $20(3\pi)$ or 60π feet.

5. (D) Area of rectangle $= b \cdot h = 36$
   Area of square $= s^2 = 36$

   Therefore $s = 6$ and perimeter $= 24$

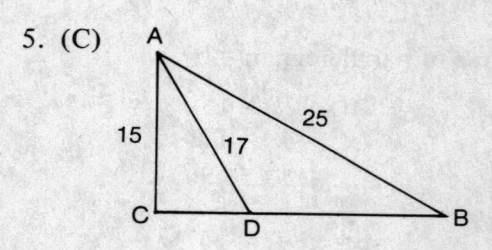

Practice 3

1. (A) $14x = 140$
   $x = 10$

   The rectangle is 30' by 40'. This is a 3, 4, 5 right triangle, so the diagonal is 50'.

2. (C) The altitude in an equilateral triangle is always $\tfrac{1}{2}$ side $\sqrt{3}$.

3. (D) This is an 8, 15, 17 triangle, making the missing side (3)17, or 51.

4. (A) The diagonal in a square is equal to the side times $\sqrt{2}$. Therefore, the side is 6 and the perimeter is 24.

5. (C) Triangle ABC is a 3, 4, 5 triangle with all sides multiplied by 5. Therefore CB = 20. Triangle ACD is an 8, 15, 17 triangle. Therefore CD = 8. CB − CD = DB = 12.

Practice 4

1. **(A)** Find the midpoint of AB by averaging the x coordinates and averaging the y coordinates.

    $$\left(\frac{6+2}{2}, \frac{2+6}{2}\right) = (4, 4)$$

2. **(C)** 0 is the midpoint of AB.

    $\frac{x+4}{2} = 2 \qquad x + 4 = 4 \qquad x = 0$

    $\frac{y+6}{2} = 1 \qquad y + 6 = 2 \qquad y = -4$

    A is the point $(0, -4)$.

3. **(A)** $d = \sqrt{(8-4)^2 + (6-3)^2} = \sqrt{4^2 + 3^2}$
    $= \sqrt{16 + 9} = \sqrt{25} = 5$

4. **(D)** Sketch the triangle and you will see it is a right triangle with legs of 4 and 3.

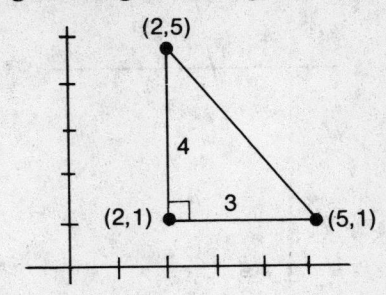

    Area $= \frac{1}{2} \cdot b \cdot h = \frac{1}{2} \cdot 4 \cdot 3 = 6$

5. **(A)** Area of a circle $= \pi r^2$

    $\pi r^2 = 16\pi \qquad r = 4$

    Points B, C, D, and E are all 4 units from the origin. Point A is not.

Practice 5

1. **(D)** Angle B = Angle C because of alternate interior angles. Then Angle C = Angle D for the same reason. Therefore, Angle D = 30°.

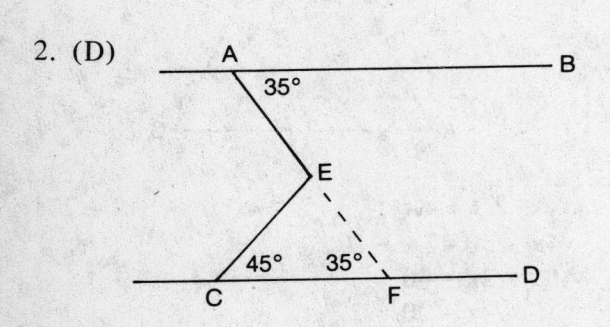

2. **(D)**

    Extend AE to F. ∡A = ∡EFC

    ∡CEF must equal 100° because there are 180° in a triangle. ∡AEC is supplementary to ∡CEF.

    ∡AEC = 80°

3. **(E)**

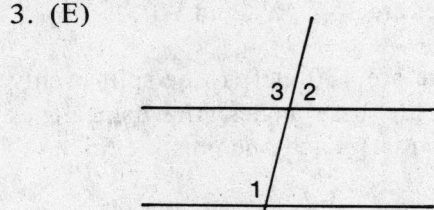

    ∡1 = ∡3
    ∡2 + ∡3 = 180°
    ∡2 = 50°

4. **(C)** Since ∡BEG and ∡EGD add to 180°, halves of these angles must add to 90°. Triangle EFG contains 180°, leaving 90° for ∡EFG.

194   GEOMETRY

5. (C)

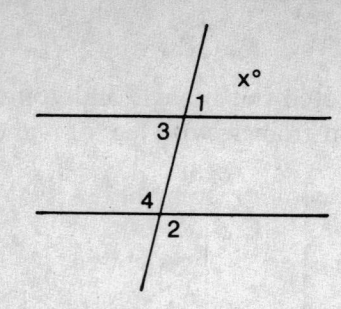

∡1 = ∡3
∡2 = ∡4
∡1 + ∡2 = ∡3 + ∡4

But ∡3 + ∡4 = 180°. Therefore, ∡1 + ∡2 = 180°

Practice 6

1. (D) Represent the angles as x, 5x, and 6x. They must add to 180°.

   $$12x = 180$$
   $$x = 15$$

   The angles are 15°, 75°, and 90°.

2. (D) There are 130° left to be split evenly between the base angles (the base angles must be equal). Each one must be 65°.

3. (E)

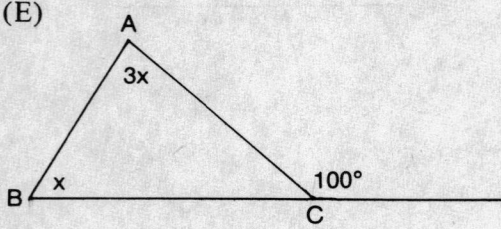

   The exterior angle is equal to the sum of the two remote interior angles.

   $$4x = 100$$
   $$x = 25$$

   Angle A = 3x = 75°

4. (D) The other base angle is also x. These two base angles add to 2x. The remaining degrees of the triangle, or 180 − 2x, are in the vertex angle.

5. (E)

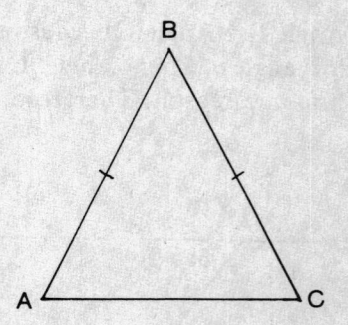

   ∡A = ∡C
   $$4x - 30 = 2x + 10$$
   $$2x = 40$$
   $$x = 20$$

   ∡A and ∡C are each 50°, leaving 80° for ∡B.

Practice 7

1. (C) A hexagon has 6 sides. Sum = (n − 2)180 = 4(180) = 720

2. (D) Opposite sides of a parallelogram are congruent, so AB = CD.

    $x + 4 = 2x - 16$
    $20 = x$

    AD = BC = x − 6 = 14

3. (B) AB = CD $x + 8 = 4x - 4$
    $12 = 3x$
    $x = 4$

    AB = 12   BC = 12   CD = 12

    If all sides are congruent, it must be a rhombus. Additional properties would be needed to make it a square.

4. (B) A rhombus has 4 sides. Sum = (n − 2)180 = 2(180) = 360

5. (C) Rectangles and rhombuses are both types of parallelograms but do not share the same special properties. A square is both a rectangle and a rhombus with *added* properties.

Practice 8

1. (C) Tangent segments drawn to a circle from the same external point are congruent. If CE = 5, then CF = 5, leaving 7 for BF. Therefore BD is also 7. If AE = 2, then AD = 2.

    BD + DA = BA = 9

2. (D) Angle O is a central angle equal to its arc, 40°. This leaves 140° for the other two angles. Since the triangle is isosceles, because the legs are equal radii, each angle is 70°.

3. (E) The remaining arc is 120°. The inscribed angle x is ½ its intercepted arc.

4. (A) $50° = \frac{1}{2}(40° + \widehat{AC})$
    $100° = 40° + \widehat{AC}$
    $60° = \widehat{AC}$

5. (D) An angle outside the circle is ½ the difference of its intercepted arcs.

Practice 9

1. (D) There are 6 equal squares in the surface of a cube. Each square will have an area of $\frac{96}{6}$ or 16. Each edge is 4.

    $V = e^3 = 4^3 = 64$

2. (C) $V = \pi r^2 h = \frac{22}{7} \cdot 49 \cdot 10 = 1540$ cubic inches

    Divide by 231 to find gallons.

3. (B) $V = \pi r^2 h = \frac{22}{7} \cdot 9 \cdot 14 = 396$ cubic inches

    Divide by 9 to find minutes.

4. (B) $V = l \cdot w \cdot h = 10 \cdot 8 \cdot 4 = 320$ cubic inches

    Each small cube = 4^3 = 64 cubic inches. Therefore it will require 5 cubes.

5. (A) Change 16 inches to $1\frac{1}{3}$ feet.
$V = 6 \cdot 5 \cdot 1\frac{1}{3} = 40$ cubic feet when full.
$\frac{5}{8} \cdot 40 = 25$

Practice 10

1. (E) If the radius is multiplied by 3, the area is multiplied by 3^2 or 9.

2. (D) If the dimensions are all doubled, the area is multiplied by 2^2 or 4. If the new area is 4 times as great as the original area, is has been *increased* by 300%.

3. (A) If the area ratio is 9:1, the linear ratio is 3:1. Therefore, the larger radius is 3 times the smaller radius.

4. (B) Ratio of circumferences is the same as ratio of radii, but the area ratio is the square of this.

5. (C) We must take the cube root of the volume ratio to find the linear ratio. This becomes much easier if you reduce the ratio first.

$$\frac{250}{128} = \frac{125}{64}$$

The linear ratio is then 5:4.

$$\frac{5}{4} = \frac{25}{x}$$

$5x = 100$
$x = 20$

Retest

1. (C) Area of trapezoid = $\frac{1}{2}h(b_1 + b_2)$
Area = $\frac{1}{2} \cdot 3(10 + 12) = 33$

2. (A) Area of circle = $\pi r^2 = 16\pi$
Therefore, $r^2 = 16$ or $r = 4$
Circumference of circle = $2\pi r = 2\pi(4) = 8\pi$

3. (D) The side of a square is equal to the diagonal times $\frac{\sqrt{2}}{2}$. Therefore, the side is $4\sqrt{2}$ and the perimeter is $16\sqrt{2}$.

4. (E) $d = \sqrt{(7-4)^2 + (-7-(-3))^2}$
$= \sqrt{(3)^2 + (-4)^2} = \sqrt{9 + 16}$
$= \sqrt{25} = 5$

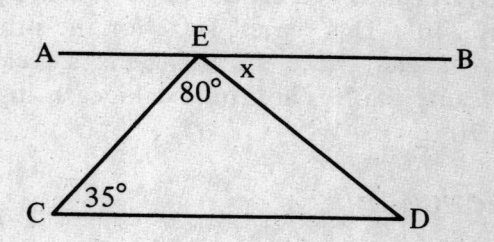

5. (D)

∡CDE must equal 65° because there are 180° in a triangle. Since AB is parallel to CD, ∡x = ∡CDE = 65°.

6. **(C)** Represent the angles as x, x, and 2x. They must add to 180°.

$$4x = 180$$
$$x = 45$$

Therefore, the largest angle is 2x = 2(45°) = 90°.

7. **(B)** A pentagon has 5 sides. Sum = (n - 20) 180 = 3(180) = 540°

In a regular pentagon, all the angles are equal. Therefore, each angle = $\frac{540}{5}$ = 108°.

8. **(D)**

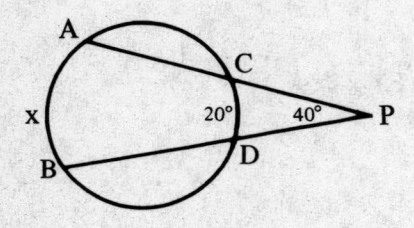

An angle outside the circle is $\frac{1}{2}$ the difference of its intercepted arcs.

$$40 = \tfrac{1}{2}(x - 20)$$
$$80 = x - 20$$
$$100 = x$$

9. **(D)** V = l · w · h = 2 · 6 · 18 = 216

The volume of a cube is equal to the cube of an edge.

$$V = e^3$$
$$216 = e^3$$
$$6 = e$$

10. **(B)** If the volume ratio is 8 : 1, the linear ratio is 2 : 1, and the area ratio is the square of this, or 4 : 1.

Inequalities

DIAGNOSTIC TEST

Answers on page 207

Work out each problem in the space provided. Circle the letter before your answer.

1. If $4x < 6$, then

   (A) $x = 1.5$ (B) $x < \frac{2}{3}$ (C) $x > \frac{2}{3}$ (D) $x < \frac{3}{2}$ (E) $x > \frac{3}{2}$

2. If $a = b$ and $c > d$, then

   (A) $a + c < b + d$ (B) $a + c > b + d$
   (C) $a - c > b - d$ (D) $ac < bd$
   (E) $a + c < b - d$

3. Which value of x will make the following expression true?

   $$\frac{3}{5} < \frac{x}{10} < \frac{4}{5}$$

   (A) 5 (B) 6 (C) 7 (D) 8 (E) 9

4. In triangle ABC, $AB = AC$ and $EC < DB$. Then

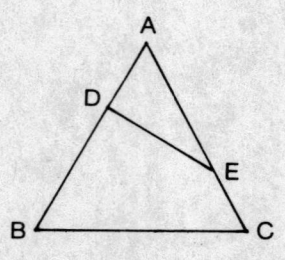

   (A) $DB < AE$ (B) $DB < AD$
   (C) $AD > AE$ (D) $AD < AE$
   (E) $AD > EC$

5. In triangle ABC, $\angle 1 > \angle 2$ and $\angle 2 > \angle 3$. Then

   (A) $AC < AB$ (B) $AC > BC$
   (C) $BC > AC$ (D) $BC < AB$
   (E) $\angle 3 > \angle 1$

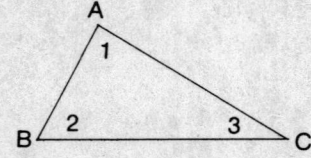

198

6. If point C lies between A and B on line segment AB, which of the following is always true?

(A) AC = CB
(B) AC > CB
(C) CB > AC
(D) AB < AC + CB
(E) AB = CB + AC

7. If AC is perpendicular to BD, which of the following is always true?

I. AC = BC
II. AC < AB
III. AB > AD

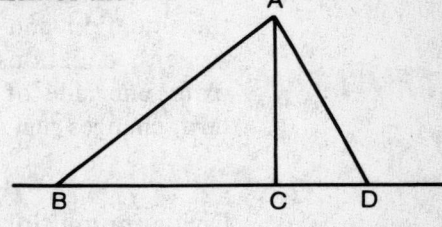

(A) I only
(B) II and III only
(C) II only
(D) III only
(E) I and II only

8. If x < 0 and y > 0, which of the following is always true?

(A) x + y > 0
(B) x + y < 0
(C) y - x < 0
(D) x - y < 0
(E) 2x > y

9. In triangle ABC, BC is extended to D. If ∡A = 50° and ∡ACD = 120°, then

(A) BC > AB
(B) AC > AB
(C) BC > AC
(D) AB > AC
(E) ∡B < ∡A

10. In right triangle ABC, ∡A < ∡B and ∡B < ∡C. Then

(A) ∡A > 45°
(B) ∡B = 90°
(C) ∡B > 90°
(D) ∡C = 90°
(E) ∡C > 90°

1. ALGEBRAIC INEQUALITIES

Algebraic inequality statements are solved in the same manner as equations. However, do not forget that whenever you multiply or divide by a negative number, the order of the inequality, that is, the inequality symbol must be reversed. In reading the inequality symbol, remember that it points to the smaller quantity. a < b is read a is less than b. a > b is read a is greater than b.

Example: Solve for x: 12 - 4x < 8

Solution: Add -12 to each side.

$$-4x < -4$$

Divide by −4, remembering to reverse the inequality sign.

x > 1

Example: 6x + 5 > 7x + 10

Solution: Collect all the terms containing x on the left side of the equation and all numerical terms on the right. As with equations, remember that if a term comes from one side of the inequality to the other, that term changes sign.

−x > 5

Divide (or multiply) by −1.

x < −5

Practice 1

Answers on page 208

Work out each problem in the space provided. Circle the letter before your answer.

1. Solve for x: 8x < 5(2x + 4)

(A) x > −10 (B) x < −10 (C) x > 10 (D) x < 10 (E) x < 18

2. Solve for x: 6x + 2 − 8x < 14

(A) x = 6 (B) x = −6 (C) x > −6 (D) x < −6 (E) x > 6

3. A number increased by 10 is greater than 50. What numbers satisfy this condition?

(A) x > 60 (B) x < 60 (C) x > −40 (D) x < 40 (E) x > 40

4. Solve for x: −.4x < 4

(A) x > −10 (B) x > 10 (C) x < 8 (D) x < −10 (E) x < 36

5. Solve for x: .03n > −.18

(A) n < −.6 (B) n > .6 (C) n > 6 (D) n > −6 (E) n < −6

6. Solve for b: 15b < 10

(A) $b < \frac{3}{2}$ (B) $b > \frac{3}{2}$ (C) $b < -\frac{3}{2}$ (D) $b < \frac{2}{3}$ (E) $b > \frac{2}{3}$

7. If $x^2 < 4$, then

(A) x > 2 (B) x < 2 (C) x > −2 (D) −2 < x < 2
(E) −2 ≦ x ≦ 2

8. Solve for n: n + 4.3 < 2.7

(A) n > 1.6 (B) n > -1.6 (C) n < 1.6 (D) n < -1.6 (E) n = 1.6

9. If x < 0 and y < 0, which of the following is always true?

(A) x + y > 0   (B) xy < 0   (C) x - y > 0
(D) x + y < 0   (E) x = y

10. If x < 0 and y > 0, which of the following will always be greater than 0?

(A) x + y   (B) x - y   (C) $\dfrac{x}{y}$ (D) xy   (E) -2x

2. GEOMETRIC INEQUALITIES

In working with geometric inequalities, certain postulates and theorems should be reviewed.

A. If unequal quantities are added to unequal quantities of the same order, the sums are unequal in the same order.

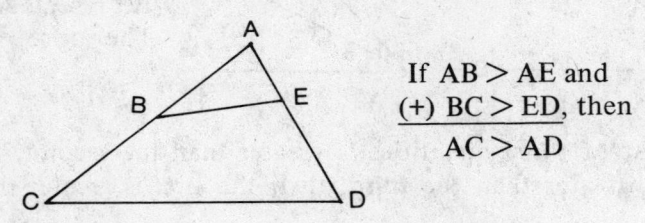

If AB > AE and
(+) BC > ED, then
AC > AD

B. If equal quantities are added to unequal quantities, the sums are unequal in the same order.

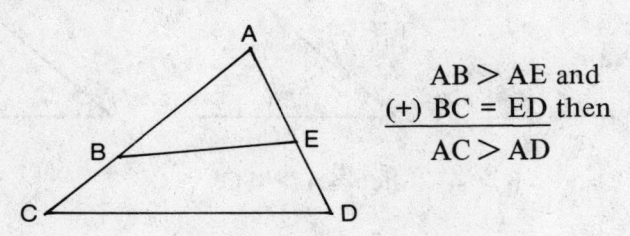

AB > AE and
(+) BC = ED then
AC > AD

C. If equal quantities are subtracted from unequal quantities, the differences are unequal in the same order.

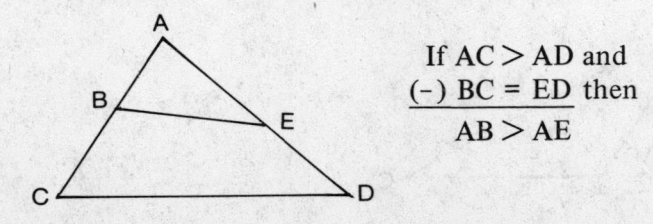

If AC > AD and
(-) BC = ED then
AB > AE

202 INEQUALITIES

D. If unequal quantities are subtracted from equal quantities, the results are unequal in the *opposite* order.

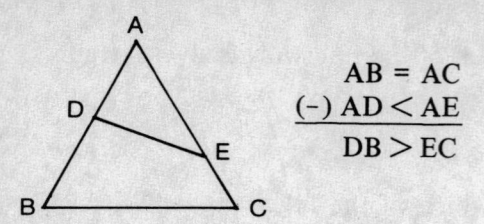

$$AB = AC$$
$$(-) \; AD < AE$$
$$\overline{DB > EC}$$

E. Doubles of unequals are unequal in the same order.

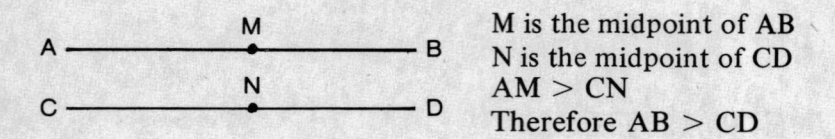

M is the midpoint of AB
N is the midpoint of CD
AM > CN
Therefore AB > CD

F. Halves of unequals are unequal in the same order.

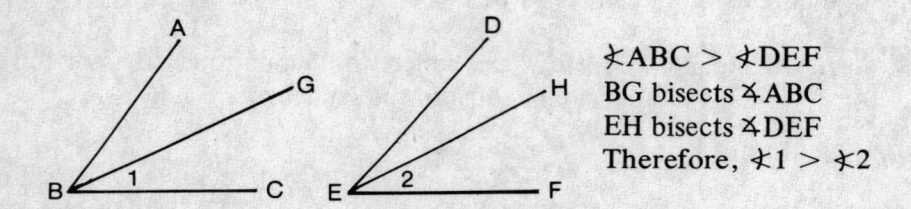

∡ABC > ∡DEF
BG bisects ∡ABC
EH bisects ∡DEF
Therefore, ∡1 > ∡2

G. If the first of three quantities is greater than the second, and the second is greater than the third, then the first is greater than the third.

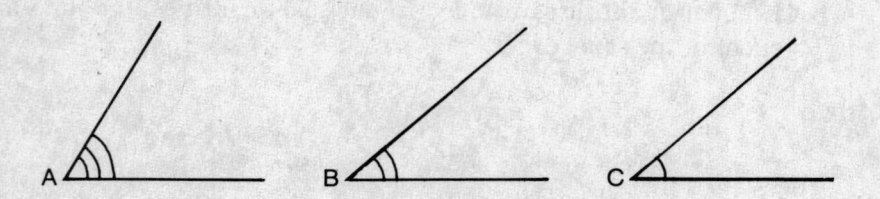

If ∡A > ∡B and ∡B > ∡C, then ∡A > ∡C.

H. The sum of two sides of a triangle must be greater than the third side.

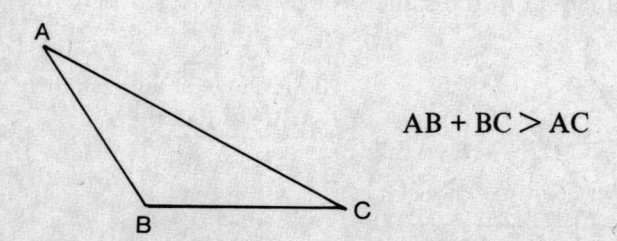

$$AB + BC > AC$$

I. If two sides of a triangle are unequal, the angles opposite are unequal, with the larger angle opposite the larger side.

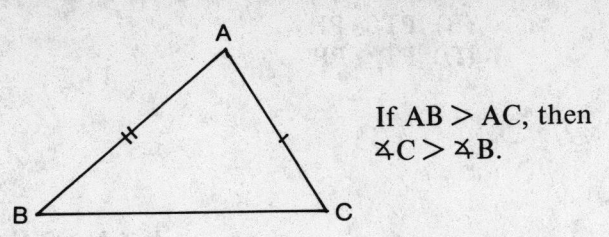

If AB > AC, then
∡C > ∡B.

J. If two angles of a triangle are unequal, the sides opposite these angles are unequal, with the larger side opposite the larger angle.

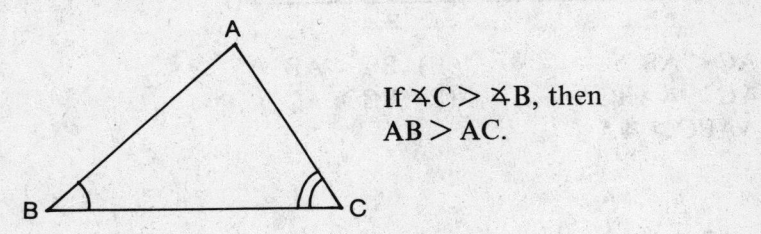

If ∡C > ∡B, then
AB > AC.

K. An exterior angle of a triangle is greater than either remote interior angle.

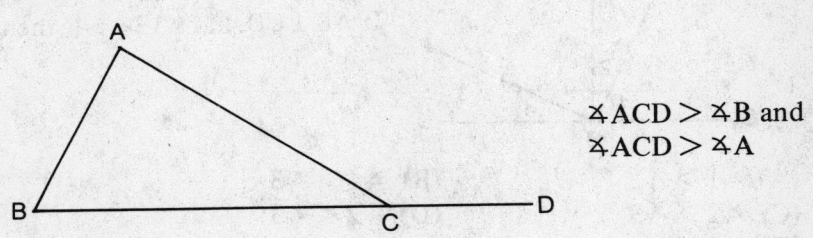

∡ACD > ∡B and
∡ACD > ∡A

Practice 2

Answers on page 208

Work out each problem in the space provided. Circle the letter before your answer.

1. Which of the following statements is true regarding triangle ABC?

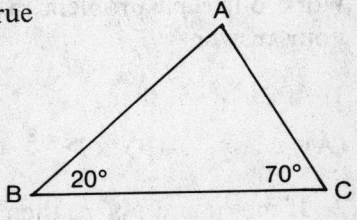

(A) AC > AB
(B) AB > BC
(C) AC > BC
(D) BC > AB
(E) BC > AB + AC

204 INEQUALITIES

2. In triangle RST, RS = ST. If P is any point on RS, which of the following statements is always true?

(A) PT < PR (B) PT > PR
(C) PT = PR (D) PT ≤ PR
(E) PT ≥ PR

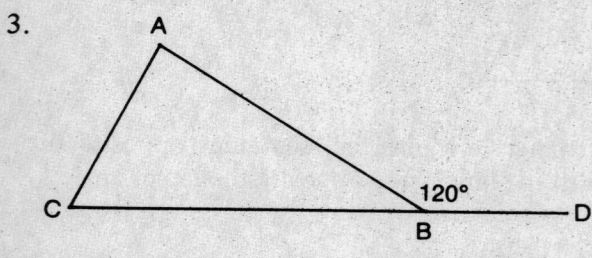

3. If ∠A > ∠C and ∠ABD = 120°, then

(A) AC < AB (B) BC < AB
(C) ∠C > ∠ABC (D) BC > AC
(E) ∠ABC > ∠A

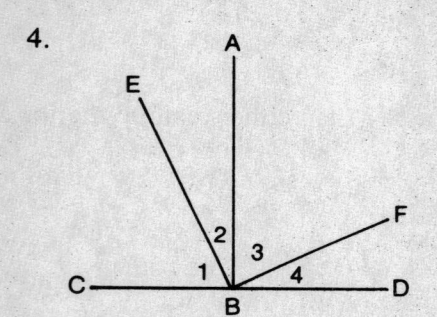

4. If AB ⊥ CD and ∠1 > ∠4, then

(A) ∠1 > ∠2 (B) ∠4 > ∠3
(C) ∠2 > ∠3 (D) ∠2 < ∠3
(E) ∠2 < ∠4

5. Which of the following sets of numbers could be the sides of a triangle?

(A) 1, 2, 3   (B) 2, 2, 4   (C) 3, 3, 6   (D) 1, 1.5, 2   (E) 5, 6, 12

Retest

Answers on page 209

Work out each problem in the space provided. Circle the letter before your answer.

1. If $2x > -5$, then

(A) $x > \frac{5}{2}$ (B) $x > -\frac{5}{2}$ (C) $x > -\frac{2}{5}$ (D) $x < \frac{5}{2}$ (E) $x < -\frac{5}{2}$

2. If $m = n$ and $p < q$, then

(A) $m - p < n - q$ (B) $p - m > q - n$
(C) $m - p > n - q$ (D) $mp > nq$
(E) $m + q < n + p$

3. If $\angle 3 > \angle 2$ and $\angle 1 = \angle 2$, then

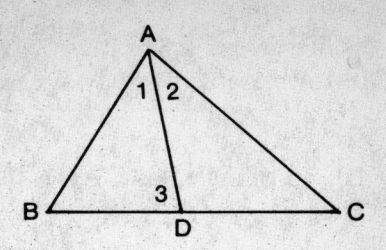

(A) AB > BD
(B) AB < BD
(C) DC = BD
(D) AD > BD
(E) AB < AC

4. If $\angle 1 > \angle 2$ and $\angle 2 > \angle 3$, then

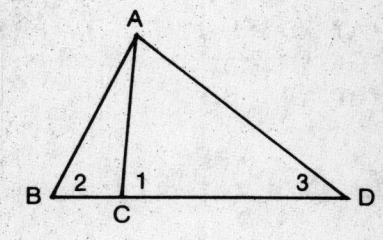

(A) AB > AD
(B) AC > AD
(C) AC < CD
(D) AD > AC
(E) AB > BC

5. If $\dfrac{x}{2} > 6$, then

(A) $x > 3$ (B) $x < 3$ (C) $x > 12$ (D) $x < 12$ (E) $x > -12$

6. If AB = AC and $\angle 1 > \angle B$, then

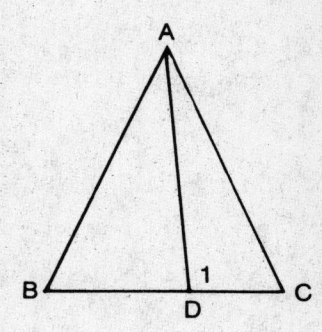

(A) $\angle B > \angle C$
(B) $\angle 1 > \angle C$
(C) BD > AD
(D) AB > AD
(E) $\angle ADC > \angle ADB$

7. Which of the following sets of numbers may be used as the sides of a triangle?

(A) 7, 8, 9   (B) 3, 5, 8   (C) 8, 5, 2   (D) 3, 10, 6   (E) 4, 5, 10

8. In isosceles triangle RST, RS = ST. If A is the midpoint of RS and B is the midpoint of ST, then

(A) SA > ST
(B) BT > BS
(C) BT = SA
(D) SR > RT
(E) RT > ST

206   INEQUALITIES

9. If $x > 0$ and $y < 0$, which of the following is always true?

(A) $x - y > y - x$ (B) $x + y > 0$ (C) $xy > 0$
(D) $y > x$ (E) $x - y < 0$

10. In triangle ABC, AD is the altitude to BC. Then

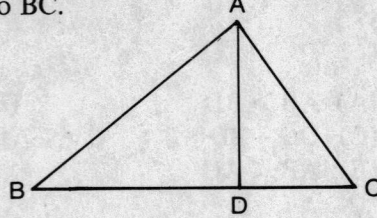

(A) $AD > DC$ (B) $AD < BD$
(C) $AD > AC$ (D) $BD > DC$
(E) $AB > BD$

INEQUALITIES 207

SOLUTIONS TO PRACTICE EXERCISES

Diagnostic Test

1. (D) $4x < 6$
   $x < \frac{6}{4}$

   Reduce to $x < \frac{3}{2}$

2. (B) If equal quantities are added to unequal quantities, the sums are unequal in the same order.

   $$\begin{array}{r} c > d \\ (+)\ a = b \\ \hline a + c > b + d \end{array}$$

3. (C) $\frac{3}{5} < \frac{x}{10} < \frac{4}{5}$

   Multiply through by 10.
   $6 < x < 8$ or x must be between 6 and 8.

4. (D)

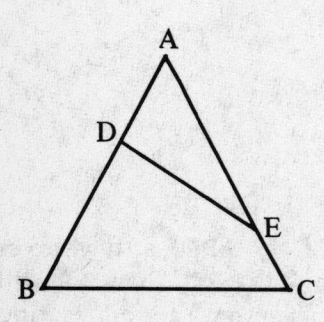

   If unequal quantities are subtracted from equal quantities, the results are unequal in the opposite order.

   $$\begin{array}{r} AC = AB \\ (-)\ EC < DB \\ \hline AE > AD \text{ or } AD < AE \end{array}$$

5. (C) If two angles of a triangle are unequal, the sides opposite these angles are unequal, with the larger side opposite the larger angle.

   Since $\angle 1 > \angle 2$, $BC > AC$.

6. (E)

   $AB = CB + AC$

7. (C) In right triangle ACB, the longest side is the hypotenuse AB. Therefore, side AC is less than AB

8. (D) A positive subtracted from a negative is always negative.

9. (B)

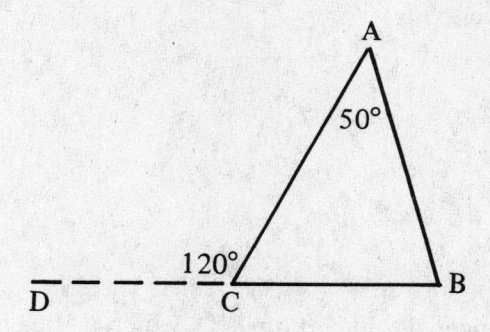

   $\angle ACB$ is the supplement of $\angle ACD$. Therefore, $\angle ACB = 60°$. $\angle ABC$ must equal $70°$ because there are $180°$ in a triangle. Since $\angle ABC$ is the largest angle in the triangle, AC must be the longest side. Therefore, $AC > AB$.

10. (D) In a right triangle, the largest angle is the right angle. Since $\angle C$ is the largest angle, $\angle C = 90°$.

Practice 1

1. (A) $8x < 10x + 20$
   $-2x < 20$
   $x > -10$

2. (C) $-2x < 12$
   $x > -6$

3. (E) $x + 10 > 50$
   $x > 40$

4. (A) $-.4x < 4$

   Multiply by 10 to remove decimals.

   $-4x < 40$
   $x > -10$

5. (D) $.03n > -.18$

   Multiply by 100

   $3n > -18$
   $n > -6$

6. (D) Divide by 15

   $b < \frac{10}{15}$

   Reduce to $b < \frac{2}{3}$

7. (D) x must be less than 2, but can go no lower than -2, as $(-3)^2$ would be greater than 4.

8. (D) $n + 4.3 < 2.7$

   Subtract 4.3 from each side.

   $n < -1.6$

9. (D) When two negative numbers are added, their sum will be negative.

10. (E) The product of two negative numbers is positive.

Practice 2

1. (D) Angle A will contain 90°, which is the largest angle of the triangle. The sides from largest to smallest will be BC, AB, AC.

2. (B) Since ∡SRT = ∡STR, ∡SRT will have to be greater than ∡PRT. Therefore, PT > PR in triangle PRT.

3. (D) Angle ABC = 60°. Since there are 120° left for ∡A and ∡C together and, also ∡A > ∡C, then ∡A must contain more than half of 120° and ∡C must contain less than half of 120°. This makes ∡A the largest angle of the triangle. The sides in order from largest to smallest are BC, AC, AB.

4. (D) ∡ABC = ∡ABD as they are both right angles. If ∡1 > ∡4, then ∡2 will be less than ∡3 because we are subtracting unequal quantities (∡1 and ∡4) from equal quantities (∡ABC and ∡ABD).

5. (D) The sum of any two sides (always try the shortest two) must be greater than the third side.

Retest

1. (B) $2x > -5$
   $x > -\frac{5}{2}$

2. (C) If unequal quantities are subtracted from equal quantities, the differences are unequal in the opposite order.

   $$\begin{array}{r} m = n \\ (-)\, p < q \\ \hline m - p > n - q \end{array}$$

3. (A) Since $\angle 3 > \angle 2$ and $\angle 1 = \angle 2$, $\angle 3 > \angle 1$. If two angles of a triangle are unequal, the sides opposite these angles are unequal, with the larger side opposite the larger angle. Therefore, $AB > BD$.

4. (D) Since $\angle 1 > \angle 2$ and $\angle 2 > \angle 3$, $\angle 1 > \angle 3$. In triangle ACB, side AD is larger than side AC, since AD is opposite the larger angle.

5. (C) $\frac{x}{2} > 6$
   $x > 12$

6. (B) If two sides of a triangle are equal, the angles opposite them are equal. Therefore $\angle C = \angle B$. Since $\angle 1 > \angle B$, $\angle 1 > \angle C$.

7. (A) The sum of any two sides (always try the shortest two) must be greater than the third side.

8. (C)

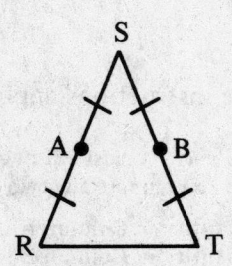

   $BT = \frac{1}{2} ST$ and $SA = \frac{1}{2} SR$. Since $ST = SR$, $BT = SA$.

9. (A) A positive minus a negative is always greater than a negative minus a positive.

10. (E) In right triangle ADB, the longest side is the hypotenuse AB. Therefore, $AB > BD$.

Quantitative Comparisons

The following instructions apply to all problems in this section.

These questions each consist of two quantities, one in Column A and one in Column B. You are to compare the two quantities and determine whether

- (A) the quantity in Column A is greater;
- (B) the quantity in Column B is greater;
- (C) the two quantities are equal;
- (D) the relationship cannot be determined from the information given.

Notes: (1) Information concerning one or both of the compared quantities will be centered above the two columns in some of the questions.
(2) Symbols that appear in both columns represent the same thing in Column A as in Column B.
(3) Letters such as x, n, and k are symbols for real numbers.

DIAGNOSTIC TEST

Answers on page 220

Write in the correct letter next to each question number.

	COLUMN A	COLUMN B
1.	$1 < X < 2$ $0 < Y < 100$	
	X	Y
2.	$x^2 = 9$ $y^2 = 144$	
	x	y
3.	$x < 0$ $y < 0$	
	x + y	xy
4.	(4) (5) (6) (7) (8)	(28) (48) (10)

QUANTITATIVE COMPARISONS 211

5. x^5 x^4

---

6. $a > b > 0$

      $\dfrac{1}{a}$ $\dfrac{1}{b}$

---

7. $a > 0, \quad b > 0, \quad c = 0$

     $2c(a + b)$ $2b(a + c)$

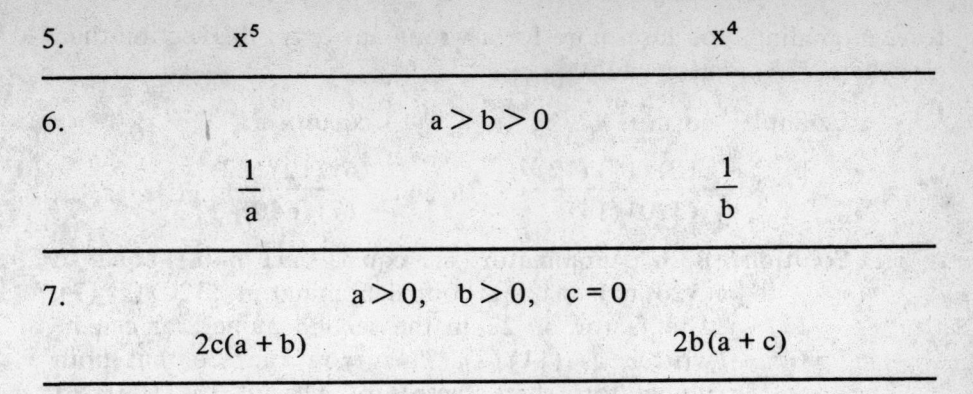

Questions 8–10 refer to this diagram.

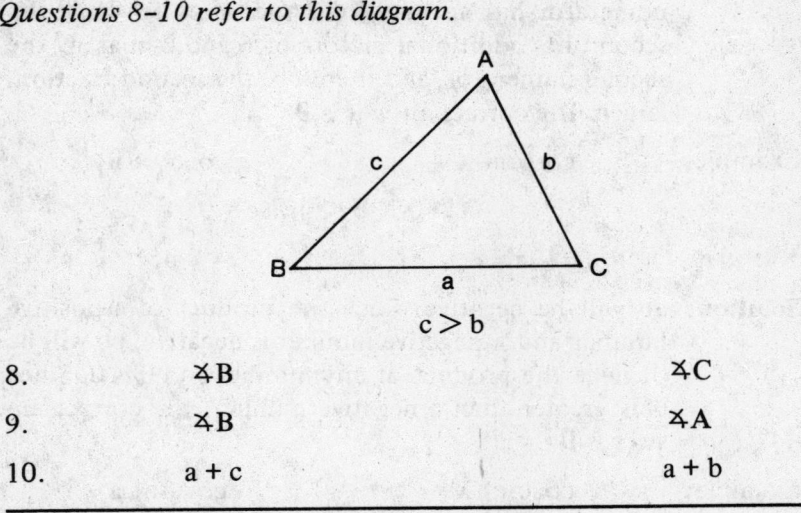

```
              A
             /\
            /  \
         c /    \ b
          /      \
         /        \
        B----------C
             a
          c > b
```

8.   ∡B   ∡C
9.   ∡B   ∡A
10. $a + c$ $a + b$

    Of increasing importance on recent examinations, this type of question can really test your ability to reason mathematically. These questions always ask you to compare two quantities to determine which, if any, is larger. Unnecessary involvement with tedious computation can really slow you down here. Always remember that if you are doing lengthy written work in finding an answer, you have missed something you should have noticed. No problems require multiplication or division by large numbers.

    By carefully studying the examples which follow, you will understand the type of reasoning which is expected and, at the same time, become aware of some of the very common student errors. At the conclusion of these examples is a set of 50 practice exercises for you to try, followed, as usual, by all solutions carefully explained. This is the last, but one of the most important sections for you to study. Do it meticulously. Thorough familiarity with these questions should really improve your confidence.

    Contrary to other questions on the examination which have five possible choices for answers, these have only four possibilities. Therefore, in grading, you lose more for a wrong answer in this section than elsewhere. Never guess wildly!

Example: COLUMN A   COLUMN B

$$\frac{(10)(11)(12)}{(320)(14)} \qquad \frac{(6)(12)(22)}{(7)(640)}$$

Solution: Both denominators are equal, since 640 is equal to (320)(2), making both denominators (320)(2)(7). The factor of 22 in the second numerator can be written as (11)(2). Then you can see that both numerators share factors of 11 and 12. The first numerator has an additional factor of 10 while the second has additional factors of 6 and 2, making the second numerator, and therefore the second fraction, larger. The correct answer is B.

Example: COLUMN A   COLUMN B

$a > 0, \quad b < 0, \quad c = 0$

ab   bc

Solution: ab will be negative, since the product of a positive number and a negative number is negative. bc will be 0, since the product of any number and 0 is 0. Since 0 is greater than a negative number, the correct answer is B.

Example: COLUMN A   COLUMN B

$a < 0, \quad b < 0$

ab   a + b

Solution: ab will be a positive number, since the product of two negative numbers is positive. a + b will be a negative number, since the sum of two negatives is negative. Therefore, the correct answer is A.

Example: COLUMN A   COLUMN B

$a > 0, \quad b < 0$

a − b   b − a

Solution: Subtracting a number is the same as adding its additive inverse. a − b will be positive, since subtracting a negative is the same as adding a positive. b − a will be negative as we will be adding two negatives. Think of 5 − (−3) compared with −3 − (+5). A is larger.

A common error in quantitative comparison questions is to think only of the first values of a variable which come to mind and not to consider *all* of the possibilities.

Example: COLUMN A   COLUMN B

$$a^2 = 4$$
$$b^2 = 100$$

a   b

Solution: Quadratic equations have two solutions. From the first equation, a could be 2 or −2. From the second equation, b could be 10 or −10. If you thought only of 2 and 10, and therefore chose B, you would have the wrong answer to the problem. For if A were −2 and B were −10, A would be larger. Therefore the correct answer here is D.

Example: COLUMN A   COLUMN B

x^2 x^3

Solution: If x is greater than 1, B is the greater quantity. If x is 0 or 1, A and B are equal. If x is a proper fraction or a negative number, A is the greater quantity. The correct answer is D.

Example: COLUMN A   COLUMN B

$$5 < x < 6$$
$$0 \leq y \leq 100$$

x   y

Solution: x and y could both be $5\frac{1}{2}$, making them equal. x could be $5\frac{1}{2}$ while y is 100, making y greater. Or, x could be $5\frac{1}{2}$ while y is 2, making x greater. The correct answer is D.

Geometry problems also lend themselves to this type of comparison question. Sometimes several questions refer to the same diagram as in the example which follows. Never judge by appearance of a diagram, but only from the given information.

Example:

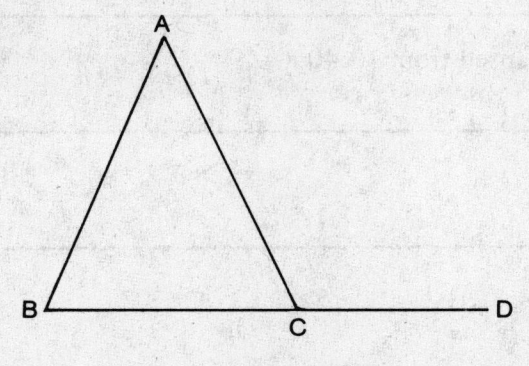

AB = AC
BC is extended to D

QUANTITATIVE COMPARISONS

	COLUMN A	COLUMN B
1.	∡B	∡C
2.	AB	BC
3.	∡ACD	∡B
4.	AB + BC	AC

Solution:
1. If two sides of a triangle are congruent, the opposite angles are congruent. The correct answer is C.
2. There is no information given about the length of BC. The correct answer is D.
3. An exterior angle of a triangle is greater than either remote interior angle. The correct answer is A.
4. The sum of any two sides of a triangle is always greater than the third side. The correct answer is A.

Practice Exercise   Answers on page 220

Write in the correct letter next to each question number.

	COLUMN A	COLUMN B
1.	$\sqrt{36.4}$	6.2
2.	$(4 + .4)(4 - .4)(\frac{2}{5})$	$(.4)(3.6)(4.4)$
3.	$\sqrt{\frac{1}{9} + \frac{1}{16}}$	$\frac{1}{3} + \frac{1}{4}$
4.	Time elapsed from 10:40 P.M. to 11:15 P.M.	$\frac{2}{3}$ hour
5. (given $x^2 > 0$)	x	0
6. (given $-1 < a < 0$)	$\frac{1}{a^2}$	$\frac{1}{a}$

QUANTITATIVE COMPARISONS

	COLUMN A	COLUMN B

7. $\quad$ $4 \cdot 4 \cdot 4 = 5 \cdot 5 \cdot a$

4	a

8. $\quad$ $a, b, c > 0$
$\quad\quad$ $4a = 2b = c$

a	c

9. $\frac{2}{3} \div 4$ $\qquad$ 20%

10. $\frac{4}{11}$ $\qquad$ $\frac{1}{3}$

11. Cost per apple if 3 dozen apples cost \$7.20 $\qquad$ Cost per orange if 5 oranges cost \$1.25

12. $\quad$ $a = 5, \quad b = 3$

$(a - b)^2$	$(b - a)^2$

13. The distance from Austin to Butte is 5 miles. The distance from Butte to Connors is 12 miles.

The distance from Austin to Connors.	13 miles

14. $4\frac{1}{2}$ expressed as a percent $\qquad$ 4.5%

15. $\quad$ $m^2 - 2 = 14 = n$

m	n

16. The circumference of a circle is 20π.

Area of the circle	400π

17. $\dfrac{1}{.2}$ $\qquad$ $\left(\dfrac{1}{.2}\right)^2$

18. $\quad$ $a = 1$

a^5	a^{25}

QUANTITATIVE COMPARISONS

	COLUMN A	COLUMN B
19.	$a > b,\ a \neq 0,\ b \neq 0$	
	$\dfrac{1}{a}$	$\dfrac{1}{b}$
20.	Area of a square with perimeter 28	Area of a circle with radius 5
21.	(32)(17)(20)	(16)(17)(40)
22.	$0 < a < 1$	
	a	$\dfrac{1}{a}$
23.	The percent of increase from $5 to $6	The percent of increase from $500 to $600
24.	$a > 0,\ b > 0,\ \dfrac{a}{b} > 1$	
	a	b
25.	$\dfrac{1}{x} < 1$	
	1	x
26.	$\dfrac{1}{2}$	$\dfrac{1}{.2}$
27.	$\sqrt{.4}$	$.2$
28.	25%	$\dfrac{1}{.04}$
29.	50% of 80	102% of 40
30.	$a > b > c > 0$	
	ab	bc
31.	$(m + n)^2$	$(m - n)^2$

COLUMN A	COLUMN B

32. The average rate of a train which travels 250 miles in $2\frac{1}{2}$ hours | The average rate of a train which travels 40 miles in 20 minutes

---

The following diagram applies to problems 33–35.

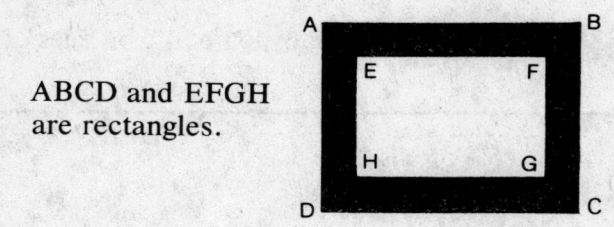

ABCD and EFGH are rectangles.

Width of shaded portion = 1
EF = 6   EH = 4

33. AB | 7
34. Perimeter ABCD | 26
35. Area of shaded portion | 24

The following diagram applies to problems 36–40.

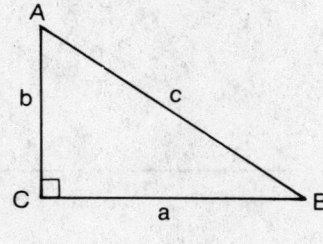

36. ∡A | ∡B
37. $a + b$ | c
38. $a^2 + c^2$ | b^2
39. ∡A + ∡B | ∡C
40. c | b

The following diagram applies to problems 41–44.

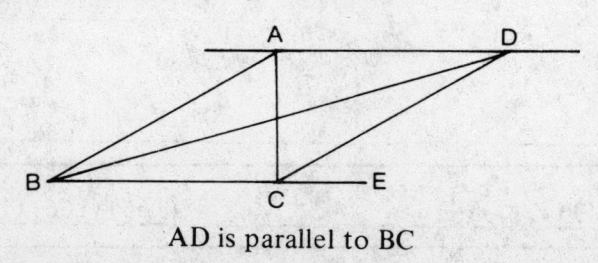

AD is parallel to BC

218   QUANTITATIVE COMPARISONS

	COLUMN A	COLUMN B
41.	Area triangle ABC	Area triangle DBC
42.	∡ADB	∡DBC
43.	∡DCE	∡DBC
44.	AB	DC

45.	A commission of 3% on sales of $400	A commission of 4% on sales of $300

46. 5% of x is 20
10% of y is 20

	COLUMN A	COLUMN B
	x	y
47.	The diagonal of a square with side 4	The altitude of an equilateral triangle with side 4
48.	The volume of a cube with edge 4	Twice the volume of a cube with edge 2

The following diagram applies to problems 49 and 50.

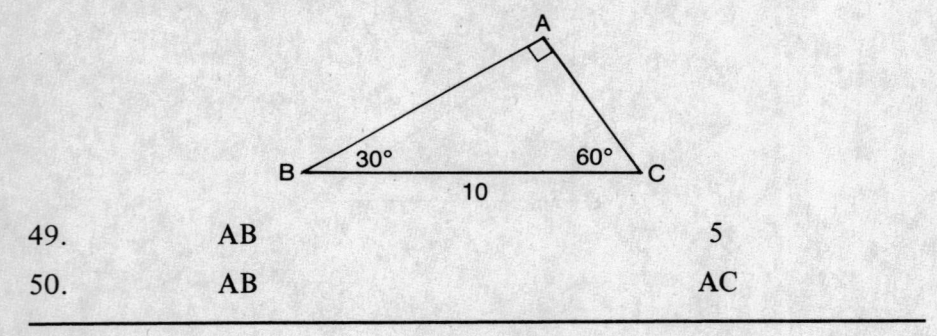

49.	AB	5
50.	AB	AC

Retest

Answers on page 223

Write in the correct letter next to each question number.

	COLUMN A	COLUMN B
1.	$a < b < -1$	
	$\dfrac{1}{a}$	$\dfrac{1}{b}$
2.	(1) (2) (3) (4)	(165) (166) (167) (0)

QUANTITATIVE COMPARISONS

COLUMN A	COLUMN B

3. $a > 0, \quad b < 0$

     $a + b$ $b + a$

---

4. $a < 0, \quad b < 0$

     $a + b$ $a - b$

---

5. $a^2 = 100$
                       $b^2 = 64$

       a   b

---

6. $8 < a < 12$
                 $10 < b < 100$

       a   b

The following diagram applies to problems 7–10.

Radius of inner circle = 2
Radius of outer circle = 4

7. Area of shaded portion 2π

8. Four times the area of outer circle   Eight times the area of inner circle

9. Half the circumference outer circle   Circumference of inner circle

10. Length of 60° arc on outer circle   Length of 120° arc on inner circle

SOLUTIONS TO PRACTICE EXERCISES

Diagnostic Test

1. (D) Y could be greater than 2, but it could also be less than 1.

2. (D) x could be +3 or −3 and y could be +12 or −12.

3. (B) The sum of two negatives is always negative and the product of two negatives is always positive. Any positive number is greater than any negative number.

4. (B) In Column A, (4)(7) = 28 and (6)(8) = 48. Since Column A has a remaining factor of 5 and Column B has a remaining factor of 10, Column B is larger.

5. (D) x^4 is positive or 0, but x^5 could be positive or negative or 0.

6. (B) The larger a denominator becomes, the smaller the fraction will be.

$$8 > 4 \qquad \tfrac{1}{8} < \tfrac{1}{4}$$

7. (B) Since c = 0, Column A equals 0 and Column B equals 2ba (a and b are positive numbers).

8. (B) ∡C is opposite the larger side.

9. (D) ∡A is opposite side a, which could be larger or smaller than side b.

10. (A) If equal quantities are added to unequal quantities, the sums are unequal in the same order.

Practice Exercise

1. (B) $(6.2)^2 = 38.44$

$$\sqrt{38.44} > \sqrt{36.4}$$

2. (C) 4 + .4 = 4.4
    4 − .4 = 3.6
    $\tfrac{2}{5} = .4$

3. (B) $\sqrt{\tfrac{1}{9} + \tfrac{1}{16}} = \sqrt{\tfrac{16+9}{144}}$

$$= \sqrt{\tfrac{25}{144}} = \tfrac{5}{12}$$

$$\tfrac{1}{3} + \tfrac{1}{4} = \tfrac{4+3}{12} = \tfrac{7}{12}$$

4. (B) A = 35 minutes
    B = $\tfrac{2}{3}$ · 60 = 40 minutes

5. (D) x could be positive or negative.

6. (A) Since a is a negative number, a^2 is positive, making Column A positive and Column B negative.

7. (A) If 25a = 64, a is between 2 and 3.

8. (B) If 4a = c, then a is only $\tfrac{1}{4}$ c.

9. (B) $\tfrac{2}{3} \div 4 = \tfrac{2}{3} \cdot \tfrac{1}{4} = \tfrac{1}{6}$

$$20\% = \tfrac{1}{5}$$

10. (A) Compare using cross multiplication.

    4 · 3 = 12   11 · 1 = 11

Therefore the first fraction is larger.

11. (B) 3 dozen = 36

    $$\frac{\$7.20}{36} = 20¢ \text{ per apple}$$

    $$\frac{\$1.25}{5} = 25¢ \text{ per orange}$$

12. (C) A = (2)² = 4
    B = (−2)² = 4

13. (D) There is no indication given of the relative directions. It could be

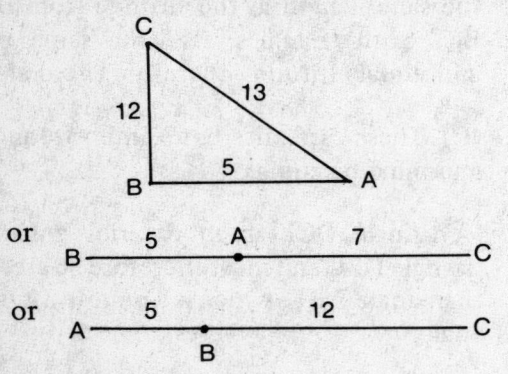

    or

    or

    or any of many others.

14. (A) $4\frac{1}{2} = 4.5$ To change a decimal to a percent, multiply by 100 and insert the percent sign.

    4.5 = 450%

15. (B) m² = 16
    m = 4 or −4
    n = 14

    Either way, n is greater.

16. (B) C = πd = 20π
    d = 20   r = 10
    A = πr² = 100π

17. (B) $\frac{1}{.2} = \frac{10}{2} = 5$

    $\left(\frac{1}{.2}\right)^2 = (5)^2 = 25$

18. (C) 1 to any power is still 1, since 1 times 1 always gives 1.

19. (B) The larger a denominator becomes, the smaller the fraction will be.

    $10 > 2 \qquad \frac{1}{10} < \frac{1}{2}$

    However, if a > 0 and b < 0, then a is still > b, but

    $$\frac{1}{a} > \frac{1}{b}$$

20. (B) Each side of square is 7
    Area of square = (7)² = 49
    Area of circle = πr² = 25π
    Since π is greater than 2, 25π is greater than 49.

21. (C) 32 = (16)(2)

    It should be clear, without any computation, that both sides are equal.

22. (B) Dividing 1 by a proper fraction gives an answer greater than 1. For example,

    $\frac{1}{\frac{1}{4}} = 4$

23. (C) Percent of increase

    $= \frac{\text{Amount of increase}}{\text{Original}} \cdot 100$

    $A = \frac{1}{5} \cdot 100 \qquad B = \frac{100}{500} = \frac{1}{5} \cdot 100$

24. (A) In order for a fraction, whose numerator and denominator are positive, to be greater than 1, the numerator must be greater than the denominator, such as $\frac{4}{3}$, $\frac{7}{4}$, etc.

25. (D) For a fraction to be less than 1, it must either be a proper fraction between 0 and 1 or be negative. In order to be a proper fraction, x would be greater than 1. In order to be a negative fraction, x would be negative, making it less than 1.

26. (B) $\frac{1}{.2} = \frac{10}{2} = 5$

27. (A) $\sqrt{.4} = \sqrt{.40}^{.6^+}$

222 QUANTITATIVE COMPARISONS

28. (B) $25\% = \frac{1}{4}$

    $\frac{1}{.04} = \frac{100}{4} = 25$

29. (B) $50\% = \frac{1}{2}$ $\frac{1}{2}$ of $80 = 40$
    102% of 40 is more than 40, since 100% of 40 would be 40.

30. (A) Since $a > c$ and a, b, and c are all positive, we can multiply both sides by b and maintain the order of the inequality.

    $ab > bc$

31. (D) If m and n are both positive, A is greater.

    $(5 + 3)^2 > (5 - 3)^2$

    However if m is positive and n is negative, B is greater.

    $[5 + (-3)]^2 = 2^2 = 4$
    $[5 - (-3)]^2 = 8^2 = 64$

32. (B) Average rate $= \dfrac{\text{Total distance}}{\text{Total time}}$

    $A = \dfrac{250}{2.5} = 100$ m.p.h.

    $B = \dfrac{40}{\frac{1}{3}} = 120$ m.p.h.

33. (A) $AB = 6 + 1$ on each end $= 8$

34. (A) The sides of ABCD are 8 and 6. Perimeter $= 8 + 6 + 8 + 6 = 28$.

35. (C) Area of shaded portion is equal to area of ABCD $(8 \cdot 6)$ minus area of EFGH $(6 \cdot 4)$.

    $48 - 24 = 24$

36. (D) There are 90° left for $\angle A$ and $\angle B$ together, but there is no indication of how this is divided.

37. (A) The sum of any two sides of a triangle is always greater than the third.

38. (A) The Pythagorean theorem states that $a^2 + b^2 = c^2$. Adding to c^2 and taking away from $a^2 + b^2$, makes A larger.

39. (C) $\angle A + \angle B$ must be the other 90° in the triangle.

40. (A) The hypotenuse is the largest side in a right triangle, as the right angle is the largest angle.

41. (C) The altitude from A to BC will be the same length as the altitude from D to BC. Both triangles have the same base and equal altitudes, therefore equal areas.

42. (C) These are alternate interior angles and must be equal.

43. (A) Angle DCE is an exterior angle of triangle DBC and must therefore be greater than angle DBC, which is a remote interior angle.

44. (D) There is no way to tell.

45. (C) $\$400(.03) = \$12$
    $\$300(.04) = \$12$

46. (A) $.05x = 20$ $.10y = 20$
    $5x = 2000$ $y = 200$
    $x = 400$

47. (A) Diagonal of a square is equal to a side times $\sqrt{2}$: $A = 4\sqrt{2}$

    Altitude of an equilateral triangle is equal to $\frac{1}{2}$ side times $\sqrt{3}$: $B = 2\sqrt{3}$

48. (A) Volume of cube $= e^3$

    $A = 4^3 = 64$
    $B = 2(2)^3 = 2(8) = 16$

49. (A) In a 30°-60°-90° triangle, the side opposite the 60° angle is equal to $\frac{1}{2}$ hypotenuse times $\sqrt{3}$.

    $AB = 5\sqrt{3}$

50. (A) $AC = \frac{1}{2}$ hypotenuse $= 5$
    $AB = \frac{1}{2}$ hypotenuse $\sqrt{3} = 5\sqrt{3}$

Retest

1. **(A)** The smaller a denominator becomes, the larger the fraction will be.

    $-5 < -3 \qquad -\frac{1}{5} > -\frac{1}{3}$

2. **(A)** Column A = 24 and Column B = 0.

3. **(C)** a + b always equals b + a, regardless of the signs of the numbers.

4. **(B)** A number plus a negative number will always be smaller than the same number minus a negative number.

5. **(D)** a could be +10 or −10 and b could be +8 or −8.

6. **(D)** b could be greater than 12, but it could also be less than 12.

7. **(A)** Area of shaded portion is equal to area of outer circle minus area of inner circle.

    $\pi(4)^2 - \pi(2)^2 = 16\pi - 4\pi = 12\pi$

8. **(A)** Area of outer circle = $\pi(4)^2 = 16\pi$
    Area of inner circle = $\pi(2)^2 = 4\pi$
    Four times the area of outer circle is 64π, and eight times the area of inner circle is 32π.

9. **(C)** Circumference of outer circle
    $= 2\pi(4) = 8\pi$
    Circumference of inner circle
    $= 2\pi(2) = 4\pi$
    Half the circumference of outer circle is 4π.

10. **(C)** Length of 60° arc on outer circle
    $= \dfrac{60°}{360°} \cdot 2\pi(4) = \dfrac{4}{3}\pi$

    Length of 120° arc on inner circle
    $= \dfrac{120°}{360°} \cdot 2\pi(2) = \dfrac{4}{3}\pi$

ANSWER SHEET

PRACTICE TEST A

PART I

1 Ⓐ Ⓑ Ⓒ Ⓓ Ⓔ	6 Ⓐ Ⓑ Ⓒ Ⓓ Ⓔ	11 Ⓐ Ⓑ Ⓒ Ⓓ Ⓔ	16 Ⓐ Ⓑ Ⓒ Ⓓ Ⓔ	21 Ⓐ Ⓑ Ⓒ Ⓓ Ⓔ
2 Ⓐ Ⓑ Ⓒ Ⓓ Ⓔ	7 Ⓐ Ⓑ Ⓒ Ⓓ Ⓔ	12 Ⓐ Ⓑ Ⓒ Ⓓ Ⓔ	17 Ⓐ Ⓑ Ⓒ Ⓓ Ⓔ	22 Ⓐ Ⓑ Ⓒ Ⓓ Ⓔ
3 Ⓐ Ⓑ Ⓒ Ⓓ Ⓔ	8 Ⓐ Ⓑ Ⓒ Ⓓ Ⓔ	13 Ⓐ Ⓑ Ⓒ Ⓓ Ⓔ	18 Ⓐ Ⓑ Ⓒ Ⓓ Ⓔ	23 Ⓐ Ⓑ Ⓒ Ⓓ Ⓔ
4 Ⓐ Ⓑ Ⓒ Ⓓ Ⓔ	9 Ⓐ Ⓑ Ⓒ Ⓓ Ⓔ	14 Ⓐ Ⓑ Ⓒ Ⓓ Ⓔ	19 Ⓐ Ⓑ Ⓒ Ⓓ Ⓔ	24 Ⓐ Ⓑ Ⓒ Ⓓ Ⓔ
5 Ⓐ Ⓑ Ⓒ Ⓓ Ⓔ	10 Ⓐ Ⓑ Ⓒ Ⓓ Ⓔ	15 Ⓐ Ⓑ Ⓒ Ⓓ Ⓔ	20 Ⓐ Ⓑ Ⓒ Ⓓ Ⓔ	25 Ⓐ Ⓑ Ⓒ Ⓓ Ⓔ

PART II

1 Ⓐ Ⓑ Ⓒ Ⓓ Ⓔ	8 Ⓐ Ⓑ Ⓒ Ⓓ Ⓔ	15 Ⓐ Ⓑ Ⓒ Ⓓ Ⓔ	22 Ⓐ Ⓑ Ⓒ Ⓓ Ⓔ	29 Ⓐ Ⓑ Ⓒ Ⓓ Ⓔ
2 Ⓐ Ⓑ Ⓒ Ⓓ Ⓔ	9 Ⓐ Ⓑ Ⓒ Ⓓ Ⓔ	16 Ⓐ Ⓑ Ⓒ Ⓓ Ⓔ	23 Ⓐ Ⓑ Ⓒ Ⓓ Ⓔ	30 Ⓐ Ⓑ Ⓒ Ⓓ Ⓔ
3 Ⓐ Ⓑ Ⓒ Ⓓ Ⓔ	10 Ⓐ Ⓑ Ⓒ Ⓓ Ⓔ	17 Ⓐ Ⓑ Ⓒ Ⓓ Ⓔ	24 Ⓐ Ⓑ Ⓒ Ⓓ Ⓔ	31 Ⓐ Ⓑ Ⓒ Ⓓ Ⓔ
4 Ⓐ Ⓑ Ⓒ Ⓓ Ⓔ	11 Ⓐ Ⓑ Ⓒ Ⓓ Ⓔ	18 Ⓐ Ⓑ Ⓒ Ⓓ Ⓔ	25 Ⓐ Ⓑ Ⓒ Ⓓ Ⓔ	32 Ⓐ Ⓑ Ⓒ Ⓓ Ⓔ
5 Ⓐ Ⓑ Ⓒ Ⓓ Ⓔ	12 Ⓐ Ⓑ Ⓒ Ⓓ Ⓔ	19 Ⓐ Ⓑ Ⓒ Ⓓ Ⓔ	26 Ⓐ Ⓑ Ⓒ Ⓓ Ⓔ	33 Ⓐ Ⓑ Ⓒ Ⓓ Ⓔ
6 Ⓐ Ⓑ Ⓒ Ⓓ Ⓔ	13 Ⓐ Ⓑ Ⓒ Ⓓ Ⓔ	20 Ⓐ Ⓑ Ⓒ Ⓓ Ⓔ	27 Ⓐ Ⓑ Ⓒ Ⓓ Ⓔ	34 Ⓐ Ⓑ Ⓒ Ⓓ Ⓔ
7 Ⓐ Ⓑ Ⓒ Ⓓ Ⓔ	14 Ⓐ Ⓑ Ⓒ Ⓓ Ⓔ	21 Ⓐ Ⓑ Ⓒ Ⓓ Ⓔ	28 Ⓐ Ⓑ Ⓒ Ⓓ Ⓔ	35 Ⓐ Ⓑ Ⓒ Ⓓ Ⓔ

PRACTICE TEST A

PART I

25 QUESTIONS

Time: 30 minutes

Directions: The problems in this section are to be solved using any available space on the page itself for scratch work. When the problem has been worked out, indicate the one appropriate answer on the answer sheet.

The information which follows should be helpful in determining the correct answers for some of the problems.

Circle of radius r: Area = πr^2 ; Circumference = $2\pi r$.
The number of degrees in a circle is 360.
The number of degrees in a straight angle is 180.

Definitions of symbols:

| is parallel to > is greater than
≤ is less than or equal to < is less than
≥ is greater than or equal to ⊥ is perpendicular to
∡ angle △ triangle

Triangle: The sum of the measures in degrees of the angles in a triangle is 180. The angle BDC is a right angle; therefore,

(1) the area of triangle ABC = $\dfrac{AC \times BD}{2}$

(2) $AB^2 = AD^2 + DB^2$

Note: The figures which accompany these problems are drawn as accurately as possible *unless* stated otherwise in specific problems. Again, unless stated otherwise, all figures lie in the same plane. All numbers used in these problems are real numbers.

1. If 20% of a number is 8, what is 25% of the number?

   (A) 2   (B) 10   (C) 12   (D) 11   (E) 15

2. If $3x + 3x - 3x = 12$, find $3x + 1$.

   (A) 4   (B) 5   (C) 10   (D) 13   (E) 37

3.

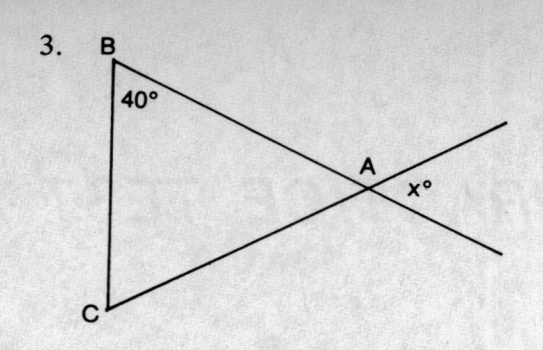

In the figure above, AB = AC. Then x =

(A) 40° (B) 80° (C) 100° (D) 60° (E) 90°

4. $(\frac{2}{5} \div \frac{2}{3}) + (\frac{1}{2} - \frac{1}{10}) =$

(A) $\frac{1}{7}$ (B) $-\frac{1}{7}$ (C) $\frac{19}{15}$ (D) $\frac{1}{5}$ (E) 1

5. The toll on the Islands Bridge is $1.00 for car and driver and $.75 for each additional passenger. How many people were riding in a car for which the toll was $3.25?

(A) 2 (B) 3 (C) 4
(D) 5 (E) none of these

6. If $y^3 = 2y^2$ and $y \neq 0$, then y must be equal to

(A) 1 (B) $\frac{1}{2}$ (C) 2 (D) 3 (E) -1

7. If x and y are negative integers and x - y = 1, what is the least possible value for xy?

(A) 0 (B) 1 (C) 2 (D) 3 (E) 4

8.

A park is in the shape of a square, a triangle and a semicircle, attached as in the diagram above. If the area of the square is 144 and the perimeter of the triangle is 20, find the perimeter of the park.

(A) $68 + 12\pi$ (B) $68 + 6\pi$ (C) $32 + 6\pi$
(D) $34 + 12\pi$ (E) $44 + 6\pi$

9. An oil tank has a capacity of 45 gallons. At the beginning of October it is 80% full. At the end of October it is $\frac{1}{3}$ full. How many gallons of oil were used in October?

(A) 21 (B) 25 (C) 41 (D) 27 (E) 30

10.

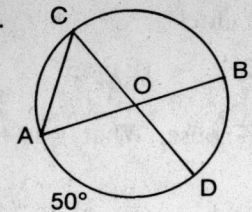

AB and CD are diameters of circle O.
The number of degrees in angle CAB is

(A) 50   (B) 100   (C) 130   (D) $12\frac{1}{2}$ (E) 25

11. If $\frac{2}{5}x = \frac{5}{2}y$ then $\frac{y}{x} =$

(A) 1   (B) -1   (C) $\frac{4}{25}$ (D) $\frac{25}{4}$ (E) $\frac{2}{5}$

12. If the sum of x and y is z and the average of m, n, and p is q, find the value of x + y + m + n + p in terms of z and q.

(A) 2z + 3q   (B) z + 3q   (C) $z + \frac{q}{3}$

(D) $\frac{z}{2} + \frac{q}{3}$ (E) none of these

13. Isosceles triangle ABC is inscribed in square BCDE as shown. If the area of BCDE is 4, the perimeter of ABC is

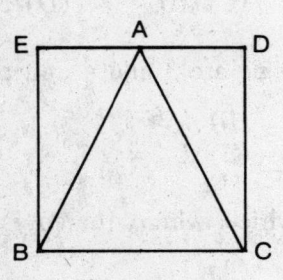

(A) 8   (B) $2 + \sqrt{5}$ (C) $2 + 2\sqrt{5}$
(D) $2 + \sqrt{10}$ (E) 12

14. If a is not 0 or 1, a fraction equivalent to $\dfrac{\frac{1}{a}}{2 - \frac{2}{a}}$ is

(A) $\frac{1}{2a - 2}$ (B) $\frac{2}{a - 2}$ (C) $\frac{1}{a - 2}$ (D) $\frac{1}{a}$ (E) $\frac{2}{2a - 1}$

15. At 3:30 P.M. the angle between the hands of a clock is

(A) 90°   (B) 80°   (C) 75°   (D) 72°   (E) 65°

16. A clerk's weekly salary is $140 after a 25% raise. What was his weekly salary before the raise?

(A) $112   (B) $110   (C) $125   (D) $105   (E) $120

17. The figure below is composed of 5 equal squares. If the area of the figure is 125, find its perimeter.

(A) 60   (B) 100   (C) 80   (D) 75   (E) 20

18. $\frac{1}{2}$ of $\frac{3}{5}$ is equal to which of the following?

(A) 3%   (B) $33\frac{1}{3}$%   (C) 30%   (D) $83\frac{1}{3}$%   (E) 120%

19. The length of an arc of a circle is equal to $\frac{1}{5}$ of the circumference of the circle. If the length of the arc is 2π, the radius of the circle is

(A) 2   (B) 1   (C) 10   (D) 5   (E) $\sqrt{10}$

20. If two sides of a triangle are 3 and 4 and the third side is x, then

(A) x = 5   (B) x > 7   (C) x < 7
(D) 1 < x < 7   (E) 1 ≦ x ≦ 7

21. The smallest integer which, when squared, is less than 5 is

(A) 0   (B) 1   (C) 2
(D) 3   (E) none of these

22. Mr. Prince takes his wife and two children to the circus. If the price of a child's ticket is $\frac{1}{2}$ the price of an adult ticket and Mr. Prince pays a total of $12.60, find the price of a child's ticket.

(A) $4.20   (B) $3.20   (C) $1.60   (D) $2.10   (E) $3.30

23. If $(_b {}^a {}_c)$ is defined as being equal to ab - c, then $(_4 {}^3 {}_5)$ + $(_6 {}^5 {}_7)$ is equal to

(A) 30   (B) 40   (C) 11   (D) 6   (E) 15

24. The diameter of a circle is increased by 50%. The area is increased by

(A) 50%   (B) 100%   (C) 125%   (D) 200%   (E) 250%

25. $\frac{1}{3}$ of the students at South High are seniors. $\frac{3}{4}$ of the seniors will go to college next year. What percent of the students at South High will go to college next year?

(A) 75   (B) 25   (C) $33\frac{1}{3}$ (D) 50   (E) 45

PART II

35 QUESTIONS
Time: 30 minutes

Directions: The problems in this section are to be solved using any available space on the page itself for scratchwork. When the problem has been worked out, indicate the one appropriate answer on the answer sheet.

The information which follows should be helpful in determining the correct answers for some of the problems.

Circle of radius r: Area = πr^2; Circumference = $2\pi r$.
The number of degrees in a circle is 360.
The number of degrees in a straight angle is 180.

Definitions of symbols:

$\parallel$ is parallel to	$>$ is greater than
$\leq$ is less than or equal to	$<$ is less than
$\geq$ is greater than or equal to	$\perp$ is perpendicular to
$\angle$ angle	$\triangle$ triangle

Triangle: The sum of the measures in degrees of the angles in a triangle is 180. The angle BDC is a right angle; therefore,

(1) the area of triangle ABC = $\dfrac{AC \times BD}{2}$

(2) $AB^2 = AD^2 + DB^2$

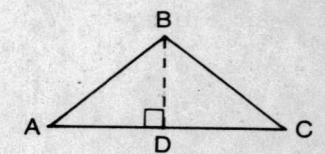

Note: The figures which accompany these problems are drawn as accurately as possible *unless* stated otherwise in specific problems. Again, unless stated otherwise, all figures lie in the same plane. All numbers used in these problems are real numbers.

1. If $a = 4$, then $\sqrt{a^2 + 9} =$

(A) 7 (B) 25 (C) 1 (D) 5 (E) -5

2. When a certain number is divided by 2, there is no remainder. If there is a remainder when the number is divided by 4, the remainder must be

(A) 5 (B) 4 (C) 3 (D) 2 (E) 1

3. If $a = x^2$ and $x = \sqrt{8}$, then $a =$

(A) $2\sqrt{2}$ (B) 2 (C) 4 (D) 64 (E) 8

4. If $\frac{a}{b} \cdot \frac{b}{c} \cdot \frac{c}{d} \cdot \frac{d}{e} \cdot x = 1$, then x must be equal to

(A) $\frac{a}{e}$ (B) $\frac{e}{a}$ (C) e
(D) $\frac{1}{a}$ (E) none of these

5. If there are 30 students at a meeting of the Forum Club, and 20 are wearing white, 17 are wearing black and 14 are wearing both black and white, how many are wearing neither black nor white?

(A) 3 (B) 5 (C) 7 (D) 9 (E) 11

6. If a □ b means a · b + (a − b), find the value of 4 □ 2.

(A) 6 (B) 8 (C) 10
(D) 12 (E) none of these

7. A drawer contains 4 red socks and 4 blue socks. Find the least number of socks that must be drawn from the drawer to be assured of having a pair of red socks.

(A) 2 (B) 3 (C) 4 (D) 5 (E) 6

8. How many 2-inch squares are needed to fill a border around the edge of the shaded square with a side of 6" as shown in the figure below?

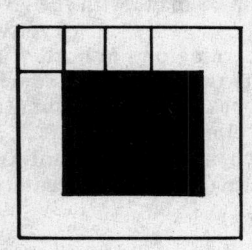

(A) 16 (B) 18 (C) 20
(D) 22 (E) none of these

9. If x + 3 is a multiple of 3, which of the following is *not* a multiple of 3?

(A) x (B) x + 6 (C) 6x + 18 (D) 2x + 6 (E) 3x + 5

10. ab = 10 $a^2 + b^2 = 30$ $(a + b)^2 =$

(A) 30 (B) 35 (C) 40 (D) 45 (E) 50

11. If a car uses $1\frac{1}{2}$ gallons of gas for 30 miles, how many miles can be driven with 6 gallons of gas?

(A) 60 (B) 80 (C) 100 (D) 120 (E) 180

12. Find the angle between the hands of a clock at 12:30 P.M.

(A) 180°   (B) 150°   (C) 165°   (D) 170°   (E) 160°

13. The distance between any 2 consecutive bases on a baseball field is 90 feet. Find, to the nearest foot, the distance, in a straight line, from home plate to second base.

(A) 90   (B) 116   (C) 127   (D) 153   (E) 180

14. If x is an even integer, what is the result when the next odd integer is added to the next even integer?

(A) 2x + 1   (B) x + 3   (C) 2x + 3   (D) x + 1   (E) x + 2

15. In triangle RST, RS = ST and angle T contains 70°. The measure of angle S is

(A) 70°   (B) 40°   (C) 50°   (D) 55°   (E) 60°

Directions: For questions 16–35, compare two quantities, one in Column A and one in Column B, and determine whether:

(A) the quantity is greater in Column A
(B) the quantity is greater in Column B
(C) both quantities are equal
(D) no comparison can be made with the given information

Notes: (1) Information concerning one or both of the compared quantities will be centered above the two columns in some of the questions.
(2) Symbols that appear in both columns represent the same thing in Column A as in Column B.
(3) Letters such as x, n, and k are symbols for real numbers.
(4) Do not mark choice (E), as there are only four choices.

COLUMN A	COLUMN B
16. $\frac{1}{2} + \frac{1}{3} + \frac{1}{4} + \frac{1}{5} + \frac{1}{6}$	1
17. $16^2 - 2(16)(17) + 17^2$	$16^2 + 2(16)(17) + 17^2$
18. 110°	number of degrees in the largest angle of an obtuse triangle

19. X is a set of 3 consecutive even integers. Y is a set of 4 consecutive odd integers.

| the largest integer in X | the largest integer in Y |

PRACTICE TEST A   233

COLUMN A	COLUMN B

20.

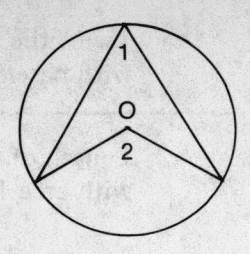

O is the center of the circle

number of degrees in angle 1	number of degrees in angle 2

---

21. $2x + 3 = 5$
     $3y + 7 = 10$

x	y

---

22. $x > 0$
     $y > 0$

$x - y$	$y - x$

---

23. $x > 0$
     $y < 0$

$x - y$	$x + y$

---

24. $\dfrac{x}{36} = \dfrac{1}{3}$

$\dfrac{4}{x}$	$\dfrac{1}{3}$

---

25. x is an integer

x	$\dfrac{x}{-1}$

---

26. | Number of seconds in one day | Number of minutes in April |
|---|---|

---

27. $9 < x < 10$
     $9 < y < 11$

x	y

	COLUMN A	COLUMN B
28.	Area of a triangle with base 5 and height 7	Twice the area of a rectangle with base 5 and height 7
29.	Length of the hypotenuse of a right triangle with legs 9 and 10	Length of the side of a square with area 180
30.	The total area of a cube with edge 6	6 times the total area of a cube with edge 2

Questions 31–35 refer to the diagram below.

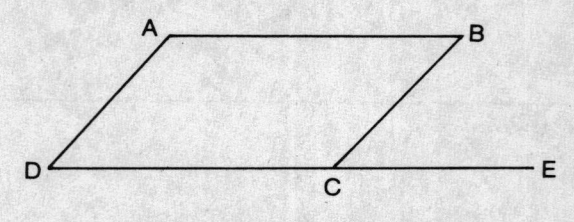

ABCD is a parallelogram

31.	AB	DC
32.	AB	BC
33.	Angle D	Angle BCE
34.	Angle D	Angle B
35.	Angle B	Angle BCE

ANSWER SHEET

PRACTICE TEST B

PART I

1 Ⓐ Ⓑ © Ⓓ Ⓔ	6 Ⓐ Ⓑ © Ⓓ Ⓔ	11 Ⓐ Ⓑ © Ⓓ Ⓔ	16 Ⓐ Ⓑ © Ⓓ Ⓔ	21 Ⓐ Ⓑ © Ⓓ Ⓔ
2 Ⓐ Ⓑ © Ⓓ Ⓔ	7 Ⓐ Ⓑ © Ⓓ Ⓔ	12 Ⓐ Ⓑ © Ⓓ Ⓔ	17 Ⓐ Ⓑ © Ⓓ Ⓔ	22 Ⓐ Ⓑ © Ⓓ Ⓔ
3 Ⓐ Ⓑ © Ⓓ Ⓔ	8 Ⓐ Ⓑ © Ⓓ Ⓔ	13 Ⓐ Ⓑ © Ⓓ Ⓔ	18 Ⓐ Ⓑ © Ⓓ Ⓔ	23 Ⓐ Ⓑ © Ⓓ Ⓔ
4 Ⓐ Ⓑ © Ⓓ Ⓔ	9 Ⓐ Ⓑ © Ⓓ Ⓔ	14 Ⓐ Ⓑ © Ⓓ Ⓔ	19 Ⓐ Ⓑ © Ⓓ Ⓔ	24 Ⓐ Ⓑ © Ⓓ Ⓔ
5 Ⓐ Ⓑ © Ⓓ Ⓔ	10 Ⓐ Ⓑ © Ⓓ Ⓔ	15 Ⓐ Ⓑ © Ⓓ Ⓔ	20 Ⓐ Ⓑ © Ⓓ Ⓔ	25 Ⓐ Ⓑ © Ⓓ Ⓔ

PART II

1 Ⓐ Ⓑ © Ⓓ Ⓔ	8 Ⓐ Ⓑ © Ⓓ Ⓔ	15 Ⓐ Ⓑ © Ⓓ Ⓔ	22 Ⓐ Ⓑ © Ⓓ Ⓔ	29 Ⓐ Ⓑ © Ⓓ Ⓔ
2 Ⓐ Ⓑ © Ⓓ Ⓔ	9 Ⓐ Ⓑ © Ⓓ Ⓔ	16 Ⓐ Ⓑ © Ⓓ Ⓔ	23 Ⓐ Ⓑ © Ⓓ Ⓔ	30 Ⓐ Ⓑ © Ⓓ Ⓔ
3 Ⓐ Ⓑ © Ⓓ Ⓔ	10 Ⓐ Ⓑ © Ⓓ Ⓔ	17 Ⓐ Ⓑ © Ⓓ Ⓔ	24 Ⓐ Ⓑ © Ⓓ Ⓔ	31 Ⓐ Ⓑ © Ⓓ Ⓔ
4 Ⓐ Ⓑ © Ⓓ Ⓔ	11 Ⓐ Ⓑ © Ⓓ Ⓔ	18 Ⓐ Ⓑ © Ⓓ Ⓔ	25 Ⓐ Ⓑ © Ⓓ Ⓔ	32 Ⓐ Ⓑ © Ⓓ Ⓔ
5 Ⓐ Ⓑ © Ⓓ Ⓔ	12 Ⓐ Ⓑ © Ⓓ Ⓔ	19 Ⓐ Ⓑ © Ⓓ Ⓔ	26 Ⓐ Ⓑ © Ⓓ Ⓔ	33 Ⓐ Ⓑ © Ⓓ Ⓔ
6 Ⓐ Ⓑ © Ⓓ Ⓔ	13 Ⓐ Ⓑ © Ⓓ Ⓔ	20 Ⓐ Ⓑ © Ⓓ Ⓔ	27 Ⓐ Ⓑ © Ⓓ Ⓔ	34 Ⓐ Ⓑ © Ⓓ Ⓔ
7 Ⓐ Ⓑ © Ⓓ Ⓔ	14 Ⓐ Ⓑ © Ⓓ Ⓔ	21 Ⓐ Ⓑ © Ⓓ Ⓔ	28 Ⓐ Ⓑ © Ⓓ Ⓔ	35 Ⓐ Ⓑ © Ⓓ Ⓔ

Practice Test B

PART I

25 QUESTIONS

Time: 30 minutes

Directions: The problems in this section are to be solved using any available space on the page itself for scratch work. When the problem has been worked out, indicate the one appropriate answer on the answer sheet.

The information which follows should be helpful in determining the correct answers for some of the problems.

Circle of radius r: Area = πr^2; Circumference = $2\pi r$.
The number of degrees in a circle is 360.
The number of degrees in a straight angle is 180.

Definitions of symbols:

$\parallel$ is parallel to	$>$ is greater than
$\leq$ is less than or equal to	$<$ is less than
$\geq$ is greater than or equal to	$\perp$ is perpendicular to
$\angle$ angle	$\triangle$ triangle

Triangle: The sum of the measures in degrees of the angles in a triangle is 180. The angle BDC is a right angle; therefore,

(1) the area of triangle ABC = $\dfrac{AC \times BD}{2}$

(2) $AB^2 = AD^2 + DB^2$

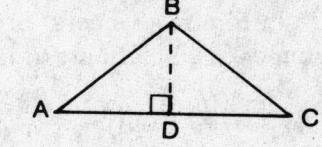

Note: The figures which accompany these problems are drawn as accurately as possible *unless* stated otherwise in specific problems. Again, unless stated otherwise, all figures lie in the same plane. All numbers used in these problems are real numbers.

1. If the outer diameter of a cylindrical oil tank is 54.28 inches and the inner diameter is 48.7 inches, the thickness of the wall of the tank, in inches, is

(A) 5.58 (B) 2.29 (C) 2.79 (D) 6.42 (E) 3.21

2. Which of the following has the largest numerical value?

(A) $\frac{3}{5}$ (B) $(\frac{2}{3})(\frac{3}{4})$ (C) $\sqrt{.25}$ (D) $(.9)^2$ (E) $\frac{2}{.3}$

3. $\frac{1}{4}$% written as a decimal is

(A) 25 (B) 2.5 (C) .25 (D) .025 (E) .0025

4. 53% of the 1000 students at Jackson High are girls. How many boys are there in the school?

(A) 470 (B) 53 (C) 47 (D) 530 (E) 540

5. How many digits are there in the square root of a perfect square of 12 digits?

(A) 4 (B) 6 (C) 10 (D) 12 (E) 24

6. The value of $\dfrac{\frac{1}{2}}{\frac{1}{3}-\frac{1}{4}}$ is

(A) 6 (B) $\frac{1}{6}$ (C) 1 (D) 3 (E) $\frac{3}{2}$

7. The sum of Alan's age and Bob's age is 40. The sum of Bob's age and Carl's age is 34. The sum of Alan's age and Carl's age is 42. How old is Bob?

(A) 18 (B) 24 (C) 20 (D) 16 (E) 12

8. On a map having a scale of $\frac{1}{4}$ inch = 20 miles, how many inches should there be between towns 325 miles apart?

(A) $4\frac{1}{16}$ (B) $16\frac{1}{4}$ (C) $81\frac{1}{4}$ (D) $32\frac{1}{2}$ (E) $6\frac{1}{4}$

9. In Simon's General Store, there are m male employees and f female employees. What part of the staff is men?

(A) $\dfrac{m+f}{m}$ (B) $\dfrac{m+f}{f}$ (C) $\dfrac{m}{f}$ (D) $\dfrac{m}{m+f}$ (E) $\dfrac{f}{m}$

10. If the angles of a triangle are in the ratio 2:3:4, the triangle is

(A) acute (B) isosceles (C) right (D) equilateral
(E) obtuse

11. If the length and width of a rectangle are each multiplied by 2, then

(A) the area and perimeter are both multiplied by 4
(B) the area is multiplied by 2 and the perimeter by 4
(C) the area is multiplied by 4 and the perimeter by 2
(D) the area and perimeter are both multiplied by 2
(E) the perimeter is multiplied by 4 and the area by 8

12. Paul needs m minutes to mow the lawn. After working for k minutes, what part of the lawn is still unmowed?

(A) $\dfrac{k}{m}$ (B) $\dfrac{m}{k}$ (C) $\dfrac{m-k}{k}$ (D) $\dfrac{m-k}{m}$ (E) $\dfrac{k-m}{m}$

13. Mr. Marcus earns $250 per week. If he spends 20% of his income for rent, 25% for food, and 10% for savings, how much is left each week for other expenses?

(A) $112.50 (B) $125 (C) $137.50 (D) $132.50 (E) $140

14. Find the value of $(3\sqrt{2})^2$

(A) $9\sqrt{2}$ (B) $6\sqrt{2}$ (C) 18 (D) 36 (E) 24

15. How far is the point (-4, -3) from the origin?

(A) 2 (B) 2.5 (C) $4\sqrt{2}$ (D) $4\sqrt{3}$ (E) 5

16. The product of 3456 and 789 is exactly

(A) 2726787 (B) 2726785 (C) 2726781 (D) 2726784 (E) 2726786

17. Susan got up one morning at 7:42 A.M. and went to bed that evening at 10:10 P.M. How much time elapsed between her getting up and going to bed that day?

(A) 18 hrs. 2 min.
(B) 14 hrs. 18 min.
(C) 15 hrs. 18 min.
(D) 9 hrs. 22 min.
(E) 14 hrs. 28 min.

18. Find the perimeter of right triangle ABC if the area of square AEDC is 100 and the area of square BCFG is 36.

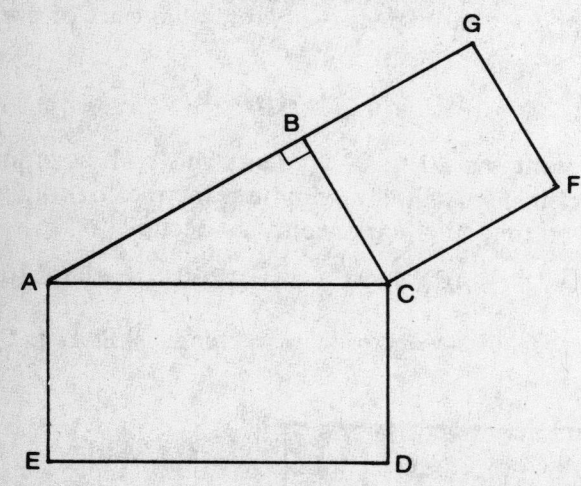

(A) 22 (B) 24 (C) $16 + 6\sqrt{3}$
(D) $16 + 6\sqrt{2}$ (E) cannot be determined from information given

19. Find the number of degrees in angle 1 if AB = AC, DE = DC, angle 2 = 40° and angle 3 = 80°.

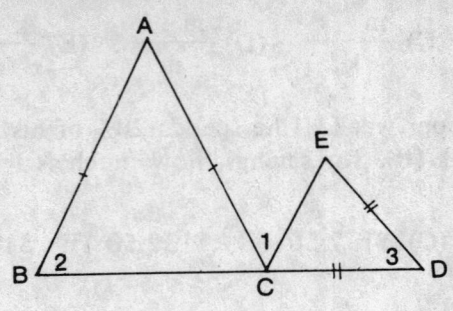

(A) 60   (B) 40   (C) 90   (D) 50   (E) 80

20. If p pencils cost 2D dollars, how many pencils can be bought for c cents?

(A) $\frac{pc}{2D}$ (B) $\frac{pc}{200D}$ (C) $\frac{50pc}{D}$ (D) $\frac{2Dp}{c}$ (E) 200pcD

21. Two trains start from the same station at 10 A.M., one traveling east at 60 m.p.h. and the other west at 70 m.p.h. At what time will they be 455 miles apart?

(A) 3:30 P.M.   (B) 12:30 P.M.   (C) 1:30 P.M.
(D) 1 P.M.   (E) 2 P.M.

22. The average of 7 consecutive even integers is 14. The sum of the first 2 integers is

(A) 18   (B) 23   (C) 14   (D) 20
(E) cannot be determined

23. If 12 inches = 1 foot and 3 feet = 1 yard, what part of a yard is 54 inches?

(A) $\frac{2}{3}$ (B) $\frac{5}{4}$ (C) $\frac{6}{5}$ (D) $\frac{3}{2}$ (E) $\frac{7}{6}$

24. If a classroom contains 20 to 24 students and each corridor contains 8 to 10 classrooms, what is the minimum number of students on one corridor at a given time, if all classrooms are occupied?

(A) 200   (B) 192   (C) 160   (D) 240   (E) 210

25. If the area of each circle enclosed in rectangle ABCD is 9π, the area of ABCD is

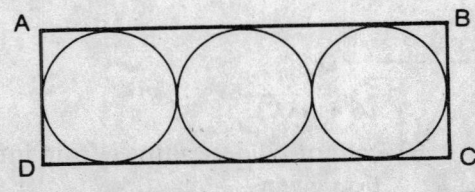

(A) 108   (B) 27   (C) 54   (D) 54π   (E) 108π

PART II

35 QUESTIONS

Time: 30 minutes

Directions: The problems in this section are to be solved using any available space on the page itself for scratch work. When the problem has been worked out, indicate the one appropriate answer on the answer sheet.

The information which follows should be helpful in determining the correct answers for some of the problems.

Circle of radius r: Area = πr^2; Circumference = $2\pi r$.
The number of degrees in a circle is 360.
The number of degrees in a straight angle is 180.

Definitions of symbols:

$\parallel$	is parallel to	$>$	is greater than
$\leq$	is less than or equal to	$<$	is less than
$\geq$	is greater than or equal to	$\perp$	is perpendicular to
$\measuredangle$	angle	$\triangle$	triangle

Triangle: The sum of the measures in degrees of the angles in a triangle is 180. The angle BDC is a right angle; therefore,

(1) the area of triangle ABC = $\dfrac{AC \times BD}{2}$

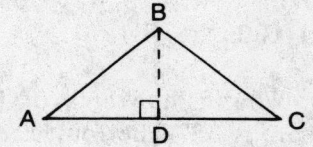

(2) $AB^2 = AD^2 + DB^2$

Note: The figures which accompany these problems are drawn as accurately as possible *unless* stated otherwise in specific problems. Again, unless stated otherwise, all figures lie in the same plane. All numbers used in these problems are real numbers.

1. What part of a dime is a quarter?

   (A) $\frac{3}{2}$ (B) $\frac{5}{2}$ (C) $\frac{2}{3}$ (D) $\frac{2}{5}$ (E) $\frac{1}{3}$

2. Marion is paid $24 for 5 hours of work in the school office. Janet works 3 hours at the same hourly wage. What is the total salary paid to the two girls?

   (A) $14.40   (B) $48   (C) $38.40   (D) $34.40   (E) $38.80

3. A musical instrument depreciates by 20% of its value each year. Find the value, after 2 years, of a piano purchased new for $1200.

   (A) $768   (B) $912   (C) $675   (D) $48   (E) $1152

4. What number added to 40% of itself is equal to 84?

   (A) 50.4   (B) 33.6   (C) 60.0   (D) 64.0   (E) 40.6

5. If r = 25 - s, then 4r + 4s =

(A) 25 (B) -25 (C) -100 (D) 100
(E) cannot be determined

6. A plane flies over Denver at 11:20 A.M. It passes over Coolidge, 120 miles from Denver, at 11:32 A.M. Find the rate of the plane in miles per hour.

(A) 480 (B) 360 (C) 600 (D) 720 (E) 540

7. Which of the following fractions is equal to $\frac{1}{4}$%?

(A) $\frac{1}{25}$ (B) $\frac{4}{25}$ (C) $\frac{1}{4}$ (D) $\frac{1}{400}$ (E) $\frac{1}{40}$

8. Roger receives a basic weekly salary of $80 plus a 5% commission. In a week in which his sales amounted to $800, the ratio of his basic salary to his commission was

(A) 2:1 (B) 1:2 (C) 2:3 (D) 3:2 (E) 3:1

9. In May, Carter's Appliances sold 40 washing machines. In June, because of a special promotion, the store sold 80 washing machines. The percent of increase in the number of washing machines sold is

(A) 100 (B) 50 (C) 200 (D) 40 (E) 80

10. What is the area of the shaded portion if the perimeter of the square is 32? The four circles are tangent to each other and the square and are congruent.

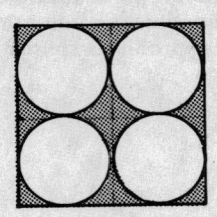

(A) $32 - 16\pi$ (B) $64 - 16\pi$
(C) $64 - 64\pi$ (D) $64 - 8\pi$ (E) $32 - 4\pi$

11. Points P, Q, and R are placed on a line segment XY so that XP = PQ = QR = RY. What percent of PR is PY?

(A) 66 (B) 200 (C) 75 (D) 125 (E) 150

12. Mr. Watts drives into the country at X miles per hour for M miles. He returns over the same route at Y miles per hour. Find his average rate, in miles per hour, for the entire trip.

(A) $\frac{M}{X+Y}$ (B) $\frac{2XY}{X+Y}$ (C) $\frac{2M}{X+Y}$ (D) $\frac{XY}{X+Y}$ (E) $\frac{X+Y}{2M}$

13. If a = 2b and 4b = 6c, then a =

(A) 3c (B) 6c (C) 2.5c (D) 4c (E) 12c

14. If x < 0 and y < 0, then

(A) x + y > 0 (B) x = -y (C) x > y (D) xy > 0
(E) xy < 0

15. Which of the following is the product of 4327 and 546?

(A) 2362541 (B) 2362542 (C) 2362543
(D) 2362546 (E) 2362548

Directions: For questions 16–35 compare two quantities, one in Column A and one in Column B, and determine whether:
- (A) the quantity is greater in Column A
- (B) the quantity is greater in Column B
- (C) both quantities are equal
- (D) no comparison can be made with the given information

Notes: (1) Information concerning one or both of the compared quantities will be centered above the two columns in some of the questions.
(2) Symbols that appear in both columns represent the same thing in Column A as in Column B.
(3) Letters such as x, n, and k are symbols for real numbers.
(4) Do not mark choice (E), as there are only four choices.

COLUMN A	COLUMN B
16. $4 \cdot a \cdot 4 \cdot 4 = 3 \cdot 3 \cdot 3 \cdot 3$	
a	3
17. $X > Y$, $W < Z$, $X > 0$, $Y > 0$, $W > 0$, $Z > 0$	
$\frac{X}{W}$	$\frac{Y}{Z}$
18. $-3 < a < -1$	
$\frac{1}{a^4}$	$\frac{1}{a^7}$
19. $18 \cdot 563 \cdot 10$	$12 \cdot 563 \cdot 16$
20. $100 - \frac{100}{.1}$	-900

	COLUMN A	COLUMN B
21.	The number of posts needed for a fence 100 feet long if the posts are placed 10 feet apart	10 posts
22.	A single discount of 10%	Two successive discounts of 5% and 5%

Questions 23–26 refer to the diagram below.

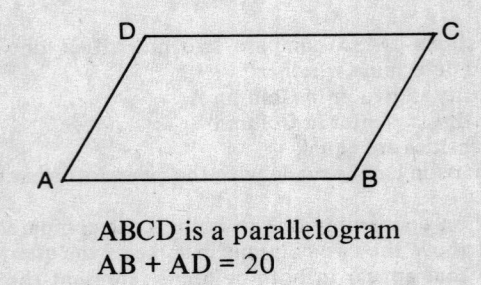

ABCD is a parallelogram
AB + AD = 20

	COLUMN A	COLUMN B
23.	DC	AB
24.	DC	DA
25.	Area ABCD	200
26.	40	Perimeter ABCD

Questions 27–30 refer to the diagram below.

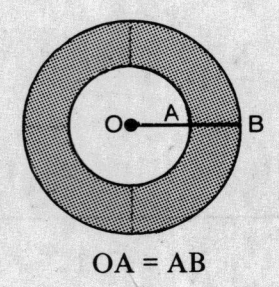

OA = AB

	COLUMN A	COLUMN B
27.	Area of outer circle	Twice the area of inner circle
28.	Area of inner circle	Area of shaded portion
29.	Diameter of inner circle	Radius of outer circle
30.	Twice the circumference of inner circle	Circumference of outer circle

Questions 31-35 refer to the diagram below.

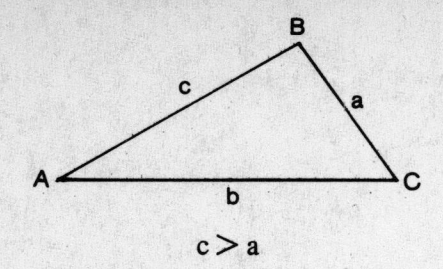

$c > a$

	COLUMN A	COLUMN B
31.	a + b	c
32.	Angle C	Angle A
33.	Angle C	Angle B
34.	a	b
35.	Area of triangle ABC in square units	Perimeter of triangle ABC in linear units

ANSWER SHEET

PRACTICE TEST C

PART I

1 Ⓐ ●　Ⓒ Ⓓ Ⓔ   6 Ⓐ Ⓑ Ⓒ Ⓓ Ⓔ   11 Ⓐ Ⓑ Ⓒ Ⓓ Ⓔ   16 Ⓐ Ⓑ Ⓒ Ⓓ Ⓔ   21 Ⓐ Ⓑ Ⓒ Ⓓ Ⓔ
2 Ⓐ ●　Ⓒ Ⓓ Ⓔ   7 Ⓐ Ⓑ Ⓒ Ⓓ Ⓔ   12 Ⓐ Ⓑ Ⓒ Ⓓ Ⓔ   17 Ⓐ Ⓑ Ⓒ Ⓓ Ⓔ   22 Ⓐ Ⓑ Ⓒ Ⓓ Ⓔ
3 Ⓐ Ⓑ Ⓒ Ⓓ Ⓔ   8 Ⓐ Ⓑ Ⓒ Ⓓ Ⓔ   13 Ⓐ Ⓑ Ⓒ Ⓓ Ⓔ   18 Ⓐ Ⓑ Ⓒ Ⓓ Ⓔ   23 Ⓐ Ⓑ Ⓒ Ⓓ Ⓔ
4 Ⓐ Ⓑ Ⓒ Ⓓ Ⓔ   9 Ⓐ Ⓑ Ⓒ Ⓓ Ⓔ   14 Ⓐ Ⓑ Ⓒ Ⓓ Ⓔ   19 Ⓐ Ⓑ Ⓒ Ⓓ Ⓔ   24 Ⓐ Ⓑ Ⓒ Ⓓ Ⓔ
5 Ⓐ Ⓑ Ⓒ Ⓓ Ⓔ   10 Ⓐ Ⓑ Ⓒ Ⓓ Ⓔ   15 Ⓐ Ⓑ Ⓒ Ⓓ Ⓔ   20 Ⓐ Ⓑ Ⓒ Ⓓ Ⓔ   25 Ⓐ Ⓑ Ⓒ Ⓓ Ⓔ

PART II

1 Ⓐ Ⓑ Ⓒ Ⓓ Ⓔ   8 Ⓐ Ⓑ Ⓒ Ⓓ Ⓔ   15 Ⓐ Ⓑ Ⓒ Ⓓ Ⓔ   22 Ⓐ Ⓑ Ⓒ Ⓓ Ⓔ   29 Ⓐ Ⓑ Ⓒ Ⓓ Ⓔ
2 Ⓐ Ⓑ Ⓒ Ⓓ Ⓔ   9 Ⓐ Ⓑ Ⓒ Ⓓ Ⓔ   16 Ⓐ Ⓑ Ⓒ Ⓓ Ⓔ   23 Ⓐ Ⓑ Ⓒ Ⓓ Ⓔ   30 Ⓐ Ⓑ Ⓒ Ⓓ Ⓔ
3 Ⓐ Ⓑ Ⓒ Ⓓ Ⓔ   10 Ⓐ Ⓑ Ⓒ Ⓓ Ⓔ   17 Ⓐ Ⓑ Ⓒ Ⓓ Ⓔ   24 Ⓐ Ⓑ Ⓒ Ⓓ Ⓔ   31 Ⓐ Ⓑ Ⓒ Ⓓ Ⓔ
4 Ⓐ Ⓑ Ⓒ Ⓓ Ⓔ   11 Ⓐ Ⓑ Ⓒ Ⓓ Ⓔ   18 Ⓐ Ⓑ Ⓒ Ⓓ Ⓔ   25 Ⓐ Ⓑ Ⓒ Ⓓ Ⓔ   32 Ⓐ Ⓑ Ⓒ Ⓓ Ⓔ
5 Ⓐ Ⓑ Ⓒ Ⓓ Ⓔ   12 Ⓐ Ⓑ Ⓒ Ⓓ Ⓔ   19 Ⓐ Ⓑ Ⓒ Ⓓ Ⓔ   26 Ⓐ Ⓑ Ⓒ Ⓓ Ⓔ   33 Ⓐ Ⓑ Ⓒ Ⓓ Ⓔ
6 Ⓐ Ⓑ Ⓒ Ⓓ Ⓔ   13 Ⓐ Ⓑ Ⓒ Ⓓ Ⓔ   20 Ⓐ Ⓑ Ⓒ Ⓓ Ⓔ   27 Ⓐ Ⓑ Ⓒ Ⓓ Ⓔ   34 Ⓐ Ⓑ Ⓒ Ⓓ Ⓔ
7 Ⓐ ●　Ⓒ Ⓓ Ⓔ   14 Ⓐ Ⓑ Ⓒ Ⓓ Ⓔ   21 Ⓐ Ⓑ Ⓒ Ⓓ Ⓔ   28 Ⓐ Ⓑ Ⓒ Ⓓ Ⓔ   35 Ⓐ Ⓑ Ⓒ Ⓓ Ⓔ

Practice Test C

PART I

25 QUESTIONS

Time: 30 minutes

Directions: The problems in this section are to be solved using any available space on the page itself for scratch work. When the problem has been worked out, indicate the one appropriate answer on the answer sheet.

The information which follows should be helpful in determining the correct answers for some of the problems.

Circle of radius r: Area = πr^2 ; Circumference = $2\pi r$.
The number of degrees in a circle is 360.
The number of degrees in a straight angle is 180.

Definitions of symbols:

		is parallel to	> is greater than
≤ is less than or equal to	< is less than
≥ is greater than or equal to	⊥ is perpendicular to
⊀ angle	△ triangle

Triangle: The sum of the measures in degrees of the angles in a triangle is 180. The angle BDC is a right angle; therefore,

(1) the area of triangle ABC = $\dfrac{AC \times BD}{2}$

(2) $AB^2 = AD^2 + DB^2$

Note: The figures which accompany these problems are drawn as accurately as possible *unless* stated otherwise in specific problems. Again, unless stated otherwise, all figures lie in the same plane. All numbers used in these problems are real numbers.

1. $8 \cdot 8 = 4^x$ Find x.

   (A) 2   (B) 3   (C) 4   (D) 5   (E) 6

2. If $2^{n-3} = 32$, then n equals

   (A) 5   (B) 6   (C) 7   (D) 8   (E) 9

247

3. Which of the following has the greatest value?

(A) $\frac{1}{2}$ (B) $\sqrt{.2}$ (C) .2 (D) $(.2)^2$ (E) $(.02)^3$

4. If $\frac{a}{b} = \frac{3}{4}$ then $12a =$

(A) 3b (B) b (C) 9b (D) 12b (E) 16b

5. If $a = b$ and $\frac{1}{c} = b$, then $c =$

(A) a (B) -a (C) b (D) $\frac{1}{a}$ (E) -b

6. If $x^2 - y^2 = 100$ and $x - y = 20$, then $x + y =$

(A) 4 (B) 5 (C) 80 (D) 300 (E) 25

7. The vertices of a triangle are (3, 1) (8, 1) and (8, 3). The area of this triangle is

(A) 5 (B) 10 (C) 7 (D) 20 (E) 14

8. Of 60 employees at the Star Manufacturing Company, x employees are female. If $\frac{2}{3}$ of the remainder are married, how many bachelors work for this company?

(A) $40 - \frac{2}{3}x$ (B) $40 - \frac{1}{3}x$ (C) $40 + \frac{1}{3}x$ (D) $20 - \frac{2}{3}x$ (E) $20 - \frac{1}{3}x$

9. A gallon of water is added to 6 quarts of a solution which is 50% acid. What percent of the new solution is acid?

(A) 30 (B) $33\frac{1}{3}$ (C) $37\frac{1}{2}$ (D) 40 (E) 45

10. In triangle ABC, AB = BC and AC is extended to D. If angle BCD contains 100°, find the number of degrees in angle B.

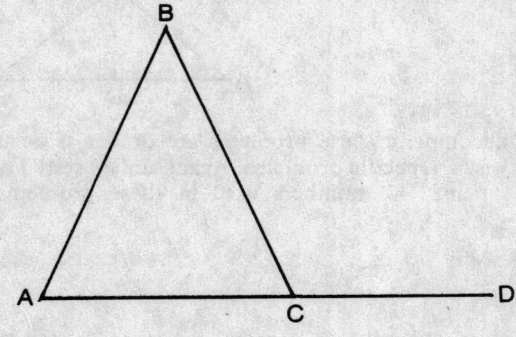

(A) 50 (B) 80 (C) 60 (D) 40 (E) 20

11. $\dfrac{4\frac{1}{2}}{10\frac{1}{8}} =$

(A) $\frac{2}{5}$ (B) $\frac{4}{9}$ (C) $\frac{4}{81}$ (D) $\frac{3}{7}$ (E) $\frac{15}{23}$

12. Which of the following is greater than $\frac{1}{3}$?

(A) .33   (B) $(\frac{1}{3})^2$ (C) $\frac{1}{4}$ (D) $\frac{1}{.3}$ (E) $\frac{.3}{2}$

13. What percent of a half dollar is a penny, a nickel, and a dime?

(A) 16   (B) 8   (C) 20   (D) 25   (E) 32

14. A gasoline tank is $\frac{1}{4}$ full. After adding 10 gallons of gasoline, the gauge indicates that the tank is $\frac{2}{3}$ full. Find the capacity of the tank in gallons.

(A) 120   (B) 48   (C) 24   (D) 20   (E) 32

15. What percent of a is b?

(A) $\frac{100b}{a}$ (B) $\frac{a}{b}$ (C) $\frac{b}{100a}$ (D) $\frac{b}{a}$ (E) $\frac{100a}{b}$

16. If the average of 5 consecutive even integers is 82, the largest of these integers is

(A) 72   (B) 76   (C) 80   (D) 84   (E) 86

17. If Danny earns $2.40 per hour, what is his salary on a day on which he punches in at 4:45 P.M. and punches out at midnight?

(A) $15.00   (B) $19.80   (C) $16.80   (D) $17.40   (E) $18.00

18. A rectangular door measures 5 feet by 6 feet 8 inches. The distance from one corner of the door to the diagonally opposite corner is

(A) 9'4"   (B) 8'4"   (C) 8'3"   (D) 9'6"   (E) 9'

19. Two ships leave from the same port at 11:30 A.M. If one sails due east at 20 miles per hour and the other due south at 15 miles per hour, how many miles apart are the ships at 2:30 P.M.?

(A) 25   (B) 50   (C) 75   (D) 80   (E) 35

20. If m men can paint a house in d days, how many days will it take m + 2 men to paint the same house?

(A) d + 2   (B) d - 2   (C) $\frac{m+2}{md}$ (D) $\frac{md}{m+2}$ (E) $\frac{md+2d}{m}$

21. Ken received grades of 90, 88, and 75 on three tests. What grade must he receive on the next test so that his average for these 4 tests is 85?

(A) 87   (B) 92   (C) 83   (D) 85   (E) 88

22. There is enough food at a picnic to feed 20 adults or 32 children. If there are 15 adults at the picnic, how many children can still be fed?

(A) 10   (B) 8   (C) 16   (D) 12   (E) 4

23. In parallelogram ABCD, angle A contains 60°. The sum of angle B and angle D must be

(A) 120°   (B) 300°   (C) 240°   (D) 60°   (E) 180°

24. The area of circle O is 64π. The perimeter of square ABCD is

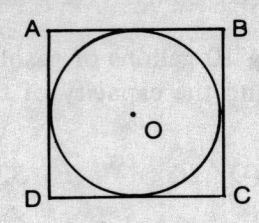

(A) 32   (B) 32π   (C) 64   (D) 16   (E) 64π

25. If a train covers 14 miles in 10 minutes, then the rate of the train in miles per hour is

(A) 140   (B) 112   (C) 84   (D) 100   (E) 98

PART II
35 QUESTIONS
Time: 30 minutes

Directions: The problems in this section are to be solved using any available space on the page itself for scratch work. When the problem has been worked out, indicate the one appropriate answer on the answer sheet.

The information which follows should be helpful in determining the correct answers for some of the problems.

Circle of radius r: Area = πr^2 ; Circumference = $2\pi r$.
The number of degrees in a circle is 360.
The number of degrees in a straight angle is 180.

Definitions of symbols:

| | is parallel to $>$ is greater than
$\leq$ is less than or equal to $<$ is less than
$\geq$ is greater than or equal to $\perp$ is perpendicular to
$\angle$ angle $\triangle$ triangle

Triangle: The sum of the measures in degrees of the angles in a triangle is 180. The angle BDC is a right angle; therefore,

(1) the area of triangle ABC = $\dfrac{AC \times BD}{2}$

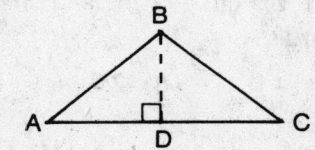

(2) $AB^2 = AD^2 + DB^2$

Note: The figures which accompany these problems are drawn as accurately as possible *unless* stated otherwise in specific problems. Again, unless stated otherwise, all figures lie in the same plane. All numbers used in these problems are real numbers.

1. If $\frac{4}{4}$ of $\frac{3}{4}$ is added to $\frac{3}{4}$, the result is

   (A) $\frac{3}{4}$ (B) $1\frac{1}{2}$ (C) $1\frac{1}{4}$ (D) 1   (E) $1\frac{3}{4}$

2. If $a > 2$, which of the following is the smallest?

   (A) $\dfrac{2}{a}$ (B) $\dfrac{a}{2}$ (C) $\dfrac{a+1}{2}$ (D) $\dfrac{2}{a+1}$ (E) $\dfrac{2}{a-1}$

3. In a group of 40 students, 25 applied to Columbia and 30 applied to Cornell. If 3 students applied to neither Columbia nor Cornell, how many students applied to both schools?

   (A) 6   (B) 12   (C) 18   (D) 19   (E) 11

252 PRACTICE TEST C

4. If a building B feet high casts a shadow F feet long, then, at the same time of day, a tree T feet high will cast a shadow how many feet long?

(A) $\dfrac{FT}{B}$ (B) $\dfrac{FB}{T}$ (C) $\dfrac{B}{FT}$ (D) $\dfrac{TB}{F}$ (E) $\dfrac{T}{FB}$

5. A circle whose center is at the origin passes through the point whose coordinates are (1, 1). The area of this circle is

(A) π (B) 2π (C) $\sqrt{2}\pi$ (D) $2\sqrt{2}\pi$ (E) 4π

6. If $\dfrac{1}{a} + \dfrac{1}{b} = \dfrac{1}{c}$ then c =

(A) $a + b$ (B) ab (C) $\dfrac{a+b}{ab}$ (D) $\dfrac{ab}{a+b}$ (E) $\tfrac{1}{2}ab$

7. $(x - y)^2 = 40$
$x^2 + y^2 = 60$
$xy =$

(A) 20   (B) -20   (C) 10   (D) 40   (E) 12

8. If 2.5 cm. = 1 in. and 36 in. = 1 yd., how many centimeters are in 1 yard?

(A) 14   (B) 25   (C) 70   (D) 90   (E) 86

9. How much more is $\tfrac{1}{4}$ of $\tfrac{1}{3}$ than $\tfrac{1}{3}$ of $\tfrac{1}{4}$?

(A) $\tfrac{1}{6}$ (B) $\tfrac{1}{12}$ (C) $\tfrac{2}{7}$ (D) $\tfrac{1}{7}$ (E) 0

10. The average of two numbers is A. If one of the numbers is x, the other number is

(A) $A - x$ (B) $\dfrac{A}{2} - x$ (C) $2A - x$ (D) $\dfrac{A+x}{2}$ (E) $x - A$

11. If $a = 5b$, then $\tfrac{3}{5}a =$

(A) $\dfrac{5b}{3}$ (B) $3b$ (C) $\dfrac{3b}{5}$ (D) $\dfrac{b}{3}$ (E) $\dfrac{b}{5}$

12. If $a + b = 9$ and $a - b = 3$, than $a^2 - b^2 =$

(A) 72   (B) 27   (C) 36   (D) 12   (E) 75

13. If John can do $\tfrac{1}{4}$ of a job in $\tfrac{3}{4}$ of a day, how many days will it take him to do the entire job?

(A) 12   (B) $1\tfrac{1}{2}$ (C) 9   (D) 6   (E) 3

14. If the area of this figure which consists of 7 equal squares is 63, find the perimeter of this figure.

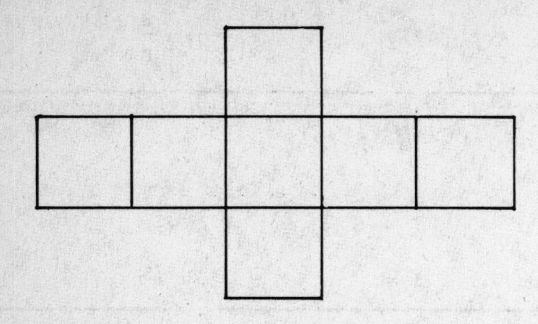

(A) 64   (B) 48   (C) 84   (D) 60   (E) 63

15. If AB = AC, DE ⊥ AB and ∡A = 40°, then ∡D =

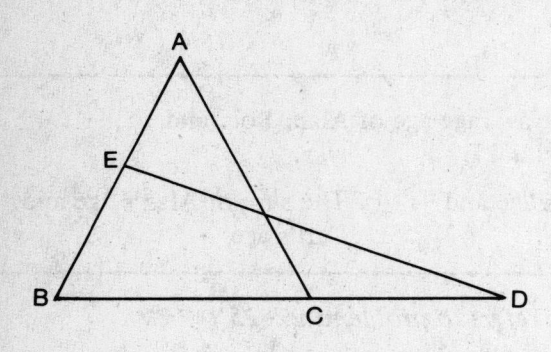

(A) 70°   (B) 40°   (C) 110°   (D) 20°   (E) 50°

Directions: For questions 16-35 compare two quantities, one in Column A and one in Column B, and determine whether:

(A) the quantity is greater in Column A
(B) the quantity is greater in Column B
(C) both quantities are equal
(D) no comparison can be made with the given information

Notes: (1) Information concerning one or both of the compared quantities will be centered above the two columns in some of the questions.
(2) Symbols that appear in both columns represent the same thing in Column A as in Column B.
(3) Letters such as x, n, and k are symbols for real numbers.
(4) Do not mark choice (E), as there are only four choices.

COLUMN A	COLUMN B
	$a = 13$, $b = 14$, $c = 0$
16. $2a(3b + 5c)$	$2c(3a + 5b)$

254 PRACTICE TEST C

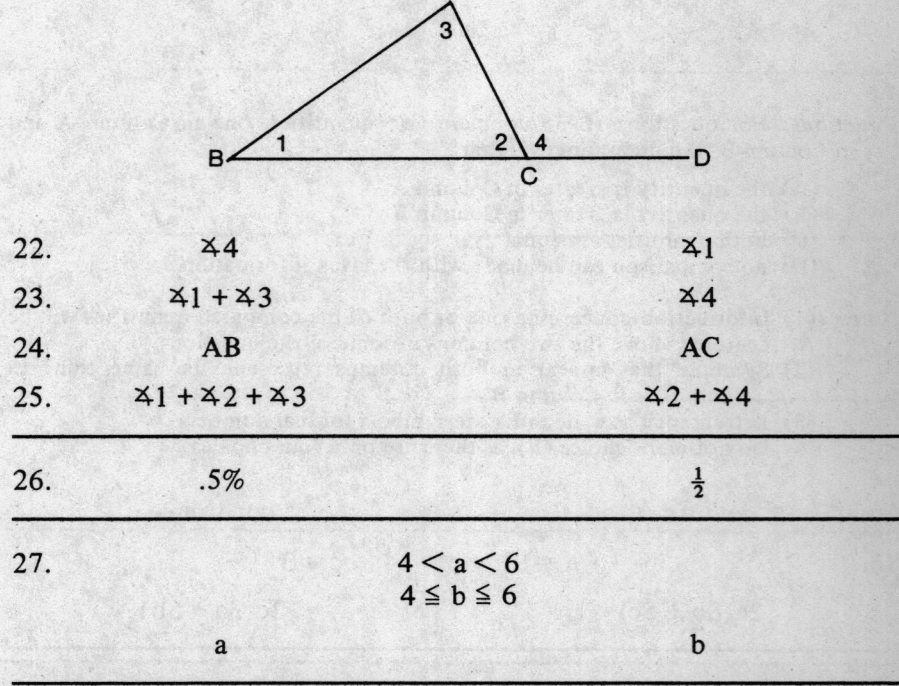

	COLUMN A		COLUMN B
17.		$a > b > c > 0$	
	$\dfrac{a}{b}$		$\dfrac{a}{c}$
18.		$r > 0, \quad s > 0$	
		$\dfrac{1}{r} > \dfrac{1}{s}$	
	r		s
19.	$\sqrt{49} + \sqrt{16}$		$\sqrt{65}$
20.		$2^{x-3} = 32$	
	5		x
21.		The average age of Alan, Bob, and Carl is 17.	
	The sum of Alan's age and Bob's age		The sum of Alan's age and Carl's age

The following diagram refers to problems 22–25.

22.	∢4	∢1
23.	∢1 + ∢3	∢4
24.	AB	AC
25.	∢1 + ∢2 + ∢3	∢2 + ∢4
26.	.5%	$\dfrac{1}{2}$
27.		$4 < a < 6$ $4 \leq b \leq 6$	
	a		b

	COLUMN A	COLUMN B
28.	Jack's salary is $\frac{3}{4}$ of Jim's salary and Joe's salary is $\frac{3}{2}$ of Jack's salary	
	Jim's salary	Joe's salary
29.	$A > 0, B > 0$ $.4A = .04B$	
	A	B
30.	$AB = AC$ $\angle A = 60°$	
	AB	BC
31.	$\angle 5 = 90°$	
	$\angle 1 + \angle 2 + \angle 3 + \angle 4$	$360°$
32.	The average of 3 consecutive even integers a, b, and c is A.	
	$a + c$	$2b$
33.	$-6 < a < -2$	
	$\dfrac{1}{a^4}$	$\dfrac{1}{a^5}$
34.	$a^2 + b^2 = 36$	
	a	b
35.	$xy = 0$	
	x	0

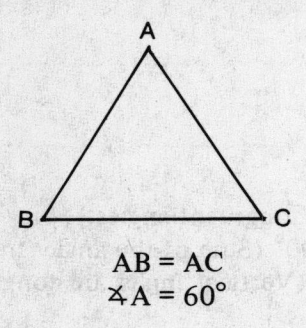

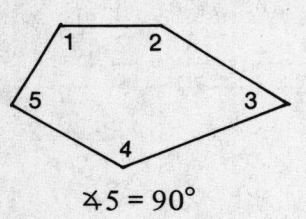

SOLUTIONS TO PRACTICE TESTS

TEST A—PART I

1. (B) $\frac{1}{5}x = 8$
   $x = 40$
   $\frac{1}{4}(40) = 10$

2. (D) $3x = 12$
   $x = 4$
   $3x + 1 = 13$

3. (C) Angle C = 40° (Congruent angles.)
   Angle BAC = 100° (Sum of the angles in a triangle is 180°.)
   Angle x = 100° (Vertical angles are congruent.)

4. (E) $\frac{2}{5} \cdot \frac{3}{2} = \frac{3}{5}$

   $\frac{1}{2} - \frac{1}{10} = \frac{10 - 2}{20} = \frac{8}{20} = \frac{2}{5}$

   $\frac{3}{5} + \frac{2}{5} = 1$

5. (C) Basic toll $1.00
   Extra toll $2.25, which is 3($.75).
   Therefore the car holds a driver and 3 extra passengers for a total of 4 persons.

6. (C) Divide by y^2. $y = 2$

7. (C) $x = y + 1$

   Using the largest negative integers will give the smallest product.
   Let $y = -2, x = -1$, then $xy = 2$

8. (C) Side of square = 12 = diameter of semicircle.
   Remaining 2 sides of triangle add to 8.
   Perimeter of semicircle = $\frac{1}{2}\pi d = \frac{1}{2} \cdot \pi \cdot 12 = 6\pi$
   2 sides of square in perimeter = 24
   Total perimeter of park = $8 + 6\pi + 24 = 32 + 6\pi$

9. (A) $80\% = \frac{4}{5}$ $\frac{4}{5} \cdot 45 = 36$
   $\frac{1}{3} \cdot 45 = 15$
   Used in October = $36 - 15 = 21$

SOLUTIONS TO PRACTICE TESTS   257

10. (E) Angle AOD = 50°
Angle COB = 50°
Arc CB = 50°
Angle CAB is an inscribed angle = 25°

11. (C) $\dfrac{y}{x} = \dfrac{\frac{2}{5}}{\frac{5}{2}} = \dfrac{2}{5} \cdot \dfrac{2}{5} = \dfrac{4}{25}$

12. (B) $\dfrac{m+n+p}{3} = q$

$\begin{array}{r} m + n + p = 3q \\ \underline{x + y = z} \\ m + n + p + x + y = 3q + z \end{array}$

13. (C) Side of square = 2
If BE = 2, EA = 1, then by the Pythagorean theorem, BA and AC each equal $\sqrt{5}$. Perimeter of triangle ABC = $2 + 2\sqrt{5}$

14. (A) Multiply every term by a.

$\dfrac{1}{2a - 2}$

15. (C) There are 30° in each of the 12 even spaces between numbers of the clock. At 3:30, the minute hand points to 6 and the hour hand is halfway between 3 and 4. The angle between the hands is $2\frac{1}{2}(30°) = 75°$.

16. (A) $140 is 125% of his former salary.

$140 = 1.25x$
$14000 = 125x$
$\$112 = x$

17. (A) Area of each square = $\frac{1}{5} \cdot 125 = 25$
Side of each square = 5
Perimeter is made up of 12 sides.   12(5) = 60

18. (C) $\frac{1}{2} \cdot \frac{3}{5} = \frac{3}{10} = 30\%$

19. (D) Circumference is 5 times arc.

$5(2\pi) = 10\pi = \pi d$
$d = 10 \qquad r = 5$

20. (D) The sum of any two sides of a triangle must be greater than the third side.
Therefore x must be less than 7 (4 + 3 > x), however x must be greater than 1, as 3 + x > 4

258 SOLUTIONS TO PRACTICE TESTS

21. **(E)** x can be negative as $(-2)^2 = 4$, which is less than 5.

22. **(D)** The two children's tickets equal one adult ticket. Mr. Prince pays the equivalent of 3 adult tickets.

    $3a = 12.60$
    $a = 4.20$

    Child's ticket = $\frac{1}{2}(4.20) = \$2.10$

23. **(A)** $(_4 \ ^3 \ _5) = 12 - 5 = 7$

    $(_6 \ ^5 \ _7) = 30 - 7 = 23$

    $7 + 23 = 30$

24. **(C)** If the linear ratio is $1:1.5$, then the area ratio is $(1)^2:(1.5)^2$ or $1:2.25$. The increase is 1.25 or 125% of the original area.

25. **(B)** $\frac{3}{4}$ of $\frac{1}{3}$ will go to college next year.

    $\frac{3}{4} \cdot \frac{1}{3} = \frac{1}{4} = 25\%$

TEST A—PART II

1. **(D)** $\sqrt{4^2 + 9} = \sqrt{25} = 5$

2. **(D)** The number must be an even number, as there is no remainder when divided by 2. If division by 4 does give a remainder, it must be 2, since even numbers are 2 apart.

3. **(E)** $(\sqrt{8})^2 = 8$

4. **(B)** $\frac{a}{\cancel{b}} \cdot \frac{\cancel{b}}{\cancel{c}} \cdot \frac{\cancel{c}}{\cancel{d}} \cdot \frac{\cancel{d}}{e} \cdot x = 1$

    $\frac{a}{e} \cdot x = 1$

    $x = \frac{e}{a}$

5. **(C)** Illustrate the given facts as follows

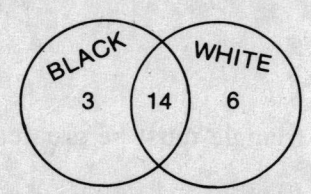

    BLACK 3 | 14 | WHITE 6

    This accounts for 23 students, leaving 7.

SOLUTIONS TO PRACTICE TESTS   259

6. (C) 4☐2 = 4 · 2 + (4 − 2) = 8 + 2 = 10

7. (E) It is possible for the first four to be blue, then the next two *must* be red. Of course it is possible that two red socks could be drawn earlier, but with 6 we are *assured* of a pair of red socks.

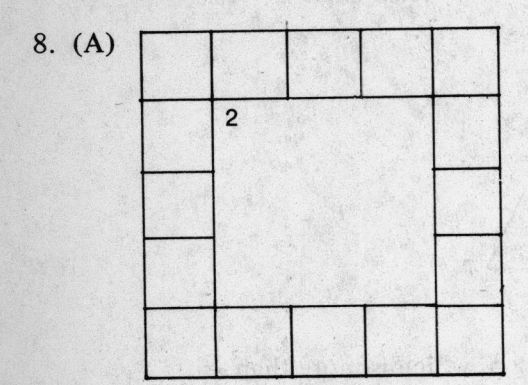

8. (A)

[grid figure with "2" label]

9. (E) Multiples of 3 are 3 apart. x is 3 below x + 3. x + 6 is 3 above x + 3. 6x + 18 = 6(x + 3), 2x + 6 = 2(x + 3). 3x + 5 does not have a factor of 3, nor can it be shown to differ from x + 3 by a multiple of 3.

10. (E) $(a + b)^2 = a^2 + 2ab + b^2$

$$\begin{array}{r} a^2 + b^2 = 30 \\ 2ab = 20 \\ \hline a^2 + 2ab + b^2 = 50 \end{array}$$

11. (D) Use a proportion comparing gallons to miles.

$$\frac{1\frac{1}{2}}{30} = \frac{6}{x}$$

$$1\frac{1}{2}x = 180$$

$$x = 120$$

12. (C) At 12:30, the hour hand is halfway between 12 and 1. Since each interval between 2 consecutive numbers on a clock contains 30°, there are $5\frac{1}{2}(30)°$ or 165° in the angle.

13. (C) The required distance is the diagonal of a square 90 feet on a side.

$$90^2 + 90^2 = x^2$$
$$8100 + 8100 = x^2$$
$$16,200 = x^2$$

Since 120^2 would be 14,400 and 130^2 would be 16,900, x is between 120 and 130.

260 SOLUTIONS TO PRACTICE TESTS

14. **(C)** Next odd integer after x is x + 1
    Next even integer after x is x + 2
    Sum = 2x + 3

15. **(B)** Angle R = 70°
    Then angle S = 40°

16. **(A)** $A = \frac{6}{12} + \frac{4}{12} + \frac{3}{12} + \frac{1}{5} + \frac{1}{6}$, which is more than $\frac{12}{12}$.

17. **(B)** Adding the middle term in this case gives a greater result than subtracting it.

18. **(D)** B can be any obtuse angle at all.

19. **(D)** There is no indication as to what the integers in X or Y are. X could be 4, 6, 8 while Y might be 101, 103, 105, 107 or Y might be -99, -97, -95, -93.

20. **(B)** Angle 2 contains the same number of degrees as the intercepted arc.
    Angle 1 contains $\frac{1}{2}$ as much.

21. **(C)** Solving the equations, x = 1, y = 1.

22. **(D)** Without an indication of which is greater, x or y, it is impossible to tell.

23. **(A)** Subtracting a negative increases a quantity. Adding a negative decreases it.

24. **(C)** Solving for x, x = 12
    $\frac{4}{12} = \frac{1}{3}$

25. **(D)** If x > 0, A is greater.
    If x < 0, B is greater.
    If x = 0, A and B are equal.

SOLUTIONS TO PRACTICE TESTS   261

26. (A) 60 seconds = 1 minute
60 minutes = 1 hour
24 hours = 1 day
Seconds in 1 day = 60 · 60 · 24
There are 30 days in April.
Number of minutes in April = 60 · 24 · 30
Without any computation, A has the greater factors.

27. (D) x and y can take on values so that A is greater, B is greater, or they are both equal.

28. (B) Area of triangle = $\frac{1}{2}$ · 5 · 7
Twice area of rectangle = 2 · 5 · 7

29. (A)

A	B
$9^2 + 10^2 = h^2$	$s^2 = 180$
$81 + 100 = h^2$	$s = \sqrt{180}$
$181 = h^2$	
$\sqrt{181} = h$	

30. (A) Area of a cube is the sum of 6 equal squares.

A	B
$6 \cdot 6^2$	$6 \cdot 6 \cdot 2^2$

The factors are greater in A.

31. (C) Opposite sides of a parallelogram are congruent.

32. (D) Not enough information is given.

33. (C) If two parallel lines are cut by a transversal, the corresponding angles are congruent.

34. (C) Opposite angles of a parallelogram are congruent.

35. (C) If two parallel lines are cut by a transversal, the alternate interior angles are congruent.

TEST B—PART I

1. (C) The difference of 5.58 must be divided between both ends. Thickness on each side is 2.79.

262 SOLUTIONS TO PRACTICE TESTS

2. (E) $\frac{3}{5} = .6$

   $(\frac{2}{3})(\frac{3}{4}) = \frac{1}{2} = .5$

   $\sqrt{.25} = .5$

   $(.9)^2 = .81$

   $\dfrac{2}{.3} = \dfrac{20}{3} = 6.\overline{6}$

3. (E) $\frac{1}{4} = .25$

   $\frac{1}{4}\% = .25\% = .0025$

4. (A) 47% of 1000 are boys.

   $(.47)(1000) = 470$ boys

5. (B) For every pair of digits in a number, there will be one digit in the square root.

6. (A) Multiply every term by 12.

   $\dfrac{6}{4-3} = 6$

7. (D) $A + B = 40$
   $B + C = 34$
   $A + C = 42$

   Subtract second equation from third.

   $A - B = 8$

   Subtract from first equation.

   $2B = 32$
   $B = 16$

8. (A) Use a proportion comparing inches to miles.

   $\dfrac{\frac{1}{4}}{20} = \dfrac{x}{325}$

   $20x = \dfrac{325}{4}$

   $x = \dfrac{325}{4} \cdot \dfrac{1}{20} = \dfrac{325}{80} = 4\dfrac{5}{80} = 4\dfrac{1}{16}$

9. (D) There are $m + f$ people on the staff. Of these, m are men.

   $\dfrac{m}{m + f}$ of the staff is men.

10. **(A)** Represent the angles as 2x, 3x, and 4x.

   9x = 180
   x = 20

   The angles are 40°, 60°, and 80°, all acute.

11. **(C)** The linear ratio stays constant, so perimeter is also multiplied by 2. The area ratio is the square of the linear ratio, so the area is multiplied by 2^2 or 4.

12. **(D)** In k minutes, $\dfrac{k}{m}$ of the lawn is mowed.

   Still undone is $1 - \dfrac{k}{m}$ or $\dfrac{m-k}{m}$

13. **(A)** 55% of his salary is spent. 45% is left.

   There is only one answer among the choices less than $\frac{1}{2}$ of his salary.

14. **(C)** $(3\sqrt{2})(3\sqrt{2}) = 9 \cdot 2 = 18$

15. **(E)** Plotting the point shows a 3, 4, 5 triangle.

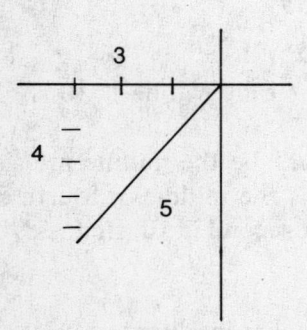

16. **(D)** Since 6 times 9 is 54, the product must end in 4.

17. **(E)** Figure the time elapsed on either side of 12 noon. From 7:42 A.M. to 12 noon is 4 hrs. 18 min. From 12 noon to 10:10 P.M. is 10 hrs. 10 min. The sum of the two is 14 hrs. 28 min.

18. **(B)** Each side of AEDC is 10.
    Each side of BCFG is 6.
    Triangle ABC is a 6, 8, 10 triangle, making the perimeter 24.

19. (C)

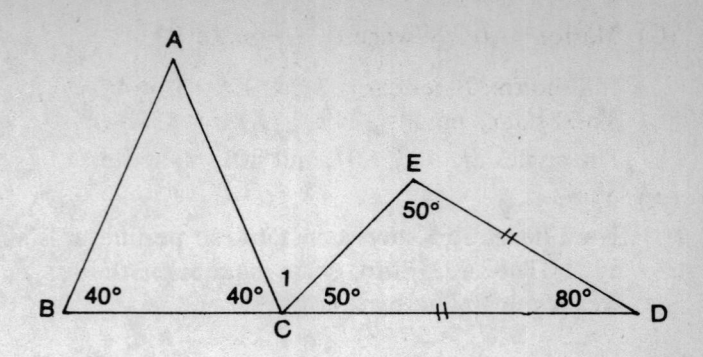

There are 90° left for angle 1 if BCD is a straight angle.

20. (B) Use a proportion comparing pencils to cents. Change 2D dollars to 200D cents.

$$\frac{p}{200D} = \frac{x}{c}$$

$$\frac{pc}{200D} = x$$

21. (C) Distance of first train = 60x
Distance of second train = 70x

$$60x + 70x = 455$$
$$130x = 455$$
$$x = 3\tfrac{1}{2}$$

In $3\tfrac{1}{2}$ hours, the time will be 1:30 P.M.

22. (A) The average will be the middle integer, since they are evenly spaced. If 14 is the middle or fourth consecutive even integer, the third is 12, second is 10, first is 8. The sum of the first two is 18.

23. (D) There are 36 inches in 1 yard.

$$\tfrac{54}{36} = \tfrac{3}{2}$$

24. (C) The minimum is 20 students in 8 classrooms.

25. (A) The radius of each circle is 3, making the dimensions of the rectangle 18 by 6, and the area (18)(6), or 108.

TEST B—PART II

1. (B) $\tfrac{25}{10} = \tfrac{5}{2}$

SOLUTIONS TO PRACTICE TESTS 265

2. (C) Marion's hourly wage is $\frac{\$24}{5}$ or $4.80.
   In 3 hours, Janet earns 3($4.80) = $14.40
   Total salary paid = $24 + $14.40 = $38.40

3. (A) 20% = $\frac{1}{5}$
   $\frac{1}{5}$ · 1200 = $240 depreciation first year.
   $1200 − $240 = $960 value after 1 year.
   $\frac{1}{5}$ · 960 = $192 depreciation second year.
   $960 − $192 = $768 value after 2 years.

4. (C) x + .40x = 84
   1.40x = 84
   14x = 840
   x = 60

5. (D) r + s = 25
   4(r + s) = 4(25) = 100

6. (C) Plane covers 120 miles in 12 minutes or $\frac{1}{5}$ hour. In $\frac{5}{5}$ or 1 hour, it covers 5(120), or 600 miles.

7. (D) $\frac{1}{4}$% = $\frac{1}{4}$ ÷ 100 = $\frac{1}{4}$ · $\frac{1}{100}$ = $\frac{1}{400}$

8. (A) .05(800) = $40 commission
   80:40 = 2:1

9. (A) Increase of 40

   Percent of Increase = $\frac{\text{Amount of increase}}{\text{Original}}$ · 100%

   $\frac{40}{40}$ · 100% = 100%

10. (B) Each side of square = 8
    Radius of circle = 2
    Area of square = 8^2 = 64
    Area of 4 circles = $4\pi r^2$ = 4 · π · 2^2 = 16π
    Shaded area = 64 − 16π

11. (E) X P Q R Y
        ├──┼──┼──┼──┤

    PR = 2 segments
    PY = 3 segments
    $\frac{3}{2}$ = 150%

12. (B) Average rate = $\dfrac{\text{Total distance}}{\text{Total time}} = \dfrac{2M}{\dfrac{M}{X} + \dfrac{M}{Y}}$

    Multiply by XY $\quad \dfrac{2MXY}{MY + MX}$

    Divide every term by M $\quad \dfrac{2XY}{Y + X}$

13. (A) If 4b = 6c, then 2b = 3c
    If a = 2b = 3c, then a = 3c

14. (D) When two negative numbers are multiplied, their product is positive.

15. (B) Since 7 times 6 is 42, the product must end in 2.

16. (B) If 64A = 81, then A = a little more than 1.

17. (A) The larger numerator with the smaller denominator will give the larger fraction.

18. (A) Since a is negative, A will be positive while B is negative.

19. (B) 18 times 10 = 180
    12 times 16 = 192

20. (C) $\dfrac{100}{.1} = 1000$

    100 − 1000 = −900

21. (A) Since a post is needed at the very beginning as well as at the end, A requires 11 posts.

22. (A) A is a greater discount since the full 10% is taken from the original price.

23. (C) Opposite sides of a parallelogram are congruent.

24. (D) Not enough information is given.

25. (B) Maximum area would be if ABCD were a square with AB = AD = 10. This area would be 100.

26. (C) If AB + AD = 20, then DC + CB is also 20.

27. (A) Let OA = AB = x
    Area outer circle = $\pi(2x)^2 = 4\pi x^2$
    Twice area inner circle = $2 \cdot \pi x^2 = 2\pi x^2$

SOLUTIONS TO PRACTICE TESTS   267

28. **(B)** See solution 27.
Area inner circle = πx^2
Area shaded portion = $4\pi x^2 - \pi x^2 = 3\pi x^2$

29. **(C)** Since OA = AB = x, radius of outer circle = 2x, diameter of inner circle = 2x

30. **(C)** Let OA = OB = x   C = πd
Circumference outer circle = $\pi(4x) = 4\pi x$
Twice circumference inner circle = $2 \cdot \pi(2x) = 4\pi x$

31. **(A)** The sum of two sides of a triangle must be greater than the third side.

32. **(A)** The larger angle is opposite the larger side.

33. **(D)** No information given about angle B.

34. **(D)** No information given about side b.

35. **(D)** Not enough information is given about lengths of sides.

TEST C—PART I

1. **(B)** $64 = 4^x$
$x = 3$ $(4 \cdot 4 \cdot 4 = 64)$

2. **(D)** $2^{n-3} = 2^5$
$n - 3 = 5$
$n = 8$

3. **(A)** $\frac{1}{2} = .5$ $\sqrt{.20} = .4^+$
$(.2)^2 = .04$ $(.02)^3 = .000008$

4. **(C)** Cross multiply.
$4a = 3b$
Multiply by 3.
$12a = 9b$

5. **(D)** $a = b = \frac{1}{c}$

$a = \frac{1}{c}$

$ac = 1$

$c = \frac{1}{a}$

268 SOLUTIONS TO PRACTICE TESTS

6. (B) $x^2 - y^2 = (x - y)(x + y)$
$100 = 20(x + y)$
$5 = (x + y)$

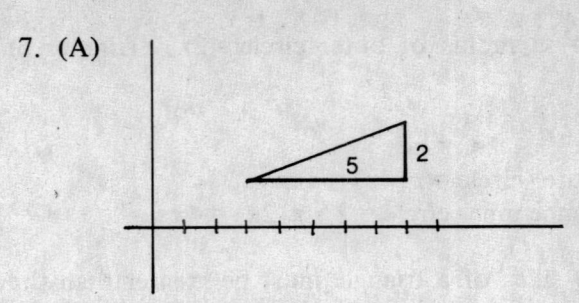

7. (A)

Right triangle area = $\frac{1}{2} \cdot 5 \cdot 2 = 5$

8. (E) $60 - x$ employees are male
$\frac{1}{3}$ of these are bachelors
$\frac{1}{3}(60 - x) = 20 - \frac{1}{3}x$

9. (A)

	No. of quarts	% acid	=	Amount of acid
Original	6	.50		3
Added	4	0		0
New	10			3

$\frac{3}{10} = 30\%$

10. (E) Angle BCA = Angle BAC = 80°
There are 20° left for angle B.

11. (B) $\frac{9}{2} \div \frac{81}{8} = \frac{9}{2} \cdot \frac{8}{81} = \frac{4}{9}$

12. (D) $\frac{1}{.3} = \frac{10}{3} = 3\frac{1}{3}$

13. (E) $\frac{16}{50} = \frac{32}{100} = 32\%$

14. (C) 10 gallons is $\frac{2}{3} - \frac{1}{4}$ of the tank.
$\frac{2}{3} - \frac{1}{4} = \frac{8 - 3}{12} = \frac{5}{12}$

$\frac{5}{12}x = 10$

$5x = 120$

$x = 24$

SOLUTIONS TO PRACTICE TESTS 269

15. (A) $\frac{b}{a} \cdot 100 = \frac{100b}{a}$

16. (E) The average is the middle integer. If 82 is the third, 86 is the last.

17. (D) From 4:45 P.M. to midnight is $7\frac{1}{4}$ hours.
    $7\frac{1}{4}(\$2.40) = \$16.80 + \$.60 = \$17.40$

18. (B) 5 feet = 60 inches
    6 feet 8 inches = 80 inches

    This is a 6, 8, 10 triangle, making the diagonal 100 inches, which is 8 feet 4 inches.

19. (C) In 3 hours, one ship went 60 miles, the other 45 miles. This is a 3, 4, 5 triangle as 45 = 3(15), 60 = 4(15). The hypotenuse will be 5(15), or 75.

20. (D) This is inverse variation.
    $m \cdot d = (m + 2) \cdot x$

    $\frac{md}{m+2} = x$

21. (A) He must score as many points above 85 as below. So far he has 8 above and 10 below. He needs another 2 above.

22. (B) If 15 adults are fed, $\frac{3}{4}$ of the food is gone. $\frac{1}{4}$ of the food will feed $\frac{1}{4} \cdot 32$ or 8 children.

23. (C) If angle A = 60°, then angle B = 120°
    Angle B = Angle D. Their sum is 240°.

24. (C) Area of circle = $64\pi = \pi r^2$
    Radius of circle = 8
    Side of square = 16
    Perimeter of square = 64

25. (C) 10 minutes = $\frac{1}{6}$ hour
    In one hour, the train will cover 6(14), or 84 miles.

TEST C—PART II

1. (B) $\frac{3}{4} + \frac{3}{4} = 1\frac{1}{2}$

2. (D) B and C are greater than 1. A, D, and E all have the same numerator. In this case, the one with the largest denominator will be the smallest fraction.

270 SOLUTIONS TO PRACTICE TESTS

3. (C)

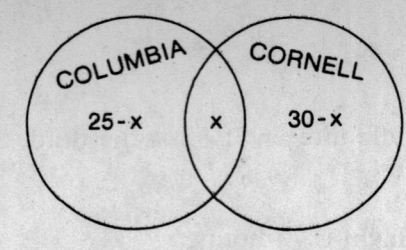

COLUMBIA 25-x | x | CORNELL 30-x

$$25 - x + x + 30 - x = 37$$
$$55 - x = 37$$
$$18 = x$$

4. (A) The ratio of height to shadow is constant.

$$\frac{B}{F} = \frac{T}{x}$$

$$Bx = FT$$

$$x = \frac{FT}{B}$$

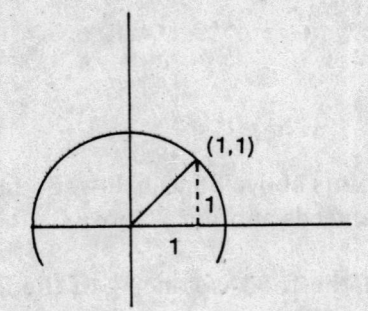

5. (B)

(1,1), 1, 1

$$1^2 + 1^2 = r^2$$
$$2 = r^2$$
$$\text{Area} = \pi r^2 = 2\pi$$

6. (D) Multiply by abc

$$bc + ac = ab$$
$$c(b + a) = ab$$
$$c = \frac{ab}{b + a}$$

7. (C) $(x - y)^2 = x^2 - 2xy + y^2$
$$40 = 60 - 2xy$$
$$2xy = 20$$
$$xy = 10$$

8. (D) $36(2.5) = 90$

9. (E) $\frac{1}{4} \cdot \frac{1}{3} = \frac{1}{12}$ $\frac{1}{3} \cdot \frac{1}{4} = \frac{1}{12}$

SOLUTIONS TO PRACTICE TESTS

10. (C) $\dfrac{x+y}{2} = A$

    $x + y = 2A$

    $y = 2A - x$

11. (B) $\dfrac{3}{8} \cdot 8b = 3b$

12. (B) $a^2 - b^2 = (a+b)(a-b) = (9)(3) = 27$

13. (E) It will take 4 times as long to do entire job. $4(\tfrac{3}{4}) = 3$

14. (B) Area of each square = 9
    Side of square = 3
    Perimeter = 16 sides $16(3) = 48$

15. (D) Angle B = Angle C = 70°

    If angle B = 70°, angle BED = 90°, then in triangle BED there are 20° left for angle D.

16. (A) In A, both factors are non-zero and will give a positive product.

    In B, 2c = 0, giving a product of 0.

17. (B) Since the numerators are the same, the fraction with the smaller denominator will be larger.

18. (B) The larger fraction has the smaller denominator.

19. (A) $\sqrt{49} + \sqrt{16} = 7 + 4 = 11$

    $\sqrt{65}$ is a little more than 8

20. (B) $2^{x-3} = 2^5$

    $x - 3 = 5$

    $x = 8$

21. (D) There is no information about the age of each.

22. (A) An exterior angle of a triangle is greater than either remote interior angle.

23. (C) An exterior angle of a triangle is equal to the sum of the two remote interior angles.

24. (D) No information given.

25. (C) Each of these is 180°.

26. (B) $\frac{1}{2} = .5$
.5% = .005

27. (D) a and b can take on values to make either one greater or to make them equal.

28. (B) If Jim's salary = 8x
then Jack's salary = 6x
and Joe's salary = 9x

29. (B) 40A = 4B
$A = \frac{1}{10} B$

30. (C) There are 120° left between angle B and angle C. Since they must be congruent, they are each 60° and the triangle is equilateral.

31. (A) The sum of the angles in a polygon is (n - 2)180.

   3(180) = 540°

   If angle 5 = 90°, there are 450° left for the other angles.

32. (C) The integers are x, x + 2, and x + 4.
The sum of the first and third is 2x + 4
Twice the second is 2x + 4
For any three consecutive even integers, these are equal.

33. (A) If a is negative, A is positive and B is negative.

34. (D) Not enough information is given.

35. (D) Either x or y must be 0. There is no indication whether it is x or y here. The other may have any value at all.

ARCO Books to Prepare for the College Board Achievement Tests

COLLEGE BOARD ACHIEVEMENT TEST IN AMERICAN HISTORY AND SOCIAL STUDIES

Nancy Woloch, Ph.D. Here is the perfect test preparation guide for the 40,000 students each year who take the College Board Achievement Test in American History and Social Studies. This book provides a complete review of the topics covered in the basic high school survey of American history and extensive practice in answering the types of questions asked on the test.
ISBN 0-668-05746-7 paper

COLLEGE BOARD ACHIEVEMENT TEST IN ENGLISH COMPOSITION

Leo Lieberman, Ph.D. and Jeffrey Spielberger, M.A. This study guide provides a complete analysis of the Achievement Test in English Composition. Diagnostic Tests pinpoint strengths and weaknesses. The Guide to Good Writing provides a concise review of the essentials of grammar and usage. Six full-length Sample Achievement Tests in English Composition with detailed explanatory answers are included.
ISBN 0-668-05728-9 paper

COLLEGE BOARD ACHIEVEMENT TEST IN BIOLOGY

Lawrence Solomon, M.D. Contains: a comprehensive, current biology review covering every subject on the exam; 3 full-length practice tests with detailed explanatory answers; mini-exams to assess strengths and weaknesses; and a glossary of biological terms.
ISBN 0-668-05861-7 paper

COLLEGE BOARD ACHIEVEMENT TEST IN CHEMISTRY

Lawrence Solomon, M.D. Provides over 1,000 practice test questions and contains three full-length practice CBATs with detailed answers, practice tests in selected areas, and comprehensive review in all subject areas covered on the exam.
ISBN 0-668-06168-5 paper

COLLEGE BOARD ACHIEVEMENT TEST: MATHEMATICS LEVEL I

Morris Bramson, M.S. New comprehensive review material and subject outlines make this an indispensable aid to studying for the Mathematics Level I Achievement Test. Six full-length sample examinations with explanatory answers provide complete examination coverage.
ISBN 0-668-05319-4 paper

COLLEGE BOARD ACHIEVEMENT TEST: MATHEMATICS LEVEL II

Morris Bramson, M.S. Containing seven full-length practice CBATs to help students score high on this test, this book provides practical information on preparing for the examination, test-taking hints, and review material covering trigonometry, algebra, and functions. Explanatory answers are provided for every problem.
ISBN 0-668-05646-0 paper

For book ordering information refer to the last page of this book.

ARCO Books For College Entrance Preparation

PREPARATION FOR THE SAT—SCHOLASTIC APTITUDE TEST
Brigitte Saunders, Gabriel P. Freedman, Leonard J. Capodice, Margaret A. Haller, and Robert Bailey. Six full-length practice exams with detailed explanatory answers to all questions. Expert review material for both verbal and mathematics sections of the exam. Comprehensive word list.
ISBN 0-668-05898-6 paper

VERBAL WORKBOOK FOR THE SAT
Gabriel P. Freedman and Margaret A. Haller. Comprehensive review for the verbal and TSWE sections of the SAT. Hundreds of graded practice questions for review in each area. Five full-length practice tests with explanatory answers. Progress charts for self-evaluation.
ISBN 0-668-04853-0 paper

MATHEMATICS WORKBOOK FOR THE SAT
Brigitte Saunders with David Frieder and Mark Weinfeld. Authoritative instructional text and extensive drill in all math areas covered on the SAT. Diagnostic tests in each area to spotlight weaknesses; post-tests to measure progress. Three sample tests with complete solutions.
ISBN 0-668-06138-3 paper.

PSAT/NMSQT PRELIMINARY SCHOLASTIC APTITUDE TEST/NATIONAL MERIT SCHOLARSHIP QUALIFYING TEST
Eve P. Steinberg. Four full-length sample exams and extensive practice with every type of examination question. Every answer fully explained to make practicing for the test a valuable learning experience.
ISBN 0-668-06100-6 paper

PAGE-A-DAY™ SAT STUDY GUIDE
Frances C. Bennett and Sunny Chang. Perforated pages to pull out and take along for study anytime, anywhere. Each page contains both verbal and math practice complete with answers to all questions.
ISBN 0-668-05196-5 paper

PRACTICE FOR THE SCHOLASTIC APTITUDE TEST
Martin McDonough and Alvin J. Hansen. The essentials of SAT preparation condensed into one compact, easy-to-use study guide that fits into pocket or purse. Complete coverage of every question type, 1000 word SAT vocabulary list, one full-length practice exam with explanatory answers for all questions.
ISBN 0-668-05425-5 paper

For book ordering information refer to the last page of this book.

AMERICAN COLLEGE TESTING PROGRAM (ACT)
Eve P. Steinberg. Four full-length practice test batteries with explanatory answers for all questions. Skills reviews and practice questions in each subject area of the exam. Detailed directions for scoring and evaluating exam results. Valuable test-taking tips.
ISBN 0-668-05957-5 Paper

VERBAL WORKBOOK FOR THE ACT
Joyce Lakritz. Intensive review for the English Usage and Reading Comprehension sections of the ACT. Three full-length sample ACT English Usage Tests with explanatory answers to help candidates assess their readiness for the ACT.
ISBN 0-668-05348-8 Paper

MATHEMATICS WORKBOOK FOR THE ACT
Barbara Erdsneker and Brigitte Saunders. In-depth review of the mathematical concepts essential to scoring high on the ACT. Diagnostic tests in each area, followed by instructional text and practice problems, with re-tests to measure progress. Three sample ACT Mathematics Tests with detailed solutions.
ISBN 0-668-05443-3 Paper

TEST OF ENGLISH AS A FOREIGN LANGUAGE (TOEFL)
Edith H. Babin, Carole V. Cordes, and Harriet H. Nichols. Complete preparation for the college entrance examination required of students whose native language is not English. Six simulated sample tests covering all sections of this important exam. Separate cassette tape available for practice with the listening comprehension section.
ISBN 0-668-05446-8 (book)
ISBN 0-668-05743-2 (cassette)

TOEFL GRAMMAR WORKBOOK
Phyllis L. Lim and Mary Kurtin; Laurie Wellman, Consulting Editor. Intensive review for the Structure and Written Expression section of the TOEFL. Concise explanations of the points of English grammar covered by the test. Diagnostic test to direct study. Three practice tests for review.
ISBN 0-668-05080-2 Paper

TOEFL READING COMPREHENSION AND VOCABULARY WORKBOOK
Elizabeth Davy and Karen Davy. Graded practice in reading comprehension and vocabulary to build these essential English skills. Numerous exercises for practice with a variety of reading materials. Three sample Reading Comprehension and Vocabulary Tests with explanatory answers for all questions.
ISBN 0-668-05594-4 Paper

For book ordering information refer to the last page of this book.

ORDER THE BOOKS DESCRIBED ON THE PREVIOUS PAGES FROM YOUR BOOKSELLER OR DIRECTLY FROM:

ARCO PUBLISHING, INC.
215 Park Avenue South
New York, N.Y. 10003

To order directly from Arco, please add $1.00 for first book and 35¢ for each additional book for packing and mailing cost. No C.O.D.'s accepted.

Residents of New York, New Jersey and California must add appropriate sales tax.

MAIL THIS COUPON TODAY!

ARCO PUBLISHING, INC., 215 Park Avenue South, New York, N.Y. 10003

Please rush the following Arco books:

NO. OF COPIES	TITLE #	TITLE	PRICE	EXTENSION
			SUB-TOTAL	
			LOCAL TAX	
			PACKING & MAILING	
			TOTAL	

I enclose check ☐, M.O. ☐ for $ _____
☐ Is there an Arco Book on any of the following subjects: _____
☐ Please send me your free Complete Catalog.

NAME _____
ADDRESS _____
CITY _____ STATE _____ ZIP _____

Every Arco book is guaranteed. Return for full refund within ten days if not completely satisfied.

NOT RESPONSIBLE FOR CASH SENT THROUGH THE MAILS